ZAYTINYA

Foreword by Aglaia Kremezi
Photography by Thomas Schauer

ZAYTINYA

Delicious Mediterranean Dishes
from Greece, Turkey, and Lebanon

JOSÉ ANDRÉS

with Michael Costa

An Imprint of HarperCollins *Publishers*

CONTENTS

turkey

lebanon

About twenty years ago on a warm fall day, José stepped out of a ferry as I waited at the port to meet him. "I am Spanish, but I look like an American," he had told me on the phone, and he was right. His tall, imposing figure was difficult to miss among the few locals arriving midweek, long after the rush of the tourist season. He flew to Athens thinking I was in the city but did not hesitate a minute when I told him I was on the island of Kea and he needed to drive south for an hour and a half to the port of Lavrion, then take the ferry if he wanted to see me. Mark Furstenberg, the legendary D.C. baker, our mutual friend, told him that I was the person to introduce him to Greek cooking.

We clicked from the very moment we met. I immediately realized that he was incredibly eager to absorb new experiences, his mind constantly rushing, thinking, and processing as he tasted the plethora of foods. I am sure he was dreaming of variations and ways to tweak the dishes he had tried in Lebanon and Istanbul, even before coming to Greece. First he visited Thessaloniki, the country's undisputed food capital, and had the great fortune to be guided by Yiannis Boutaris, the renowned fourth-generation wine producer. Founder of Kir-Yianni wines, Boutaris is a rare visionary with vast knowledge of the multiethnic culinary traditions of Northern Greece, and the one who started and inspired the renaissance of Greek wines in the 1980s. In Thessaloniki, José tasted amazing meze—I use the word "meze," as we do in Greece, in America it's commonly spelled mezze—the little dishes of hot and cold foods shared around a table. There were different versions of saganaki, like the classic garides saganaki (shrimp saganaki, *left*), and a variety of htipiti (whipped feta and roasted pepper spread), along with lots of other memorable dishes.

As we sat at a tavern on the port, he showed me on his iPhone—the first such device I saw—vibrant photos of the beautiful meze plates he had created; I was truly amazed!

I don't remember what we ate at the various restaurants we visited, but I am sure we had kolokythokeftedes (zucchini fritters). I think we had taramosalata somewhere because we had a long discussion about the ubiquitous spread he kept trying in various Greek taverns all over the world; he didn't limit his experiences to Greece or Turkey but felt that he had to also try the meze served in England, in Turkish restaurants in Germany, and Greek taverns in Astoria, in Queens, New York, where expats have transported their traditional dishes.

After the success of Jaleo, his first Spanish tapas restaurant, in Washington, D.C., it seems to me only natural that José chose to look east, toward Greece, Cyprus, Turkey, and Lebanon, for inspiration as he created Zaytinya, his second venture.

But it was a tall order, as the mostly frugal, ingredient-based cooking of our region is not easily interpreted in restaurant kitchens and is badly abused in most cases. Traditionally, it is practiced in the home by women who learned the often-intricate dishes from their mothers and grandmothers. It entails iconic preparations like the stuffing of grape leaves to make dolmades, the meticulous shaping of tiny mantı—a kind of Turkish "tortellini"— or the rolling of paper-thin phyllo, which needs special training even for experienced cooks and bakers. But José was up to the challenge. I emphatically told him that he absolutely needed

to make phyllo in the kitchen in order to serve perfectly flaky spanakopita, kleftiko, and other sweet and savory pies, and also that to serve perfect pita, the region's iconic flatbread, which accompanies spreads and other meze, the dough and baking had to be done on the spot, so that the pita would arrive at the table warm and irresistibly crunchy. That same dough is the base for several kinds of enticing, light, and spicy pide—the Turkish boat-shaped "pizza."

Although José didn't aspire to offer authentic, traditional Eastern Mediterranean meze, he absolutely wanted to keep the core of the various foods he chose to serve, creating his own brilliant dishes inspired by the region's cuisines. He mostly wanted to continue the joy of sharing small plates of food around a table, much like the tapas that had been served in Jaleo for years. His efforts did not go unnoticed. Not long after opening, Zaytinya

became a nominee for the 2003 James Beard Award's Best New Restaurant, and José would go home with that year's award for Best Chef: Mid-Atlantic for Jaleo, the first of many James Beard Foundation awards.

Bringing a variety of small plates to the table for guests to accompany their wine is an ancient tradition, as this passage from the comedy *Centaur* by Lynceus, written in the fourth or third century BC, explained:

❝ ...the cook sets before you a large tray on which are five small plates. One of these holds garlic, another a pair of sea-urchins, another a sweet wine sop, another ten cockles, the last a small piece of sturgeon. While I'm eating this, another is eating that; and while he is eating that, I have made away with this. What I want, good sir, is both the one and the other, but my wish is impossible. For I have neither five mouths nor five hands... ❞

The scene describes the frustration slow eaters like me may feel when they fail to taste all the different meze; obviously an age-old problem!

In Zaytinya's kitchen, all the painstaking Eastern Mediterranean preparations are done every day following the old home traditions, and every dish is made from scratch, with the best seasonal ingredients, and this long before the notion became almost cliché.

Over the years, as Zaytinya's "Greek grandmother," I have had the privilege to work often with the wonderful kitchen team, led by concept chef Michael Costa (*above*). He is one of the rare people I know so obsessively dedicated to making everything as it should be, never cutting corners, on the contrary insisting, for example, that fresh chickpeas are used in the spring for the special green hommus, although it is such a pain to peel the tiny pods. He makes sure that everything that comes out of the kitchen is absolutely as it should be, as José originally imagined it.

Chef Costa, whom I am proud to consider my friend, crossed the Atlantic and came to my rescue when I undertook the challenge of preparing a Greek dinner for 280 participants of the Oxford Food Symposium in 2019. These were not ordinary diners, but well-known authors and scholars, all with deep knowledge and experience in food. Working with him in the large college kitchen, designed to serve meals to a dining hall of students, was an unforgettable experience. The symposium participants, Claudia Roden, Harold McGee, and David Tanis among them, were thrilled with the dishes we served.

Zaytinya, more than twenty years after it opened, is still one of the best-loved places for both the locals and tourists visiting the U.S. capital. And it became instantly popular in New York when it opened in 2022. Both José and Chef Costa told me that they are particularly proud when they are praised by people who come from Eastern Mediterranean countries and have experienced the foods in their original settings, and who are therefore quite difficult to please.

The restaurant's fun, convivial atmosphere and of course the delicious dishes that are passed around and shared, creating a celebration at every table, seem to be addictive. Patrons love Zaytinya and keep returning to the restaurant.

The concept of meze served in the middle of the table, self-evident all over the Eastern Mediterranean, was far from attractive to Americans when I started advising Greek restaurants in the mid-1990s. Chefs had warned me then that Americans wanted each to have his or her own plate of food and hated the idea of dipping their forks in the same plate, even with family or close friends.

I think that José helped make sharing food fashionable and fun. Zaytinya proved those doubters wrong: the spirit of the Eastern Mediterranean, as you will find in these pages, is irresistible.

Long after the city's restaurants have gone to bed, I'm standing on the Galata Bridge in Istanbul watching a young man turn simple ingredients into a masterpiece past midnight. He stuffs a soft roll with shredded lettuce and pickled sweet peppers, then slides a just-grilled meat köfte into the roll. He wraps it all in paper and hands it to me. It's hot and juicy and just what I need after a night walking through the city streets. The stalls under the bridge that sell the city's famous fish sandwich, balık ekmek, are all closed. But up top, on the street, the bridge is alive with people, mostly men, with their long fishing poles hanging into the water below, hoping to catch sardines and bluefish.

From here I can see the old city of Istanbul, the home of the sultans and the Ottoman Topkapi Palace, and across the bridge to the more modern heart of Europe's busiest city. Farther out lies the Bosphorus Strait, where Europe and Asia come together. In this moment, I find myself just where I love to be, one foot in the old and one foot in the new—eating an old recipe that survives in the hands of a young cook. In this part of the world, the curve of the Eastern Mediterranean where east meets west, I am humbled and inspired by how tradition and modernity connect.

These connections, these shared cultures that speak through our food, are at the heart of Zaytinya.

The best stories to share are the authentic ones, the ones that come from a place and a community with its own history and culture. I always say that I don't open restaurants, I tell stories. Of course, in restaurants we tell our own versions of those stories, using our own accents—while always aiming to be truthful and respectful. We strive to share those stories with love and joy, with appreciation and admiration.

I came to understand the importance of storytelling more than twenty years ago with the creation of Zaytinya, my restaurant celebrating the food of Greece, Turkey, and Lebanon through the delicious little dishes known as mezze.

Everyone knows I'm from Spain and ultimately that will always be my identity. It's where I come from. When I first arrived in Washington, D.C., I told my story through the food from my home country in my first restaurant, Jaleo. Through small plates of garlic shrimp, jamón, and piquillo peppers, I introduced the beauty of Spain's tapas to America. But that was not enough for me or my partners, Roberto Alvarez and Rob Wilder. We had bigger appetites. We wanted to see if we could tell the stories of another place, across the Mediterranean.

In one of the richest parts of the culinary world, I set out to discover the traditions of mezze: small plates of spreads like hommus and labneh, olives, mussels, grape leaves filled with rice, and salads of wild greens to share around a table. I was amazed by how much the ingredients and the recipes—and the people who cooked them—connected to my soul.

"IT'S IMPORTANT TO UNDERSTAND JUST HOW ANCIENT, AND HOW CONNECTED, THESE PARTS OF THE WORLD ARE."

The foods of the Eastern Mediterranean have always been fascinating to me. There are so many familiar flavors: olive oil, citrus, lots of fish and seafood, peppers, eggplant, olives, chickpeas, lentils, and rice. I wanted to discover the stories behind the classic dishes, to understand the origins of shared ingredients, and how recipes and techniques traveled across the Mediterranean and the Middle East. You see, the history of the Eastern Mediterranean shares some of the same DNA as the history of Spain—if you go back far enough, we have some of the same ancestors and many of the same cultural roots.

It's important to understand just how ancient, and how connected, these parts of the world are. The famous Fertile Crescent of Western Asia, the birthplace of what we call civilization, included parts of Lebanon and southeastern Turkey. Centuries and generations of empire-building and conquest, victories and defeats, led to the rise and fall of different groups of people, each leaving their own imprint on the culture, the food, the society. The Phoenicians (who made it as far west as Spain), the Persians, the ancient Greeks, the Macedonians, the Byzantines, the Roman Empire, the Islamic Caliphate (and, of course, its Spanish stronghold, al-Andalus)—all left their mark.

Maybe the most consequential culture, the one that informs much of the food in the Eastern Mediterranean, emerged in the Ottoman Empire. Many of the dishes we think of as Turkish, and some of the ones that are Greek and Lebanese, have their origins in the six-hundred-year Islamic dynasty. What started as a powerful local tribe in Anatolia, the central plain of Turkey, ended up becoming a cross-continent powerhouse ranging from current-day Algeria in the west to Saudi Arabia in the east, from Ukraine to Egypt. Constantinople—Istanbul today—was its capital, a bridge from Asia to Europe and ultimately a bridge from the tribal rulers of the fifteenth century to the modern ones of the twentieth. The Ottomans were great assimilators, creating a giant melting pot of the many cultures they dominated: the royal tastes of the Persian nobility, the pastries of the Levant, the stuffed dishes of Armenia, the seafood of Greece, the meat dishes of the Eurasian steppe, the spice trade that helped fuel the economy. When the Ottoman Empire finally fell, just a hundred years ago, its impact remained in what came next. Modern Turkey was founded, while Lebanon became a French colony before gaining independence in 1943. The Greeks won their independence in the 1830s, but retained many cultural influences from their four hundred years of Ottoman rule.

Today we might look at this part of the world and think of instability and conflict at the edge of the Middle East. But the borders and politics that have sparked so many problems are relatively new. The connections between the people of this region are old and deep—and their shared food traditions prove that what brings us together is more powerful than what separates us. Neighboring communities have been sharing their food traditions since the beginning of time, whether or not there's

a border between them. So you'll see again and again in this book that the same dish might have three different names in Greek, Turkish, and Arabic, or that an ingredient plays a similar role in all three cultures.

We opened Zaytinya in the nation's capital in 2002, just a year after we had plunged into the darkness of the post-9/11 era. The restaurant was a burst of Eastern Mediterranean sunshine, bringing people together around shared plates, at a restaurant whose name was inspired by the Turkish word for olive oil, "zeytinyağı." It was not a neighborhood Greek tavern or a Turkish kebab house or a fine Lebanese restaurant. It was all of them together, at a time when the world felt like it was falling apart.

We set out to explore the classic flavors of the region and discovered not just wonderful food but incredible generosity. One of our very first steps was to turn to our good friend Dany Abi-Najm and his family. As the owners of the celebrated Lebanese Taverna restaurants in the Washington, D.C., area, they offered their knowledge, recipes, and kitchens to help us come to understand the multilayered cuisine of Lebanon and the Levant, the region stretching from Syria to Egypt. Dany guided us to discover and master the key dishes that all good Lebanese cooks are judged by—hommus, fattoush, tabbouleh, falafel, baba ghannouge, kibbeh— and then to make them our own.

My wife, Patricia, and I traveled through Greece, eating our way through Santorini, Thessaloniki, and Athens, taking notes and drinking in all the flavors, including the astonishing wines that surprised me with their variety and finesse. We went on to explore Istanbul, its markets and bazaars, not to mention countless spots for fried mussels, or midye tava, which quickly became my favorite street snack. We found a merchant to provide the copper platters that would later fill the restaurant, and I would learn, after many cups of Turkish tea in the merchant's shop, that Tichi (as my wife is known) could be a fierce negotiator when she wanted to be.

For a chef like me, there was nothing quite like walking through the Topkapi Palace kitchens in Istanbul, imagining what it must have been like to see the huge complex of buildings, larger than a football field, filled with an army of cooks and kitchen staff. More than eight hundred people stocked the pantry, mended the cookware, prepared the ingredients, and baked bread. The famous chefs of the Ottoman palace created meals and confections for thousands of people, from the sultan and his family, to military leaders and so many more; many of their dishes and recipes we know then traveled from within the palace walls to the far reaches of the vast Ottoman Empire. It was astonishing and inspiring.

Before we opened the doors at Zaytinya, I set out to experience restaurants like the Black Olive in Baltimore, Molyvos and Milos in New York, the Real Greek in London, and the Turkish markets in Berlin. I wanted to taste the many interpretations of Mediterranean ingredients. Back in Washington, I visited Neyla, the Mediterranean restaurant from renowned Lebanese restaurateur Bechara Nammour of Capital Restaurant Concepts, and Kazan, the iconic Turkish restaurant from Chef Zeynel Uzun across the Potomac in northern Virginia. I had a small team of cooks and managers help me research culinary traditions, recipes, and wines, like Sotiris Bafitis and Alex Zeppos, cousins whose Greek

book *Greek Cookery*, first published in English in 1950, was a special find. We filled Ghillie Başan's *Classic Turkish Cooking* with Post-it notes, tagging dishes to explore further.

Above all, we admired Aglaia Kremezi, award-winning Greek cookbook author, teacher, journalist, and expert on Mediterranean cooking. I had studied her books *The Foods of Greece* and *The Foods of the Greek Islands*, and through an introduction by my longtime friend, chef and master baker Mark Furstenberg, I traveled to meet Aglaia on her home island of Kea, a one-hour ferry ride south of Athens. I spent days cooking by her side, learning, laughing, and eating everything. This would be the beginning of a friendship that has had the most profound effect on Zaytinya, on the dishes we serve and the stories we tell. Over the years, Aglaia has spent time with our team in Washington and beyond, teaching us about the essential flavors and ingredients of not only Greece but the Eastern Mediterranean, and showing us how to master the elements of classic dishes. She has welcomed our chefs to cook with her in Greece; an amazing experience to better understand the recipes we prepare at Zaytinya. As our mentor and guide, she keeps me and my team deeply connected to the Mediterranean as we explore new techniques, expanding our menu and our locations.

No man is an island. I am who I am today because of the people who have shared their knowledge, their passion, their creativity, and their generous spirit with me. This is particularly true for the people who have helped me build Zaytinya; so many that I cannot possibly mention them all—chefs, cooks, servers, managers, winemakers, importers, farmers, purveyors, partners, and friends. I am forever grateful to them all. There are a few you will meet in the pages of this book, including Chef Michael Costa, who has been leading our Zaytinya family for more than a dozen years. I am amazed by his determination, his willingness to learn and to teach. He is methodical and unwavering in his commitment to understand

heritage was not only a great resource but a point of immense pride for both. There were others who shared their history and knowledge to train our team on dishes and service, such as manager Selçuk Önce, a native of Turkey who knew how to find anything and anybody, including someone to teach us to make the tiny mantı I adored; Pastry Chef Steve Klc who created desserts that remain favorites to this day; and Abdelrazzaq Hashhoush, a talented cook from Lebanon who could make lighter-than-air phyllo and shape kibbeh by the hundreds. We pored through books by Claudia Roden, Clifford A. Wright, Mary Salloum, Diane Kochilas, and Paula Wolfert. The father of modern Greek cooking Nikolaos Tselementes's

"WHAT YOU WILL FIND ARE RECIPES THAT HONOR THOSE TRADITIONS BUT ARE CREATED IN A NEW WAY."

authentic flavors and create inspired dishes. At the same time as developing new Zaytinyas in New York, Las Vegas, and Miami, he was instrumental in helping me pull together the recipes and stories we share in this cookbook.

The recipes here are many of Zaytinya's most popular dishes, including ones that guests have asked me for years to share. Yes, my friends, our havuç köftesi (carrot fritters) and hünkâr beğendi (eggplant puree and braised lamb) are here, plus so many more that you can make at home to enjoy with family and friends. Nearly all of the dishes you'll find here are made for sharing, with a few exceptions designed for individual portions. Most recipes are perfect for four people, while one chapter focuses on dishes to prepare for six or more.

There are recipes for everyone in this book. A new cook just learning their way around a kitchen can easily put together a bright, flavorful fattoush salad and skewers of marinated grilled chicken. For those who want to up their culinary game, we have step-by-step instructions on making Turkish pide and mantı (dumplings), Lebanese kibbeh, and Greek-style roasted leg of lamb. Some recipes are easy and quick; others will take more time. Some require two days to allow for beans to soak or meats to marinate, but it will be worth it. The amazing thing about these dishes, really about the cooking of this region, is that as long as you start with the best ingredients possible, and treat them with care and respect, you will create something astonishing and delicious.

To be clear, these recipes are not the traditional dishes you might find on menus in Greek tavernas or Turkish lokantas. What you will find are recipes that honor those traditions but are created in a new way. You can call it José's way: using ingredients and techniques that inspire me and my team. That's what gives Zaytinya its unique style, and what has filled the restaurant from the first day it opened, two decades ago.

This is where the old and new come together, where the east and west meet, where the people of the Eastern Mediterranean share their flavors, their food, and their stories. This is where I love to find myself, with a just-grilled meat köfte in my hand, watching the fishermen as they try to catch something fresh to eat.

— JOSÉ ANDRÉS

01

THE FUNDAMENTALS & THE FLAVORS

hat has always fascinated me most about this region of the Mediterranean is how east and west come together; thousands of years of spice trading have shaped the cooking and flavors and so much more. Seeds, nuts, and herbs from China and India, carried by Persian and Arab traders, made their way to Greek and Roman shores. When you first start to cook some of the incredible dishes, you too might be surprised at just how much Greece, Turkey, and Lebanon use the same ingredients in different ways, and call them different names. It's not only their location along the spice and trading routes in the Eastern Mediterranean that connects these countries but also a common history under Ottoman rule, which dominated the region for hundreds of years. Traveling through the region, and learning from chefs and friends, I came to understand how their cooking is rooted in the ingredients of the mountains and the seas, but is then transformed into something unique and complex by deftly layering in spices and herbs.

Any food lover will tell you that one of the best things about traveling is visiting local grocery stores. In every aisle is something tantalizingly new—a rare kind of honey, a spicy chili paste, or an unfamiliar cheese. When we started Zaytinya twenty years ago, we crammed our suitcases with spices and oils and whatever else we could legally carry to make the dishes taste just like the ones we had savored across the Eastern Mediterranean.

We've come a long way! Many of these once "exotic" ingredients are now on supermarket shelves. Labneh, that deliciously thick strained yogurt, sits next to the peach and blueberry flavors. Tart, ruby-colored sumac is stashed between star anise and Szechuan peppercorns. And, of course, you can find everything online.

I will tell you that the recipes in this book are generally forgiving. Don't turn back if you realize you are missing one little ingredient. (We do share substitutions when we think it won't compromise the dish.) But I will also tell you that a little Kefalograviera cheese grated into zucchini fritters really brings the taste of the region home.

And, of course, have fun! New herbs and spices can often be used in whatever you are cooking. Try sprinkling smoky Urfa biber chili pepper over chicken instead of black pepper. By adding these regional flavors to your pantry, you are joining in an age-old tradition: the mixing of cultures and ingredients to create new dishes with delicious stories to tell.

YOGURT AND LABNEH

CHEESES

No one can deny that yogurt is one of the most useful ingredients in the Eastern Mediterranean pantry. On Turkish and Greek tables, you'll find a bowl of thick **strained plain yogurt** right next to a basket of pide bread, and the best thing to do is to spoon it on everything from dolmades to kebabs. Yogurt is also the star in some of our favorite mezze, like Crispy Brussels Sprouts Afelia (page 186), Tzatziki (page 52), and of course, our Chilled Yogurt Soup (page 119). Use plain whole-milk **Greek yogurt** for these recipes. It's thicker than domestic yogurt and is higher in protein and lower in sugar. In parts of the Mediterranean, you might come across sheep's-, goat's-, cow's-, and even camel's-milk yogurt. But for the purposes of this book, full-fat Greek cow's-milk yogurt is the way to go. **Labneh** is like super Greek yogurt. It's extra-strained, very tangy, and has a cream cheese–like texture. I use labneh to add body to a yogurt sauce, like tzatziki. We also whip it up with olive oil and salt to make a sauce for beets or asparagus, or to just dip with pita bread.

We could write a whole book on Mediterranean cheeses. To get the best out of these recipes, there are a few important ones to know:

Feta is traditionally made in Greece with sheep's milk and a small addition of goat's milk. Outside Europe, you can find it made with goat's milk and, more commonly, cow's milk. The milk is curdled to separate the curds and whey, drained, and then cut into large slices before being brined. (The word "feta" means "slices" in Greek.) Feta can be sharp or mild, tangy or creamy. At the restaurant we prefer the traditional, mostly sheep's-milk feta of Dodoni and Roussas brands because they are creamier and less salty. But there's something for everyone.

In choosing a feta, we recommend that you skip crumbled feta. The blocks tend to have more flavor and can be stored almost indefinitely in the brine they come in, or in a brine you make yourself at home: Just mix 2 teaspoons of salt with 1½ cups water or enough to submerge the cheese. The brine is useful too. We use it to season our cold yogurt soup.

Halloumi hails from the island of Cyprus and is traditionally made with a mix of goat's and sheep's milk. But what makes it stand out is its squeaky

(in a good way!) texture and its very high melting point, which makes it ideal for grilling or frying. We cut it into slabs and sear it, but we also turn up the heat on halloumi and melt it over Turkish flatbreads called pide.

Kefalograviera is a hard yellow cheese that is smooth, slightly nutty, and easy to grate, making it handy to stir into fritters or baked dishes like Chicken Youvetsi (page 264). It's available online, but aged Manchego can work as a substitute.

Kaşar, as it's known in Turkey, or Kasseri, as it's called in Greece, is a semihard yellow cheese that melts beautifully, making it a great choice for saganaki or, for that matter, a grilled cheese. At Zaytinya, we dice the cheese and melt it on pide. If you can't easily find it, try provolone instead.

Cooking with these cheeses is one way to get to know them. Another is to simply put together a regional cheese plate—no cooking required! See page 78 for a variety of cheeses and accompaniments that will make your next wine-and-cheese hour unforgettable.

RICE, BEANS, LEGUMES, AND GRAINS

I am a great believer in the humble bean. My life has been shaped by Spanish stews where beans play a starring role, like fabada (alongside chorizo and blood sausage). Beans are no less fundamental in the Eastern Mediterranean. I have no problem with canned beans. They are fast and healthy and easy and cheap. What is there to grumble about? But dried beans, soaked and cooked with a few aromatics like carrots, onions, and celery, deliver better texture in our dishes.

We make our White Bean Stew (page 162) with buttery Greek **gigantes beans**. Meaty and creamy, they can stand up to strong flavors, which is why the Greeks bake them in tomato sauce with plenty of herbs in a delicious dish called plaki. **Dried chickpeas** are a must for Falafel (page 161) and our Chicken Stock (page 113). We also love **dried yellow split peas**. We use a variety of yellow split pea from Santorini that is called fava, which are larger than American yellow split peas but definitely not what we call fava beans! You can sometimes find them at Mediterranean markets or online, but grocery-store yellow split peas, also called dal, will work too. At Zaytinya, we also use two types of lentils: **Red lentils**, for mercimek çorbası (page 114), the iconic Turkish soup; **French green lentils**, also called Le

Puy lentils, are for mujadara (page 159), because they hold their shape as they cook to a creamy soft center and mix beautifully with seasoned rice.

Bulgur is a parboiled, dried wheat grain, and tastes much better than that sounds! It was a staple of the Ottoman Empire, embraced as a cheaper alternative to rice, but also for its texture and its light, nutty flavor. Note: Different recipes call for different sizes of bulgur. Fine grains are best for mezze like Tabbouleh (page 97), because they absorb more flavor and are less chewy, or for stuffing peppers and tomatoes. I cook the coarse, thicker bulgur to stand up to meat or vegetables and use it in kisir (page 164), which is like a slightly spicy, tart version of tabbouleh.

Freekeh and **wheat berries** are two more of those "ancient grains" that are so popular these days, and for good reason. They are whole grains and therefore more nutritious than the refined ones that so often fill our plates. Freekeh is a toasted green wheat kernel, while wheat berries include the kernel as well as the wheat's germ and bran. Both grains have a chewy texture and a subtle nuttiness that you will love. But plan ahead: they do take a bit longer to cook than other grains and pasta.

Rice deserves a book of its own, and yes, they exist, and you should read them. But here's what you need to know about rice to cook the food of Zaytinya: If you want grains to stick together, use short-grain rice. If you want more texture and separate grains that don't clump together, use long-grain rice. For dishes like dolmades (page 154), which use short-grain rice, we prefer **Valencia rice**. For pilafs (page 156), we use aromatic **basmati rice**. One note: Be sure to check the cooking times on the variety you choose and adjust our recipes to follow the package recommendations.

Kritharaki is tiny oval pasta—the Greek version of what you may know as orzo. If you can't find a Greek brand, like Misko, grocery-store orzo will work just fine. Kritharaki is used widely in Greek home cooking in dishes ranging from Chicken Youvetsi (page 264) to lemony chicken soup (page 110).

DRIED AND FRESH HERBS

SPICES

Dried herbs sadly often have the same flavor as freeze-dried dust. But this is not the fault of the dried herbs. It is ours. We let them sit around for years! We store them near the stove where the heat drains away their flavor. People, it's time to respect dried herbs! Which, by the way, is exactly what they do in the Mediterranean.

High-quality dried herbs have very intense flavors, and indeed they sometimes differ from the ones you find when the herbs are fresh. **Dried oregano** is in fact more intense, and often lacks the unpleasant bitterness that fresh oregano sometimes has. The name "oregano" comes from the Greek word "origanum," which means "joy of the mountain," a reference to the fantastic aroma that floats across Greek hillsides in spring. At Mediterranean markets, you can sometimes find dried Greek oregano that is still on its stem, which is potent stuff. Fresh mint has a tendency to release its flavor in a dish immediately, while **dried mint** is more subtle and warms up slowly, which is why we use it in our tomato ezme spread and to flavor ground meats like Adana kebabs. If you are lucky enough to be shopping in a store that has different types of mint, you'll want peppermint for a stronger, brighter mint flavor, or spearmint for a sweeter, milder taste.

In Greece and Turkey, they use **fresh herbs** much like we do, as garnishes, such as some mint in a classic Greek salad. But in Lebanon, and throughout the Arab world, fresh herbs are treated more like salad greens. Think of how much parsley goes into tabbouleh! I love this approach. Throw them into summer salads by the handful. You'll be amazed at how fresh dill can add earthy sweetness, and how parsley brings just the right level of bitter to your bowl.

❀ ❀ ❀ ❀ ❀ ❀ ❀ ❀ ❀ ❀

"THE NAME 'OREGANO' COMES FROM THE GREEK WORD 'ORIGANUM,' WHICH MEANS 'JOY OF THE MOUNTAIN.'"

Spices, I always say, are like flowers—as soon as you separate them from the earth, they start to fade. This is why it's important to buy fresh spices and treat them with care. Rule number one: Keep them in a cool, dry place. Rule number two: Buy them in small quantities so they don't linger too long in your pantry. Rule number three: Where possible, buy whole spices that you can grind or grate when you need them. This will give you a fresher, purer flavor and, conveniently, also ends in less waste. At home I always have sticks of **cinnamon**, **cardamom pods**, **whole nutmeg**, **cumin**, **caraway seeds**, and **allspice**. All of the spices described in the pages that follow are used frequently in the book, so you'll finish them off in no time. And if you don't, it's time to invite a few people over for dinner!

If you've ever had a glass of rakı (Turkish) or ouzo (Greek) or arak (Lebanese), you know the intense, sweet licorice flavor of **anise**. We use ouzo to flambé our tomato saganaki but we also use a pinch of ground anise to reinforce the fennel flavor once the alcohol in the ouzo burns off. Another unique flavor of the region is **mastic**, the aromatic resin from an evergreen that grows on the Greek island of Chios. How anyone figured out how to use it, I don't know! But each summer, tiny cuts are made

into the branches. This releases the resin, which is then dried into crystal-like tear-shaped balls. The classic preparation of mastic is to grind it with a bit of sugar in a mortar and pestle, to keep it from clumping together. In the restaurant, we put mastic in a plastic bag and then freeze it. We then go over it with a rolling pin, in the bag, to crush it to a powder, making cleanup much easier. When heated, the mastic delivers a warm, subtle piney flavor, and makes an amazing ice cream (page 325). You will love it!

It may surprise you to know that we use more white pepper than black at the restaurant because it is milder and avoids black flecks in delicate dishes like our avgolemono soup. Even more than other spices, it's essential to buy **whole white peppercorns** and grind them fresh. White peppercorns oxidize as soon as they are ground and lose their funk and fruitiness, leaving you with not much more than spicy sawdust. **Aleppo pepper** or **Marash pepper** is a bright, fruity chili flake that is used throughout Turkey much as we use salt and pepper here; in other words, on everything. We refer to this type of chili as Aleppo pepper in the book, though it's been a long time since any pepper came out of Aleppo. The brutal civil war in Syria put an end to most production and any export. Instead,

most of what you find sold as Aleppo pepper is actually the Turkish version, Marash, which is grown near the Syrian border, dried in the sun, and equally delicious. Another chili to add to your cabinet is **Urfa pepper**, also called Urfa biber. It has a wonderful smoky flavor and a tad more heat than Aleppo pepper. Try it on your next batch of scrambled eggs. You won't be sorry.

Where tomato paste is a go-to in American kitchens, so **pepper paste** is in Turkey and other parts of the Mediterranean. Just a dab adds a deep, sweet pepper flavor and richness and a boost of umami to sauces, grilled meats, and grain dishes like kisir.

❀ ❀ ❀ ❀ ❀ ❀ ❀ ❀ ❀ ❀

"A DAB OF PEPPER PASTE ADDS A DEEP, SWEET PEPPER FLAVOR AND RICHNESS AND A BOOST OF UMAMI."

We all take salt for granted, but it's really the most important "spice" in any kitchen. Okay, it's not a spice. It's a mineral and the world's greatest

flavor enhancer, making anything, from steak to eggs to beets, taste more like itself. We use three varieties at the restaurant, and it's useful to have all of them at home too. **Kosher salt** is your basic cooking salt. It's a type of salt with slightly bigger flakes than what is called table salt. The trick with kosher salt is to pick a brand and stick with it because different brands have varying textures and levels of salinity. And you want to know your salt! We are Diamond Crystal people because we like its fine texture and balance. Morton's, another popular brand, has larger flakes and is a bit saltier. For fried foods, we use **fine sea salt** because it clings so well to the hot oil. And to finish a dish, we sprinkle **flaky sea salt**, like Maldon. The crystals don't dissolve as easily as other salts, adding texture and pops of flavor.

Saffron is expensive for a reason. The scarlet threads are stigmas from *Crocus sativus*—and each flower produces just three. Thought to hail from Greece, saffron has long been a culinary star, though it is also said to have been scattered on the floors of ancient theaters and public halls to perfume the air. It must have cost less back then! The good news is it takes only a few threads to infuse that warm, fragrant sunshine into a sauce or pan of rice.

FRUITS, VEGETABLES, AND NUTS

The rest of the world is finally starting to see how much magic lives inside a jar of cured **sumac**! First used in ancient Greece as a fabric dye (you'll see why as soon as you open a jar), powdered sumac is made from dried, crushed, and fermented sumac berries, which grow along the Caspian Sea (and in many parts of America!). This bright purple garnish spice adds tartness, acidity, and a hint of sweetness to everything from a bowl of Fattoush (page 94) to a pide with soujouk.

Renowned for its glorious golden color, **turmeric** has a flavor that is often underestimated. But it has a subtle spiciness, akin to ginger or mustard, that we love. We use it in our Hawayej and Golden Baharat spice blends (page 27), which are used to season our lamb kebabs (page 248) and in our popular Golden Spice Cauliflower (page 192).

Za'atar can refer to a particular herb—a relative of oregano that grows in the Levant—or to a spice blend that usually includes thyme, oregano, and sesame seeds. (Some people also throw in a bit of sumac for good measure.) When we talk about za'atar in this book, we mean the blend. We import ours from Jordan, and still marvel at how it manages to be somehow nutty, herbaceous, and earthy all at the same time.

Barberries are small, tart berries that resemble red currants. I like to think of them as the love child of sumac and a cranberry. They used to be relatively difficult to find, but they have had a bit of a renaissance lately and now are much more widely available. (Though if you can't find them, you can substitute dried cranberries.) We use barberries to add punch to our crispy Brussels sprouts, and you should use them too. One important note: You must inspect barberries very carefully before cooking. They grow on thorny bushes, so spread them out on a tray and look closely for gnarly thorns before serving.

Dates and **dried apricots** are usually reserved for sweets here, but in the Mediterranean they are paired with savory flavors, creating an alluring contrast. We use dates—fat, chewy medjools preferably—with our seared halloumi cheese, and plump Turkish apricots, which we soak overnight with lemon and cardamom, to serve with pastirma, a Turkish cured loin of beef.

You'll be hard-pressed to find a Turkish, Lebanese, or Greek breakfast spread without a bowl or two of marinated **olives**, either bright green and cured in brine with fresh herbs, or fleshy and black with a mellow, smooth flavor. For a region covered in ancient olive trees,

cured olives are an elemental part of any mezze table, ready to be shared whenever people gather. You'll find them added to salads, vegetables, and fish dishes as well. We use Kalamata olives most often, even smoking them (page 205), but also find ourselves reaching for wrinkly black Moroccan cured olives. Greek cracked green olives add meatiness and flavor. They are cracked with a stone or sliced with a knife to allow the curing liquid and herbs to infuse the olive, but remember they are whole and you have to watch out for the pits.

For a punch of briny goodness, we keep a few ingredients on hand: **capers**, which add bite to fava Santorini (page 61) and beef soutzoukakia (page 270), are the unopened flower buds of a prickly bush native to the Mediterranean, which are then plucked, dried, and cured with salt or pickled in brine. Brined capers are cheaper and great for everyday use. But for a treat, splurge on the salt-cured ones, which have a hint of a floral aroma and better texture. Make sure to rinse the salt-cured ones before using. Long, thin whole green **pickled peppers** are the classic accompaniment to kebabs and grilled meats; they also add a hit of acid to salads, and are just as good eaten right out of the jar.

Sun-dried tomatoes preserve the intense flavor of ripe summer tomatoes, a long-held tradition in the Mediterranean. In Turkey, that means sun-drying plum tomatoes so that even in the dull winter months of tasteless produce you can add rich tomato flavor to your soups and sauces. The best versions have the texture of a good dried apricot and a balance of sweetness and acidity that makes them hard to stop snacking on. At Zaytinya, we use **Turkish sun-dried tomatoes** to create a rich, flavorful sauce (page 74) used on pide, blending grated fresh tomatoes with hydrated, chopped sun-dried ones. These vacuum-packed, dried tomatoes add an intensity that you will not find in any canned or jarred sauce.

"PRESERVING THE INTENSE FLAVOR OF RIPE SUMMER TOMATOES IS A LONG-HELD TRADITON IN THE MEDITERRANEAN."

Unless you are friends with a winemaker or grape grower, don't bother to make your **grape leaves**. A jar of leaves works just fine—plus you don't need to precook them to get them nice and soft. All you do is rinse them in hot water, drain, and you're ready to stuff and roll! A sixteen-ounce jar will give you enough to make our dolmades recipe (page 154).

Flaky pastries and desserts may be the first thing that springs to mind when you think about nuts in the Eastern Mediterranean. And yes, these sweets laden with honey and pistachios are a signature of the region. But nuts are not reserved just for desserts. You'll find **pine nuts** in Kibbeh (page 257) and dolmas, **walnuts** in a red-pepper muhammara dip (page 57), **pistachios** in salads, and **almonds** in pilaf. Be sure to toast them before using them (see: A Toast to Good Taste, page 23) and store nuts in airtight containers in your refrigerator to extend their shelf life.

SWEETENERS

Using honey is like traveling the world. You can taste the flavor of local flowers and herbs and see how they change from season to season. In Greece, we found Attiki **thyme flower honey** with an herbaceous, minty flavor, and that's become our go-to honey. Another way to add floral notes and a touch of sweetness to a dish is with **orange blossom water**, which is easily found online or in Middle Eastern grocery stores. It's made by steaming the flower petals and then condensing the steam into an intense liquid in a copper still. But use these distillates carefully! Their flavor is meant to be subtle. My rule: If a dish tastes like orange blossom water, you used too much!

There is no fruit more beautiful than a pomegranate. The ruby seeds look like gems and it's obvious, even to people like me who never studied art history, why they have long been seen as a symbol of fertility. I love scooping out pomegranate seeds to garnish salads or rice. But for a hit of sweet-and-sour flavor, nothing beats a bottle of **pomegranate molasses**. This thick, tangy syrup is made by boiling the juices of sour pomegranates. Think of it as tamarind meets balsamic glaze, and use it in salad dressings, drizzled on meat, or over ice cream! Pomegranate molasses is available in Middle Eastern groceries and

some large supermarkets. (It may also be called grenadine molasses.) There's no reason to splurge on a fancy brand. The main idea is to choose one without added sugars; you don't want to lose the tartness you are seeking. **Unsweetened pomegranate juice** is also a favorite at our bar. The color is irresistible, and you're in control of the sweetness of your cocktail, like in our refreshing Pom-Fili (page 335), made with red wine, vodka, and pomegranate juice.

A TOAST TO GOOD TASTE

It makes sense that nuts and seeds add extra flavor and crunch to a dish. But if you're not toasting them first, you're only getting half their value. Toasting nuts takes away any raw green flavor and brings their natural oils to the surface, which makes them nuttier (or seedier), and crunchier. It takes minutes and you (almost) can't screw it up.

Here are the rules:
For small nuts and seeds (and spices!), put a small, dry sauté pan on the stove top over medium-low heat. Add the seeds or nuts so they rest in a single layer and occasionally stir or shake the pan.

Of course, it wouldn't be a real Mediterranean pantry without **tahini**, that silky, bittersweet paste made from toasted ground sesame seeds. Sesame is a uniquely drought-tolerant crop, which is just one reason why the people of the Levant have been making tahini for centuries. It's easy to find tahini in most American grocery stores today, and the best tahini is made with nothing more than 100 percent premium sesame seeds.

They are ready when they are golden and aromatic: usually 2 minutes for whole spices, 3 to 4 minutes for sesame seeds, and 5 minutes for pine nuts. But remember, it can take just seconds to screw them up. The tricky part is that small nuts and seeds go from underdone to burnt in a flash. So as soon as you start to smell them, keep your eyes on the stove. (If they burn, you have to start again.)

For bigger, meatier nuts like pistachios, walnuts, and almonds, the oven is a better bet. Preheat the oven to 300°F. Spread the nuts out across a rimmed baking sheet and roast until just fragrant, 4 to 5 minutes for slivered almonds, 7 to 8 minutes for pistachios, 8 to 10 minutes for whole almonds, and 10 to 12 minutes for walnuts.

OLIVE OIL

Olive oil might as well run through the pipes of Zaytinya! It's the life and soul of so many of our favorite recipes, and even the name of the restaurant is derived from the Turkish word for olive oil, "zeytinyağı." When it comes to using olive oil from the Eastern Mediterranean, Greek olive oil is usually easy to find, but try exploring bottles from Turkey and Lebanon as well. We like to use **extra-virgin olive oil** from Crete, made from the Koroneiki olive, which has a fruity, herbaceous flavor. Organic extra-virgin olive oil from Turkey, made with Memecik olives, is also a favorite for its grassy, green-almond flavor.

* See **RESOURCES** (page 341) to find some of our favorite producers and shops for many of these ingredients.

HELP IN THE KITCHEN

One of the perks of being a chef is having a team to support you. At Zaytinya, our cooks arrive early to slice and dice and grind ingredients fresh. At home, you need your own team: a set of tools that will help things come together quickly and easily.

Many of our favorite tools are found in many home kitchens these days. But there are a few, especially for grinding spices and making delicate doughs, that you might consider adding to your collection as you cook your way through this book.

IMMERSION BLENDER

You'll find this power-packed magic wand in every single one of my restaurants, and a couple more in my home kitchen. Lightweight, portable, and quick to clean, an immersion blender is the easiest way to emulsify oil and dressings or puree a pot of vegetables.

FOOD PROCESSOR

This kitchen workhorse can combine ingredients in a few quick pulses or create an ultra-smooth puree, making it your best friend as you prepare many of the spreads and sauces of Zaytinya.

STAND MIXER, WITH ATTACHMENTS

If you like to bake, you probably already have a stand mixer. If you don't, and want to make pita bread or phyllo, it's a worthwhile investment. Why? Well, a stand mixer can do more than mix. We use its meat grinder attachment to run through our chickpea mixture for falafel and to grind beef for kibbeh nayeh. The pasta-rolling attachment can help in stretching out sheets of phyllo.

SPICE GRINDERS

I love to crush spices. You'll find a mortar and pestle on my kitchen counter, just like in many kitchens in my native Spain. I actuallyhave several types at home, including a Mexican molcajete and a Thai mortar that I use to smash herbs and spices and make salsas and pesto. If you don't have one, don't worry! For many spice blends in this book, you can also grind up toasted spices and seeds in a spice grinder—or a well-rinsed coffee grinder.

MICROPLANE

If you buy one tool on this list, make it a Microplane! Every kitchen needs one for grating garlic, zesting citrus, or creating an airy mountain of hard cheese.

SPRAY BOTTLES AND SQUEEZE BOTTLES

Inexpensive spray and squeeze bottles got some bad press in the 1990s, with every chef putting dots of this or that on a plate. But give them a chance and you'll see how useful they can be! We use spray bottles to evenly cover phyllo with a film of olive oil and squeeze bottles to drizzle our herbaceous mint oil (page 31) around grilled fish. Just remember to give them a good wash in hot, soapy water.

KITCHEN SCALE

We've worked to keep ingredient measurements as straightforward as possible, sticking mostly to cups and tablespoons. (Because, let's face it, it is not a tragedy if you end up with a bit more carrot or tomato in a dish.) But for some recipes—particularly breads and desserts—being precise is essential. You'll see we give measurements in weights in those recipes. A digital kitchen scale lets you measure to the gram, and they are both affordable and small enough to tuck away in a kitchen drawer. Once you get one, you won't know how you ever lived without it.

RECIPES: SPICES, PICKLES, AND CONDIMENTS

Okay, people. Let me be clear: Condiments deserve our respect! Yes, they are often used to dress up a plate, but they are not just for show. They are an integral part of a dish, the drizzle or sprinkle or crunch that takes a plate from good to great!

Many of these condiments, pickles, and spice blends show up in recipes throughout the book. So it's not a bad idea to make more than you need. I also highly recommend that you experiment with them! Use baharat on roast potatoes or green mint oil on grilled fish or finely chop some preserved lemons and stir them into a pot of lentils. Sometimes the little things make all the difference.

LEBANESE SEVEN SPICE

The only rule for making a seven-spice mix is to include at least seven spices; the proportions are up to you. We've tried countless versions, but our hands-down favorite is this one from the great Lebanese cook Anissa Helou. (Pssst. Pass it on.)

Makes ¼ cup

1 tablespoon finely ground black pepper • 1 tablespoon ground allspice • 1 tablespoon ground cinnamon • 1 teaspoon ground nutmeg • 1 teaspoon ground coriander seeds • 1 teaspoon ground cloves • 1 teaspoon ground ginger

○ Mix all of the spices in a small bowl until well combined. Store in an airtight container, preferably in a dark, cool spot, for up to 2 months.

GOLDEN BAHARAT

The Arabic word "baharat" translates simply to "spices." This aromatic mix has a golden hue from the turmeric and a hit of heat from Aleppo pepper. It's designed to season meats, but it's so good we also use it in rice dishes, even to flavor candied walnuts (page 38).

Makes ¼ cup

1 tablespoon Aleppo pepper • 2 teaspoons ground turmeric • ¼ teaspoon ground ginger • ¼ teaspoon ground clove • ¼ teaspoon ground nutmeg • 2 tablespoons cumin seeds • ¼ teaspoon fenugreek seeds • ¼ teaspoon whole allspice • 2 whole cardamom pods

○ Put the Aleppo pepper, turmeric, ginger, clove, and nutmeg in a small mixing bowl.

○ Lightly toast the cumin, fenugreek, allspice, and cardamom in a dry sauté pan over medium heat until fragrant, about 2 minutes. Transfer the toasted spices to a spice grinder and finely grind, then stir into the bowl with the other spices. Store for up to a month.

SUMAC ROSE SPICE

With tiny pink petals scattered throughout, this blend (*left*) is almost too pretty to eat. But not quite! A classic flavoring of Persian cuisine that spread across the Middle East, rose petals are often found in desserts and spice mixes from Morocco to Turkey to India. We love what our friend and chef Lior Lev Sercarz does with rose petals and aromatics at his La Boîte spice shop; it inspired us to create our own mixture. I for one cannot resist this combination of sweet, tart, and spicy.

Makes about ½ cup

2 tablespoons pink peppercorns • ¼ cup rose petals • 3 tablespoons sumac • 1 teaspoon coarsely ground cumin • 2 teaspoons Urfa pepper • 1 tablespoon sesame seeds, toasted

○ Grind peppercorns in a spice grinder or food processor until finely ground. Add the rose petals and pulse to crush them into very small pieces. Transfer the pepper and rose petals to a mixing bowl and add the sumac, cumin, Urfa pepper, and sesame seeds. Stir together until well combined and store in an airtight container for up to 3 weeks.

HAWAYEJ

This Yemeni spice mix is traditionally used to season soups, but it's not the only way to put it to good use. Our version is the dominant flavor in our Golden Spice Cauliflower (page 192).

Makes about ⅓ cup

2 tablespoons ground cumin • 2½ teaspoons ground cardamom • 1½ tablespoons ground turmeric • 1½ teaspoons ground coriander • 2 teaspoons ground black pepper

○ Stir together all of the spices, then store in an airtight container for up to 6 months.

MUSHROOM GARLIC SALT

At first, this seasoned salt may seem like a lot of effort. But I promise you, once you get a taste of its savory umami, you'll want to put it on everything from lamb and pork to simple scrambled eggs. At Zaytinya, it makes our Mushroom Flatbread (page 138) even more mushroomy. It's also the not-so-secret seasoning on our famous fries.

Makes 1 cup

½ pound medium cremini mushrooms, cleaned

¾ cup kosher salt

1 teaspoon canola oil

4 garlic cloves, peeled

○ Separate the mushroom stems from the caps and thinly slice the stems. Cut the caps into ¼-inch wedges. Lay the mushrooms in one layer in a large, dry sauté pan and sprinkle with some of the salt. Set the pan over medium-low heat and allow the mushrooms to cook, slowly releasing their liquid and simmering in the pan. Stir the mushrooms so they don't stick to the pan and continue to cook until the mushrooms are soft and the pan is nearly dry, about 5 minutes.

○ Push the mushrooms to the edge of one side of the pan and carefully wipe off any remaining liquid in the pan with a paper towel. Increase the heat to medium-high and add the oil. Once the oil is sizzling, spread the mushrooms back across the hot pan and sear them until nicely browned, about 7 minutes. Transfer the mushrooms to a paper towel-lined plate to drain and cool.

○ Preheat the oven to 250°F. Combine the mushrooms, garlic, and remaining salt in a small food processor and blend until the texture is similar to coarse sand. Spread the mixture out on a parchment-lined baking sheet and bake for 2 hours, or until totally dry and brittle. Wipe the bowl of the food processor completely clean.

○ Let the mushroom mixture cool, then transfer to the food processor again, breaking up any large pieces that have formed, and pulse until the mixture's texture resembles that of kosher salt.

○ Store at room temperature in an airtight container for up to 3 months.

GARLIC CONFIT

Slowly cooking garlic in olive oil may be the best trick in the history of mankind. It takes away all the garlic's bite and amps up its natural sweetness. A tub of this in your fridge is a culinary secret weapon. We like to mash a clove or two into yogurt for a quick sauce. Just be sure to keep the oil and garlic cloves stored separately in your refrigerator.

Makes ½ cup garlic cloves and 1 cup garlic oil

2 heads garlic, separated into cloves, peeled, ends trimmed

1 cup olive oil, plus more if needed

○ Combine the garlic and oil in a small pot, making sure to fully submerge the cloves in the oil. Warm slowly over medium heat, until the oil begins to barely simmer. Reduce heat to low and cook until the garlic is very soft and lightly browned, about 1 hour.

○ Strain the garlic, reserving the oil for other uses (such as Harissa Chili Crisp, page 30). Put the garlic in a container, cover, and refrigerate. Refrigerate the oil in a separate container.

○ The garlic and garlic oil may be refrigerated for up to 2 weeks.

CHEF MOVE Garlic cloves can also be slow-roasted in a 250°F oven. Put the garlic in a small baking dish, cover with oil, and roast until tender, about 45 minutes.

HARISSA CHILI CRISP

Chili crisp is the condiment of the moment, so it didn't take long for us to invent our own Turkish take on this spicy, crunchy Chinese condiment with Aleppo chilis, crispy onions, garlic, and spices. Spoon over çilbir eggs (page 174) or Grilled Lamb Chops (page 250).

Makes 1 cup

½ teaspoon cumin seeds

1 teaspoon coriander seeds

¼ teaspoon caraway seeds

¾ cup Garlic Confit oil (page 29)

¾ teaspoon kosher salt

1 teaspoon smoked sweet paprika

1 teaspoon Aleppo pepper

¼ cup sesame seeds, toasted

½ cup store-bought crispy fried onions, chopped

○ Set a medium frying pan over medium-low heat. Add the cumin, coriander, and caraway seeds and cook, stirring occasionally, until they are fragrant and lightly toasted, about 2 minutes. Transfer the seeds to a spice grinder or mortar and pestle and grind into a powder.

○ Put the garlic oil in a small mixing bowl and allow it to warm to room temperature. Add the toasted spices, salt, paprika, and Aleppo pepper and briskly whisk to combine. Then stir in the sesame seeds and fried onions.

○ Transfer the mixture to a container and cover with a tight-fitting lid until ready to use. Keep refrigerated for up to a week. Bring to room temperature before using.

GREEN MINT OIL

Oh my god. I love this oil! Its color is astonishing and the intensity of the flavor is electric. This, my friends, will up your cooking game. Two notes: Do not skip the blanching of the mint; mint oxidizes quickly and if it does, you will not get that deep green you are looking for. Store the oil in the refrigerator and pull it out a half hour before you are ready to use.

Makes 1¼ cup oil

1 cup loosely packed fresh mint leaves

1 bunch parsley

¼ teaspoon dried mint

1 cup extra-virgin olive oil

○ Fill a mixing bowl with ice water. Bring a pot of water to a boil, add the fresh mint, and blanch for 20 seconds. Immediately transfer the mint to the ice water and set aside to cool.

○ Put the parsley, blanched mint, and dried mint in a blender. Blend on medium speed and, with the motor running, drizzle in the oil. The herbs should puree and the mixture emulsify. Increase the speed to high and continue to blend for 2 more minutes, until

you begin to see steam rise and the emulsion begins to break, with the green oil separating from the herbs.

○ Pour the herbed oil into a mixing bowl set in a large bowl of ice so that it cools quickly. Once it has cooled, about 5 minutes, strain the oil through a coffee filter. (Note: This may take several hours.) Discard the herb pulp and transfer the oil to a sealed container. Refrigerate for up to a week.

SUMAC ONIONS

Sumac is ubiquitous in Turkish cuisine, adding color and a bright acidity. No wonder it's a key ingredient in this colorful, raw onion salad that pairs perfectly with grilled meats and kebabs (page 247). Many cooks will use red onions for this dish, but use a sweet variety of onions, such as Vidalia or Maui, for best results.

❀❀❀❀❀❀❀❀❀❀❀❀❀❀❀❀

Makes 2 cups

1 large sweet onion, quartered lengthwise and thinly sliced • 1 tablespoon red wine vinegar • 1 tablespoon sumac • Pinch ground allspice • 1 tablespoon finely chopped parsley leaves • 2 tablespoons extra-virgin olive oil • Kosher salt

○ Put the onions in a mixing bowl, sprinkle with vinegar, sumac, allspice, and parsley and drizzle with the olive oil. Toss well and season with salt.

○ The onions can be kept covered and refrigerated for 1 week.

PICKLED RED ONIONS

Why do pickled cucumbers get all the love? It's not fair, so I am taking up the case of the pickled onion (*right*) an underappreciated pickle that adds bite and, here, a gorgeous ruby color to our Greek Mixed Lettuce Salad (page 99) or alongside Octopus Santorini (page 219). Hint: To get an even deeper red shade, add a few slices of raw red beets to the pot with the vinegar.

❀❀❀❀❀❀❀❀❀❀❀❀❀❀❀❀

Makes 1½ cups

¼ cup red wine vinegar • 1 tablespoon kosher salt • 1 tablespoon granulated sugar • ½ small red beet, peeled and sliced (optional) • 1 medium red onion, quartered lengthwise and thinly sliced

○ Combine the vinegar, salt, sugar, beet slices (if using), and 1 cup of water in a medium saucepan over medium-high heat. Bring to a boil, stirring occasionally to dissolve the salt and sugar.

○ Put the onions in a heatproof container or jars, packing them tightly. Once the liquid comes to a boil, strain through a fine-mesh sieve and discard the beet slices. Pour the hot liquid over the onions, making sure to completely cover. Let it sit at room temperature for an hour, then, for best results, cover and refrigerate overnight.

○ The onions can be kept covered and refrigerated for at least 1 week.

FOR PICKLED ANISE ONIONS:
Start by using a yellow onion and substitute white wine vinegar for the red wine vinegar and add a star anise instead of beets. Follow the remaining steps. These onions are a perfect accompaniment to Pastirma with Apricots (page 261).

PRESERVED LEMONS

Preserved lemons are a staple of Eastern Mediterranean and North African cooking. You can buy them, of course, but I like the floral notes that come from adding verbena and orange blossom water to the brine, plus an extra golden hue from a touch of turmeric. These beauties add zing to braised artichokes (page 183) and Golden Spice Cauliflower (page 192); they also add a little acid and salt to shakshouka (page 168). Before you start, find a quart-size jar and see how many lemons you can tightly pack inside. You may want to wear plastic gloves when salting the lemons as the turmeric can stain your hands.

**Makes 5 to 6
preserved lemons**

5 to 6 lemons

½ cup kosher salt, or more as needed

1 teaspoon ground turmeric

4 to 5 lemon verbena leaves, bay leaves, or sprigs of lemon thyme

½ teaspoon orange blossom water

¼ to ½ cup fresh lemon juice (from 2 to 3 lemons), or more as needed

Extra-virgin olive oil

○ Clean and sterilize a quart-size glass jar. Rinse the lemons in warm water, gently scrubbing them to remove any waxy coating. Pat dry, then roll them on a cutting board, pressing down with the palm of your hand to soften and break up the membranes.

○ Stir the salt and turmeric together in a small bowl.

○ Carefully cut the lemons lengthwise in quarters without cutting all the way through to the end—you want to keep the lemons connected at one end. Holding a lemon over the salt mixture (you should put gloves on for this), pack in about a tablespoon of the turmeric salt, pushing the salt into the creases of the lemon quarters. Repeat with the remaining lemons, layering the lemons and herbs into the glass jar as you go. Press down on the lemons as you add them; they should fit tightly and will shrink later.

○ Press down on the lemons again to make sure they are tightly packed. Add the orange blossom water, lemon juice, and any salt and lemon juice that accumulated in the bowl to barely cover the lemons.

○ Seal the jar tightly with a lid, set on a plate (to catch any spills), and let sit for twenty-four hours at room temperature. The lemons should release enough juice to be completely covered in liquid. If not, add a bit more lemon juice, then pour a thin layer of olive oil on top to create a seal. Tightly close the jar again and let the lemons cure at room temperature for 4 to 6 weeks, or until the lemon peels are quite soft. Store in the refrigerator for up to a year.

CARDAMOM APRICOTS

We try not to pick favorites at the restaurant, but these syrupy apricots are up there as one of our best inventions. The apricots give a bright juiciness to dishes like Crispy Fried Eggplant (page 197) and pastirma (page 261), but they will also blow your mind in desserts. Even better, after steeping the apricots, preferably overnight, you can reduce the liquid over medium heat and use it to flavor sodas or cocktails or drizzle it over ice cream. Honestly, it's not a bad idea to double the recipe. That way, like me, you can snack on some while you're cooking, eat a few more from the cheese board before dinner, and still have some left over to serve with yogurt for breakfast.

❀ ❀ ❀ ❀ ❀ ❀ ❀ ❀ ❀ ❀ ❀ ❀ ❀ ❀ ❀ ❀

Makes 1 cup apricots, plus syrup

1½ teaspoons whole green cardamom pods • 1 cup dried apricots • 1 cup granulated sugar • 1 cup fresh lemon juice (from 5 to 6 lemons) • 1½ teaspoons turmeric • Kosher salt

○ Toast the cardamom pods over medium heat in a 2-quart saucepan for a few minutes, until fragrant.

○ Turn off the heat and tip the cardamom into a mortar and pestle; crack the pods, then pound to crush the seeds. (If you don't have a mortar and pestle, wrap the pods in a clean towel and use the handle of a wooden spoon to crush the pods on a cutting board.)

○ Return the seeds and shell fragments to the pot, add the apricots, sugar, lemon juice, turmeric, and a pinch of salt, and cover with 4 cups of water. Bring to just a gentle simmer over medium-high heat, then reduce heat to maintain a low simmer, cover, and cook for 10 minutes, until the apricots are soft but not mushy. Allow the apricots to cool in the liquid in the pot, then transfer the apricots and liquid to a container, cover, and refrigerate for at least a few hours before using.

○ Refrigerate the apricots in enough liquid to cover them and store for up to 2 weeks.

TURMERIC PICKLED VEGETABLES

Pickling vegetables is a simple way to preserve the season's bounty. But pickles play an essential role in a mezze spread, providing contrast and crunch and brightness to the feast of creamy spreads and cheeses. We serve these sunshine-yellow pickles with Hommus with Spiced Lamb (page 51) and with our selection of cheeses and cured meats.

❀ ❀ ❀ ❀ ❀ ❀ ❀ ❀ ❀ ❀ ❀ ❀ ❀ ❀ ❀ ❀

Makes 2 ½ cups

1 medium carrot, peeled and sliced (about ½ cup) • 1 celery stalk, trimmed and sliced (about ½ cup) • ½ small sweet onion, sliced (about ½ cup) • 1 cup small cauliflower florets • 1 cup white wine vinegar • 2 tablespoons sugar • 2 tablespoons salt • ¾ teaspoon ground turmeric • 2 tablespoons golden raisins

○ Put the carrots, celery, onions, and cauliflower in a large glass jar (or evenly distribute among small jars or heatproof containers). The vegetables should be packed in tightly.

○ Combine the vinegar, sugar, salt, and turmeric with 2 cups of water in a small pot and bring to a boil over medium-high heat. Stir to dissolve the sugar and salt. Pour the hot pickling liquid over the vegetables until they are completely covered, using a spoon to push all the vegetables under.

○ Let the vegetables come to room temperature and pickle for at least 1 hour. When ready to serve, garnish with golden raisins.

○ For best results, cover tightly and refrigerate overnight. The vegetables can be kept refrigerated for 1 week.

FOR SUMMER PICKLED VEGETABLES:
In warm-weather months, we like to mix up the vegetables. Instead of carrots, celery, and cauliflower, try sliced cucumbers, sweet Vidalia onions, and yellow and red bell peppers. Then follow the steps above.

OVEN-ROASTED CHERRY TOMATOES

While we can't get the intensely flavored tomatoes from the Greek island of Santorini here in the U.S., we like to give cherry tomatoes a boost of flavor by doing a low-and-slow roast in the oven. Peeling the skin off a tomato gives you the velvety texture and smooth bite we want in these recipes. A quick blanching in hot water makes it super easy. Blanching works for all sizes of tomatoes: just score the round bottoms of larger tomatoes with a sharp knife and cut a small circle around the stem end to remove the core.

Makes 24 tomatoes

24 grape or cherry tomatoes • Pinch of kosher salt • Pinch of sugar • 1 tablespoon extra-virgin olive oil, plus more for storing

○ Preheat the oven to 200°F.

○ Bring a pot of water to a boil. Add the tomatoes for just a few seconds—5 seconds for cherry tomatoes, or up to 30 seconds for large heirloom or beefsteak tomatoes—then remove and immediately transfer to an ice bath. As the tomatoes cool, their skins loosen and slip right off. (Remove the peel from larger tomatoes with a knife in sections.)

○ Toss the cherry tomatoes with salt, sugar, and olive oil in a mixing bowl. Transfer to a rimmed baking sheet lined with parchment paper. Slow roast the tomatoes until they start to shrivel, about 1 hour and 15 minutes, then let cool.

○ Use immediately or transfer tomatoes to a container with a lid. Drizzle with just enough olive oil to cover and store in refrigerator for up to 2 weeks. Bring to room temperature before using.

CYPRIOT OLIVE MIX

You can marinate olives with almost anything—citrus peel, garlic, rosemary, bay leaves—and they'll turn out delicious. We serve a traditional Cypriot olive mix where the dominant note is coriander seed. If you can't find cracked green olives from Greece, look for large, firm, green olives to give a meaty texture to the mix.

❀ ❀ ❀ ❀ ❀ ❀ ❀ ❀ ❀ ❀ ❀ ❀ ❀ ❀ ❀ ❀ ❀ ❀

Makes 3 cups

2 tablespoons coriander seeds • 1 cup Kalamata olives • 1 cup oil-cured Thassos olives, or other black oil-cured olive • 1 cup large cracked green olives, preferably from Greece • 2 teaspoons Aleppo pepper • ¼ cup extra-virgin olive oil • 1 small lemon

○ Lightly toast the coriander seeds in a dry sauté pan over medium heat until fragrant, about 1 minute. Tip onto a cutting board, let cool slightly, then cover with a dish towel and use a rolling pin or the side of a chef's knife to coarsely crack the seeds.

○ Combine the olives, coriander seeds, Aleppo pepper, and olive oil in a mixing bowl. Zest the lemon over the bowl, then stir well. Reserve the rest of the lemon for another use.

○ Transfer the olive mix to a container, cover, and keep refrigerated for up to 2 weeks. Allow the olives to come to room temperature before serving.

SPICED SMOKED WALNUTS

Spiced nuts are great. Smoked nuts are great. Nuts that are spiced *and* smoked are out of this world! Eat them as a snack or serve them, like we do, as part of a mezze spread.

❀ ❀ ❀ ❀ ❀ ❀ ❀ ❀ ❀ ❀ ❀ ❀ ❀ ❀ ❀ ❀ ❀ ❀

Makes 2 cups

2 cups walnut halves • ½ tablespoon extra-virgin olive oil • 1 teaspoon fine sea salt • ½ teaspoon Lebanese Seven Spice (page 27)

○ Smoke the walnuts by following manufacturer's instructions for a stove-top smoker or outdoor smoker. (For an alternate technique for stove-top smoking, see page 205.)

○ Preheat the oven to 300°F. Spread the smoked walnuts on a baking sheet and warm for 10 minutes. (If not smoking the walnuts first, roast them at 350°F for 8 to 10 minutes, or until lightly toasted and fragrant.)

○ Transfer to a bowl and toss with olive oil, salt, and spice mixture. Store the nuts, covered, at room temperature and use within 3 days.

CANDIED WALNUTS

These sweet treats add crunch to creamy Circassian Chicken Salad (page 108). Or try crumbling them over our Walnut Ice Cream (page 325). Keep a splatter screen nearby as these syrup-soaked nuts can bubble and pop when they hit the hot oil.

❀ ❀ ❀ ❀ ❀ ❀ ❀ ❀ ❀ ❀ ❀ ❀ ❀ ❀ ❀ ❀ ❀ ❀

Makes 1 cup

2 cups sugar • 1 cup walnut halves • Canola oil • 1 teaspoon Golden Baharat (page 27) • 1 teaspoon fine sea salt

○ Combine the sugar and 2 cups of water in a medium pot and bring to a boil over medium-high heat. Add the walnuts and boil for 5 minutes, then remove with a slotted spoon or mesh spider and spread them out on a cooling rack set in a parchment-lined baking sheet. (Reserve the syrup for another use.)

○ Meanwhile, warm 2 to 3 cups of canola oil in a medium pot until it reaches 350°F. Quickly fry the sugared walnuts, a few at a time, in the hot oil until nicely browned, about 1 minute.

○ Transfer the fried walnuts back to the cooling rack and immediately sprinkle with Golden Baharat and fine sea salt. Be sure to spread the walnuts apart on the cooling rack so they won't stick together.

○ Keep the candied walnuts at room temperature, sealed in a storage container, for up to 2 weeks.

02

SPREADS,
SAUCES
&
CHEESE

If you ask my friend Dany Abi-Najm about his hommus, he'll tell you, "It's simple, but not easy." With just a few ingredients—lemon juice, chickpeas, tahini, garlic—there's no way to cut corners without compromising flavor, and everything has an important role to play. "We squeeze all of our lemons, we soak our chickpeas overnight with a bit of baking soda, we peel our garlic every day, and we cook our chickpeas slowly," he says with pride. The hommus that Dany's family has been serving for more than forty years at their restaurant Lebanese Taverna has a strong lemon flavor, more than what you might find at your local grocery store, and that, my friends, is just how I like it! It makes sense, I guess, since it was Dany's family who taught me and my cooks how to make and master this most essential dish of Lebanon.

When my partners and I first began to dream of Zaytinya's menu, a celebration of mezze from the eastern side of the Mediterranean, our friends the Abi-Najm family opened their doors and welcomed my team into their kitchen at Lebanese Taverna, willing to show us the techniques and traditions of their native cuisine. In this moment, my eyes were opened to the generous spirit and legendary hospitality of the Lebanese people. I would come to know it well in the decades that followed.

Standing shoulder to shoulder in the kitchen in those very early days, we took the beauty of burnt eggplant and its silky center, and with the help of garlic and tahini, transformed it into batch after batch of baba ghannouge until we got the flavors just right. We crushed walnuts and red peppers and swirled them with sweet pomegranate molasses to make muhammara. We studied their techniques of whipping garlic into a creamy emulsion to make toum, not unlike the allioli of Spain that I love so much. We learned how a simple bowl of labneh drizzled with olive oil and served with warm, steaming pita bread could be so welcoming and comforting.

It's no surprise that Dany and his sisters, Gladys and Grace, and brothers, Dory and David, have such a passion for sharing the food of their home country. It runs in their family; their grandfather, Tabeet Abi-Aad, was a chef who helped create one of Lebanon's first cookbooks, *Rayess' Art of Lebanese Cooking*, published in 1966 in Beirut with Chef George Rayess of the city's Hotel Bristol. But it was the courage of Dany's parents, Marie and Tanios (known to everyone as Tony), that put the family on the path to becoming celebrated restaurateurs and champions

of Mediterranean cooking in America. In 1976, Tony and Marie boarded a cargo ship with their five young children to escape the civil war in Lebanon. They made their way to Arlington, Virginia, right outside Washington, D.C., where some of Tony's family had already settled. For years, the family worked in restaurants, either cooking like Tony and Marie or busing tables like teenagers Dory and Dany, and in 1979, they were able to open their first restaurant, Lebanese Taverna. Decades later, with a business built around family and community, sharing authentic mezze and Lebanese traditions, they have more than twelve locations.

In recent years, I've traveled with Dany back to Beirut. He joined our World Central Kitchen team in 2020 after the massive explosion in the port in Beirut, helping guide us through the city and connecting us with local family and friends as we worked to set up kitchens to provide meals to those affected by the blast. Then a few years later we were able to visit again, this time exploring the city and coastal towns with my wife, Patricia; Dany's wife, Jenifer; and my good friend Aline Kamakian of Beirut's Mayrig restaurant. Breakfasts included fried eggs and bowls of hommus at the legendary El Soussi (*top left*) in West Beirut, while lunches of manousheh were devoured standing on the street corner at Abu Shadi in the Ras Beirut neighborhood or sitting at seaside tables filled with fried fish in Batroun (*far left*). A special surprise was the chance to see my old friend, Dany's father, Tony (*bottom left*, with his son Dany) who had retired to Lebanon years ago and was now living near the beautiful town of Byblos, considered the oldest port in the world by many. Walking through this ancient town, he reminded us how far we have come, but also how much has stayed the same—the importance of family, of friends, and of making lasting connections through food.

HOMMUS

Hommus is a true food of the people and the essential mezze spread. It transcends borders and tables from Lebanon to Los Angeles, and while it calls for just a few ingredients, there are a couple of things to keep in mind when making your own. First, you need to plan ahead and let the dried chickpeas soak overnight—canned chickpeas can be great in some dishes, but I would skip them when making hommus. Second, you want to keep your eyes on these chickpeas as they cook, making sure they simmer gently and stirring them occasionally so they cook evenly. The goal is to cook the liquid almost all the way off—you shouldn't be able to strain any liquid when it's done. We like a tart lemon flavor here, just like our friends the Abi-Najm family taught us. "A pop of lemon is the key to the flavor," says Dany Abi-Najm. I couldn't agree more!

Makes about 3 cups

½ teaspoon baking soda, divided

1 cup dried chickpeas

½ cup tahini

½ cup fresh lemon juice (from 2 to 3 lemons), plus more to taste

1 small garlic clove, mashed to a paste

Salt to taste

Smoked sweet paprika, for garnish

Extra-virgin olive oil, for drizzling

○ Dissolve ¼ teaspoon baking soda in 1 cup room-temperature water in a medium mixing bowl, then add the chickpeas and cover with water by 2 inches. Cover and let soak overnight, or for at least 8 hours.

○ The next day, drain and rinse the chickpeas, then put in a medium pot and completely cover with water, leaving only ½ inch (yes, only ½ inch!) of water on top of the chickpeas. Stir in the remaining ¼ teaspoon baking soda and bring the chickpeas to a boil over medium-high heat. Reduce heat to medium or medium-low to maintain a gentle simmer and cook uncovered, stirring occasionally, skimming off any foam and skins from the surface of the water. When done, the chickpeas will be extremely soft and some of their skins shed. The water should be mostly evaporated, with the mixture resembling a thick porridge. This will take an hour or two, depending on the chickpeas' freshness (older beans take longer to cook).

○ Remove from the heat and let cool, then chill in the refrigerator until cold. The cooked mixture will firm up as the pectin in the chickpeas sets.

○ Reserve a few whole chickpeas to be used for garnish, then put the rest (with their thick cooking liquid) in a food processor with the tahini, lemon juice, and garlic. Blend until pureed, about 1 minute, then scrape down the sides. Taste, seasoning with salt and more lemon if needed, then blend for another 30 seconds. The finished hommus should be fluffy and smooth. Blend in a little cold water if it's too thick.

○ To serve, put the hommus in the middle of a serving bowl. Using a large kitchen spoon, push down on the center and slowly turn the bowl while spreading the hommus along the sides of the bowl, to make a large circular well in the center. Sprinkle the paprika in lines along the edge of the bowl. Garnish with the reserved whole cooked chickpeas (or green chickpeas, when in season, as we do at the restaurant) and a generous drizzle of olive oil.

○ Cover any remaining hommus and refrigerate for up to a week.

BUTTERNUT HOMMUS

There seem to be endless variations on hommus these days, from what gets pureed to what goes on top. I love this version, a take on a classic Lebanese dish of pumpkin with tahini. We make ours with butternut squash—a perfect fall ingredient that's a little easier to cook with. We also look for kabocha, honeynut, acorn, or whatever seasonal squash happens to be at the farmers' market in our neighborhood. With no chickpeas in this dish, maybe this is not technically "hommus," which is Arabic for chickpea, but with its rich creamy flavor from the tahini, I love it all the same. We elevate this dish by garnishing it with za'atar, pepitas (a variety of pumpkin seeds), and intensely nutty pumpkin seed oil. Our photographer, Thomas Schauer, will tell you that the best pumpkin seed oil comes from his native Austria . . . I agree!

Makes about 3 ½ cups

1 small butternut squash, (1½ to 2 pounds)

Kosher salt

½ cup plus 1 teaspoon extra-virgin olive oil

¼ cup tahini

¼ cup pumpkin seeds (pepitas), roasted and salted

2 tablespoons za'atar

1 to 2 teaspoons pumpkin seed oil

○ Preheat the oven to 400°F. Split the butternut squash in half lengthwise. Scoop out and reserve the seeds for another use. Season the squash with salt and rub the cut surfaces with 1 teaspoon of the olive oil. Place the squash cut side up in a roasting pan, then pour ½ cup water into the pan and roast until tender, 45 minutes to 1 hour. Allow to cool.

○ Once cool enough to handle, scoop out the squash flesh and put into the bowl of a food processor. Add ½ cup olive oil and the tahini. Process until you have a nice, fluffy puree, stopping to scrape down the sides as necessary. Add cold water if needed to get the right consistency, then taste and adjust salt to your liking.

○ To serve, spread the puree in a serving bowl. Sprinkle with the crispy pumpkin seeds, and za'atar, and drizzle with pumpkin seed oil.

○ Cover any remaining hommus and refrigerate for up to a week; bring to room temperature before serving.

HOMMUS WITH SPICED LAMB
HOMMUS MA LAHM

This dish, Lebanese comfort food at its very best, is a lesson in layering flavors; combining velvety spiced meat with creamy hommus, then punching it up with pickles, fresh mint, and crunchy toasted pine nuts. A warm hommus dish may surprise you, but you will be fighting over every last bite. Be sure to allow the spread to come to room temperature before adding the spiced lamb mixture. Serve with pita bread so you can scoop up all the saucy meat. Look for tips on toasting nuts and seeds on page 23.

Serves 4 to 6

1 teaspoon extra-virgin olive oil, plus more for drizzling

½ pound ground lamb

1 tablespoon tomato paste

1 teaspoon flour

½ teaspoon freshly ground black pepper

½ teaspoon ground allspice

½ teaspoon ground cumin

1 cup Chicken Stock (page 113)

Salt to taste

3 cups Hommus (page 46), at room temperature

½ cup Turmeric Pickled Vegetables (page 36)

2 tablespoons pine nuts, toasted

3 tablespoons chopped fresh mint leaves

1 teaspoon sesame seeds, toasted

○ Warm the olive oil in a medium sauté pan over medium-high heat, until it shimmers. Add the ground lamb (it will spatter!) and cook, stirring often and breaking up the lamb with your spatula, until well browned, 4 to 5 minutes.

○ Scrape the lamb into a bowl and reduce the heat to medium-low. Add the tomato paste, spread it around the pan, and cook until a nice crust forms, about 2 minutes. Sprinkle in the flour and lightly toast, about 1 minute, then stir in the spices and cook until fragrant, about 30 seconds more. Add half of the chicken stock and scrape the bottom of the pan. All of the browned bits that come up are the secret to deep flavor.

○ Cook while stirring until the stock thickens and is more or less smooth, then add the browned lamb and stir in the remaining chicken stock. Increase the heat as needed to maintain a simmer and cook until you have a thick rich lamb sauce, about 5 minutes. Season to taste with salt. Reduce the heat to low and cover to keep warm.

○ To serve, spread the hommus in a large, wide, shallow bowl. Spoon the lamb into the center and add the pickled vegetables. Top with the pine nuts, mint leaves, sesame seeds, and a drizzle of olive oil.

○ Cover any leftovers and refrigerate for up to 3 days.

TZATZIKI

Tzatziki is one of those dishes that really shows just how much Turkish, Lebanese, and Greek cuisines have in common. In Turkey, you'll see a thinner, lighter version known as cacik; in Lebanon, a similar dish is called laban wa khayar. Like ezme (page 64), tzatziki is extremely flexible. You can eat it as a dressing on lamb and beef gyros, as a dip for warm pita, or make a salad out of a version loaded with seasonal vegetables (page 105). For me, tzatziki is best when it's thick and creamy, so we use a combination of yogurt and labneh. Salting and draining the cucumber will also help get rid of extra moisture that can turn your mixture watery. We use tzatziki as a way to play with the best produce of the season: try tender English peas or nutty white asparagus in the spring, corn in the summer, apples in the fall, and celery root in the winter.

Makes about 2½ cups

1 English cucumber, peeled, seeded, and finely diced

1 teaspoon kosher salt, plus more to taste

2 cloves Garlic Confit (page 29)

¾ cup Greek yogurt

¾ cup labneh

¼ cup extra-virgin olive oil, plus more for drizzling

2 tablespoons minced fresh mint

2 tablespoons minced fresh dill

Freshly ground white pepper to taste

○ Season the cucumber with a teaspoon of salt and let sit for 1 hour. Wring out the cucumbers in a clean dish towel to remove excess liquid.

○ Put the garlic into a medium bowl and smash into a paste with a fork or the back of a wooden spoon. Whisk in the yogurt and labneh, then slowly drizzle in the olive oil while continuing to whisk. Fold in the cucumbers and herbs, then season to taste with salt and white pepper.

○ Spoon into a serving dish and garnish with a drizzle of oil.

○ Cover any remaining tzatziki and refrigerate for up to a week.

FOR SPRING PEA TZATZIKI:
Instead of cucumbers, add ½ cup of fresh English peas (or frozen peas) to a pot of heavily salted boiling water and cook until soft and tender, 2 to 5 minutes. Roughly chop 10 sugar snap peas, add them to the boiling water, and cook for 1 more minute. Drain the vegetables, then chill them in an ice bath. Once cool, drain them again very well and add to the garlic-yogurt mixture, along with the dill and mint, then season to taste with salt and white pepper. Spoon the tzatziki into a serving

dish and garnish with 2 tablespoons of roasted pistachios, ½ cup pea tendrils, and a drizzle of olive oil.

FOR WHITE ASPARAGUS TZATZIKI:
Trim and peel 1 bunch of white asparagus and add to a pot of heavily salted boiling water. Remember, salt is the secret to balancing the natural bitterness of asparagus, especially white asparagus. Blanch the asparagus until tender but firm, about 2 minutes depending on the thickness of the asparagus. Drain and transfer to an ice bath until cold, then remove the asparagus and dry on a clean kitchen towel. Dice the asparagus into ¼-inch pieces, reserving a few of the asparagus tips. Add the asparagus to the garlic-yogurt mixture along with the mint and dill, then season to taste with salt and white pepper. Spoon the tzatziki into a serving dish, garnish with the asparagus tips, and drizzle with olive oil. You can also combine green and white asparagus for this variation.

BABA GHANNOUGE

Walking into Zaytinya's kitchen in the mornings, you're hit with the sweet and smoky scent of eggplants burning over flames. Charring eggplants is serious business when you are making batches of baba ghannouge to feed hundreds of people. We roast eggplant until they are completely blackened, when the flesh inside has softened and taken on a deep, smoky flavor. With simple recipes like this, it's always important to use the best available products—fresh garlic, good olive oil, and tahini. When shopping for eggplant, look for Holland or Italian eggplants, which tend to be a little smaller, sweeter, and have fewer seeds than the larger globe (American) ones, but either will work fine as long as you roast them till they are charcoal black. If it makes you nervous to cook them them over a flame in your kitchen, you can roast them in your oven under the broiler or outside on your grill, just be sure to turn them to get black all over and soft inside.

Makes about 2½ cups

2 to 3 small eggplants (about 1⅔ pounds pounds)

½ teaspoon extra-virgin olive oil, plus more for drizzling

½ cup tahini

1 teaspoon minced garlic

1 teaspoon kosher salt, plus more to taste

3 tablespoons fresh lemon juice, plus more to taste

1 tablespoon chopped fresh parsley

1 tablespoon pomegranate seeds

○ Rinse and dry the eggplant, then lightly brush with the oil. Set the eggplant directly on the grate of a gas burner set to medium heat. Cook the eggplant for 20 to 30 minutes, turning with tongs about every 5 minutes. When done, the skin should be charred, black, and flaky, the flesh collapsing and easily pierced with a sharp knife. (Be sure to turn your vents on to keep your kitchen from getting smoky). Transfer the eggplant to a cooling rack set over a baking sheet to cool and drain.

○ When the eggplant is cool enough to handle, slice it in half lengthwise and scoop the flesh onto the cooling rack so it continues to drain, then put into a food processor with the tahini, garlic, salt, and lemon juice. Process until smooth, light, and airy, 1 to 2 minutes. Taste and adjust the salt and lemon as needed.

○ Spread about 1½ cups eggplant mixture into a serving bowl and garnish with parsley, pomegranate seeds, and a drizzle of olive oil.

○ Cover any remaining baba ghannouge and refrigerate for up to a week.

ROASTED PEPPER AND WALNUT SPREAD
MUHAMMARA

Delicious and addictive, this vibrant red spread pulls on my Catalan heart with a combination of roasted peppers and walnuts, not all that different from the almond-and-pepper romesco sauce of my native Spain. With smoky spice from Aleppo pepper, this dish is often associated with Syria, but it's also claimed by Lebanon and Turkey, where the dish is made with the very similar Marash pepper. The result is a beautiful, border-transcending balance of sweet, sour, savory, salty, and bitter. Serve as a dip, or with grilled vegetables or chicken.

Makes about 1 cup

3 large red bell peppers, cored, seeded, and sliced

1 teaspoon granulated sugar

Kosher salt

1 teaspoon canola oil

1 cup walnut halves and pieces

¼ teaspoon Aleppo pepper

1 teaspoon ground cumin

1 tablespoon fresh lemon juice

1½ tablespoons pomegranate molasses

2 tablespoons extra-virgin olive oil

○ Preheat the oven to 350°F and line a rimmed baking sheet with parchment paper.

○ Toss the peppers, sugar, 1 teaspoon of salt, and canola oil together on the baking sheet, then roast for 20 minutes, until sizzling around the edges.

○ Keeping the oven at 350°F, spread the walnuts over the peppers and roast until fragrant and lightly browned, about 7 minutes. Sprinkle the Aleppo pepper and cumin over the roasting peppers and walnuts and continue to cook for 3 more minutes.

○ Transfer the peppers and walnuts to a food processor, add the lemon juice and pomegranate molasses, and puree until smooth. Continue blending and slowly drizzle in the olive oil until the puree becomes emulsified and resembles a creamy sauce that's almost as thick as hommus; add a little water if needed, then season to taste with salt.

○ To serve, spread on a platter and top with grilled chicken or vegetables or spoon into bowls as a dip.

○ Cover any remaining muhammara and refrigerate for up to a week.

CREAMY CAVIAR SPREAD
TARAMOSALATA

My first taste of this light, savory spread, rich in carp roe, did not take place sitting next to the sea in Greece. I was actually in a café in London called the Real Greek, run at that time by chef Theodore Kyriakou. As I traveled to research the kinds of dishes we wanted to create for Zaytinya, a friend brought me to experience what was considered some of the best Greek food outside of Greece. The taramosalata was a revelation . . . I abandoned my pita and dove in with a spoon. I could not get enough of this creamy taste of the sea. Known as a classic Lenten dish in Greece, but equally loved in Turkey, taramosalata gets its smooth texture from pureeing the roe with bread, or sometimes potatoes. We like to make the spread extra light and silky by folding in a bit of whipped cream. You can find jars of high-quality tarama in specialty Mediterranean and Greek markets or online; be sure it's only the roe caviar and not a spread and try to avoid varieties that are bright pink in color, which is a sign of added dyes.

Makes about 2 cups

⅔ cup panko (Japanese bread crumbs)

½ cup whole milk

1¼ tablespoons lemon juice

⅛ teaspoon (or a pinch) freshly ground white pepper

2 tablespoons extra-virgin olive oil, divided

½ cup heavy cream

3½ tablespoons plus 2 teaspoons tarama (carp roe)

Kosher salt

○ Put the bread crumbs in a mixing bowl and stir in the milk, then let soak for 5 minutes. Drain in a fine-mesh sieve, pressing with the back of a spoon to squeeze as much milk out as possible. Pulse in a food processor with the lemon juice and white pepper until evenly blended, then continue pulsing while drizzling in 1 tablespoon of the olive oil. Be careful not to overdo it, as this could make the mixture gluey. Scrape back into the mixing bowl.

○ Whip the heavy cream to stiff peaks using a handheld mixer or whisk. Gently stir the 3½ tablespoons of tarama into the bread mixture, then fold in the whipped cream. Taste and season with salt if needed (it rarely needs salt because the roe can be quite salty).

○ When ready to serve, combine the remaining 2 teaspoons of tarama with ½ tablespoon of the remaining olive oil in a small bowl and stir with the prongs of a fork to break up the roe. Spread the taramosalata in a serving bowl and spoon the roe oil over the top. Drizzle with the remaining ½ tablespoon of olive oil and serve.

○ Cover any remaining taramosalata and refrigerate for up to 3 days.

LEMON-HONEY DRESSING
LADOLEMONO

We use gallons of this lemony dressing (*right*) to flavor many dishes on our menu. It has the power to make a good salad great, though in Greece you'll most often find it as a marinade for chicken or lamb. Mixing it into Greek yogurt (like for our Crispy Brussels Sprouts Afelia—page 186) takes this dressing into sauce territory, or drizzle it over fish for a touch of sweet and sour. Keep a container of it in your refrigerator, to be ready to go at any time, just give it a shake or blend to emulsify it again.

Makes 2 cups

1 cup canola oil • ⅓ cup extra-virgin olive oil • ⅔ cup fresh lemon juice (from 3 to 4 lemons) • 2 tablespoons Greek honey • 1½ teaspoons kosher salt • Freshly ground white pepper

○ Put the oils in a mixing bowl or tall container. Add the lemon juice, honey, salt, and pinch of pepper. Blend the mixture with an immersion blender, or with a handheld mixer on high speed, until emulsified and creamy.

○ Keep refrigerated in an airtight container—a dressing-specific glass bottle is ideal—for about a week. The sauce will separate as it sits; blend again to emulsify.

WHIPPED LABNEH

Traditionally, labneh is yogurt strained through muslin (or cheesecloth) to remove the whey, producing a thick, tart spread. Some even consider it a cheese. I love my labneh to be super thick, so if it looks a little loose, I'll strain it for a few hours before flavoring it with olive oil and salt. You'll be surprised by how many ways you'll use this Lebanese classic, which is just as delicious served with beet salad (page 102) and dolmades (page 154) or as

a simple spread drizzled with olive oil and a generous sprinkle of za'atar. Chef Costa likes to smoke labneh (page 205) to create a more complex flavor. Labneh can now be found in grocery stores nationwide. Isn't that amazing?

Makes about 2 cups

2 cups labneh • ¼ cup extra-virgin olive oil, plus more for drizzling • 1 teaspoon kosher salt • 1 tablespoon za'atar

○ Put the labneh in a large mixing bowl (drain it first in a cheesecloth-lined colander if it looks loose or watery), and add the ¼ cup of olive oil and the salt. Whisk them together until well combined.

○ To serve, spoon about 1 cup of labneh into a shallow bowl, sprinkle with za'atar, and drizzle with olive oil.

○ Cover and refrigerate leftover whipped labneh for up to a week.

YELLOW SPLIT PEA SPREAD
FAVA SANTORINI

I can't get enough of this vibrant yellow spread. I've been known to eat so many spoonfuls of it while cooking that there isn't any left for the plate of grilled octopus. What can I say, it's that good, people! Some years ago, our Greek mentor Aglaia Kremezi asked Chef Costa to help her prepare a meal celebrating the power of frugal Greek cooking at the Oxford Food Symposium in England, an academic gathering for food research. On the menu was, of course, a dish of fava Santorini. This fava is not to be confused with fava beans you find in your grocery's produce section. Instead, these creamy pureed yellow split peas are a modern take on a native variety of split pea from the island of Santorini, a type of grass pea (*Lathyrus sativus*) that was once one of the few grains that could survive the harsh conditions of the rocky Cycladic islands. Today, some

places in Greece are starting to prepare dishes using the traditional split pea, but most often fava Santorini is made with easy-to-find yellow split peas as we do here in the U.S. We serve it as a spread with pickled onions and briny capers, or alongside grilled octopus (page 219) and horta salata (page 93).

Makes about 2½ cups

1 cup dried yellow split peas, rinsed and picked over • ¼ cup minced yellow onion • 2 garlic cloves, minced • ½ teaspoon (or large pinch) saffron • Pinch of cayenne or other chile powder, plus more to taste • Kosher salt • ½ cup fresh lemon juice (from 2 to 3 lemons), plus more to taste • ¼ cup extra-virgin olive oil, plus more to taste

○ Put the split peas in a pot with 3 cups of water. Bring to a simmer over medium-high heat, skimming any froth that rises to the top.

○ Reduce the heat to medium-low, to maintain a gentle simmer, and add the onions, garlic, saffron, cayenne, and 1 teaspoon of salt. Simmer uncovered for about 30 minutes, adding more water if necessary, until the split peas are completely cooked and soft. Drain, reserving the cooking liquid.

○ Pour the still-warm split peas into a food processor. Start processing while drizzling in the lemon juice, 2 tablespoons of the olive oil, and cooking liquid as necessary to achieve a smooth, thick puree. (You can also return the split peas to the pot and use an immersion blender.) Season to taste with salt and additional olive oil, cayenne, and/or lemon juice.

○ Refrigerate for up to a week.

ROASTED RED PEPPER AND FETA SPREAD
HTIPITI

I can't tell you the number of friends and guests who have stopped me in the restaurant, pointed to a plate of our htipiti, ruby red peppers tumbled together with feta, and exclaimed, "I don't know how to say it, but I love it!" Okay people, let me help you: tee-pee-TEE, that's it, simple—and incredibly delicious. It means "beaten" in Greek; traditionally the peppers and cheese were crushed together in a mortar and pestle. What we make at Zaytinya is the opposite of a traditional recipe, which is spicy and very smooth in Greece, while our interpretation is sweet and chunky. We like to serve it by first creating a layer of pureed peppers and feta, then topping it with the chunky mixture and thyme leaves to give you two different textures. If you're short on time, you can skip the puree and dive right into a heaping bowl with pita or lettuce leaves.

Makes about 2 cups

4 medium red bell peppers, halved and seeded

1 teaspoon canola oil

Kosher salt

½ small shallot, minced

½ garlic clove, minced or grated

1 tablespoon red wine vinegar

½ teaspoon freshly ground white pepper

¼ cup extra-virgin olive oil

½ teaspoon chopped fresh thyme, plus more for garnish

2 tablespoons finely diced red onion

3 ounces feta cheese, preferably a block in brine

○ Preheat the oven to 425°F. Line a rimmed baking sheet with parchment paper.

○ Put peppers cut side down on the baking sheet, rub with the oil, season with a pinch of salt, and roast for 10 minutes. Reduce the temperature to 325°F and roast for another 20 to 25 minutes, or until the peppers are very tender and lightly colored around the edges. (Don't let the peppers cook too long and begin to brown; you want to keep the bright red color but be able to easily remove the skins.)

○ Meanwhile, put the shallots, garlic, vinegar, 1 teaspoon of salt, and the white pepper in a mixing bowl and whisk to combine. Continue whisking and add the olive oil in a slow, steady stream, blending until the vinaigrette emulsifies.

○ Once cool enough to handle but still warm, carefully peel away the pepper skins, then dice and add to the vinaigrette. Stir in the thyme and red onions. Break the feta into pieces and, using your fingers, crumble it into the bowl, making sure there are no large chunks. Stir together so the feta is well incorporated, then season to taste with salt. Chill, covered, for at least 15 minutes before serving.

○ To serve, take half of the mixture and puree in a mini food processor until smooth. Spoon the puree into a serving bowl and spread around the bottom of the bowl. Top with the remaining chunky pepper-feta mixture. Garnish with thyme.

○ Cover any remaining htipiti and refrigerate for up to a week.

VEGETABLE EZME SAUCE

Think of ezme, which literally translates to "mashed," as a Turkish meeting between a salsa and a salad. Chef Costa first came across this dish on a trip to Gaziantep, in the southern part of Turkey, near Syria, where you traditionally find it served with kebab and pide. He also brought back an impressive zirh knife (*right*), which he watched cooks use to mince vegetables and meats in shop after shop. Its curved blade rocks back and forth to quickly chop herbs, tomatoes, even lamb. In this dish, we use the juices from the minced vegetables to hydrate sun-dried tomatoes, giving the sauce a unique intensity and sweetness. Look for Turkish sun-dried tomatoes, which are as soft as dried apricots.

You'll notice this recipe makes a good amount (three cups) of ezme, but luckily, it won't take much to use it all up. Try it as a sandwich spread, a dip for potatoes or asparagus, or on grilled sausages and meats.

Makes 3 cups

¼ cup dry-packed sun-dried tomatoes

1 cup chopped seedless cucumber

¾ cup chopped ripe beefsteak tomato

½ cup chopped red onion

¼ cup chopped red bell pepper

½ Fresno chili, seeded and diced (about 1 tablespoon), seeds reserved

1 teaspoon kosher salt, plus more to taste

½ teaspoon dried mint

½ teaspoon Urfa pepper

¼ teaspoon Aleppo pepper

¼ teaspoon smoked sweet paprika

1 teaspoon red wine vinegar

1 teaspoon pomegranate molasses

1½ tablespoons extra-virgin olive oil

○ Working on a large cutting board, mince the sun-dried tomatoes, removing any dried core pieces, and push to one side. Add the chopped cucumbers, tomatoes, onions, bell peppers, and Fresno chili to the same cutting board, piling each vegetable onto the board. Season the chopped vegetables with salt.

○ Using a large kitchen knife, scrape the vegetables together in the center of the cutting board and chop them to combine. Sprinkle with the mint, Urfa pepper, Aleppo pepper, and smoked paprika over the chopped vegetables, and continue to chop the vegetables, mixing in the spices as you go. (You can also add all the vegetables and spices to a food processor and pulse until a chunky, salsa-like sauce forms.)

○ Scrape the chopped vegetables into a mixing bowl, add the vinegar, pomegranate molasses, and olive oil, and stir until well combined. Taste and adjust salt and seasoning as needed, adding more vinegar or pomegranate molasses if you like.

○ Keep the sauce refrigerated in an airtight container for up to a week.

TAHINI SAUCE

Tahini is an essential ingredient of Lebanese cooking. This thick paste made from sesame seeds flavors hommus and baba ghannouge, but it also quickly becomes a sauce with just a few ingredients. This recipe is the perfect companion to Falafel (page 161), either spread on the serving plate or spooned into a pita for a sandwich, and grilled lamb baharat (page 248). Adding very cold water as the sauce purees helps keep it from turning bitter and adds some body to lighten the mixture; you can even add a few ice cubes if you like. Blending in herbs like mint and parsley (see below) makes it an excellent sauce for vegetables and fish.

Makes about 2 cups

⅓ cup fresh lemon juice
(from 1 to 2 lemons)

4 garlic cloves, peeled

2 teaspoons kosher salt,
plus more to taste

¾ teaspoon ground cumin

1 cup tahini

○ Pulse the lemon juice and garlic for 30 seconds in a blender. It should still be chunky. Let the mixture macerate for 10 minutes.

○ Strain the garlic-lemon juice through a fine-mesh sieve, pressing on the garlic with the back of a wooden spoon to release all the juice, then discard the garlic. Pour the juice back into the blender and add the salt, the cumin, and ½ cup of very cold water. Start the blender on low speed and slowly drizzle in the tahini. Turn the blender up to medium speed and drizzle in 2 to 4 tablespoons more of very cold water to create a creamy sauce that can hold a soft peak. Taste and add more salt if you like.

○ Keep the sauce refrigerated in an airtight container for up to a week.

FOR HERBED TAHINI SAUCE:
Put ¼ cup of packed mint leaves, 1 packed cup of parsley leaves, 1 bunch of chives, and ¼ teaspoon of ground cumin in a blender along with ¼ cup of cold water and blend on low. Add 2 cups of tahini sauce (see left), ¼ cup of fresh lemon juice, and a generous pinch of salt, then blend until smooth, adding more water (up to ½ cup) if the sauce is too thick to blend. Season to taste with salt and transfer to a container. This recipe will make about 3½ cups. Refrigerate, covered, for up to a week.

TOUM
WHIPPED GARLIC SAUCE

There's really one main rule for making a very good toum: Use the best garlic you can find. Look for a firm, tightly packed head of garlic. If you see that green sprouts (germ) have started to form in the clove, save those cloves for another use, and only use garlic without them. This classic Lebanese sauce is perfect for nearly everything . . . meat, fish, and vegetables. We always serve it alongside our spicy kebabs and shish taouk, as well as spread on the lavash that wraps our chicken shawarma. When you're making the sauce, chilling the lemon juice and oil, as well as the bowl and the blade of the food processor, helps it emulsify nicely, and so does slowly drizzling in the oil (we prefer canola oil over olive oil for a smoother flavor) and lemon juice. You can keep a jar in the fridge for up to 30 days or so, but know that the garlic flavor will get more and more intense as the days go by—in a week or two, you'll have a super-garlicky sauce!

Makes about 2 cups

½ cup garlic cloves (10 to 15, depending on size), peeled

2¼ teaspoons kosher salt

4 tablespoons fresh lemon juice (from 1 lemon), chilled, divided

2 cups canola oil, chilled

○ Put the garlic into the bowl of a small (3- to 9-cup) food processor, then add the salt and 2 tablespoons of the lemon juice. Pulse to mix. Then, with the motor running, slowly trickle in 1 cup of the oil. Be patient and take your time, or the sauce will not emulsify. A fluffy, light, white paste should start forming within 1 minute; keep slowly drizzling in the oil over the course of about 4 minutes.

○ Turn off the motor, scrape down the sides of the bowl, then turn the motor on again and drizzle in the remaining 2 tablespoons of lemon juice, followed by the remaining 1 cup of oil. The whole process will take 7 to 8 minutes.

○ Scrape into a container and let sit uncovered at room temperature to cool. Keep the sauce refrigerated in an airtight container for up to a month.

HARISSA

It seems everyone is in love with harissa. You see this red chili sauce everywhere. I'm not normally a person who likes a lot of hot chilis; most Spaniards don't, but I keep finding myself reaching for this spicy mix—a classic of North Africa. It adds an intense flavor to rich meats, especially when a cool, creamy labneh is there beside it. While most harissa recipes are loaded with garlic, I like it less pungent and more aromatic with spices. Using a food processor is an easy way to bring this mixture together, but if you have a meat grinder attachment for a stand mixer, you will get a more complex sauce with more texture, I promise. If you want it spicier, keep the seeds in one of the Fresno chilis or add cayenne or pepper flakes to the chilis before grinding them. I like the sweet notes that Spanish piquillo peppers can add to this sauce to balance out the spice; if you can find jarred Greek florina peppers, even better, but you can easily roast large red bell peppers to add instead.

Makes about 2 cups

1 medium carrot, scrubbed and ends trimmed

1½ teaspoons canola oil, divided

Kosher salt

3 medium red bell peppers, cored, seeded, and sliced

2½ teaspoons cumin seeds

2 teaspoons coriander seeds

1½ teaspoons caraway seeds

2 to 3 red Fresno chilis (to taste), stemmed, seeded, and chopped

¼ cup fresh lemon juice (from 1 lemon)

○ Preheat the oven to 425°F.

○ Rub the carrot with ½ teaspoon of the oil, season with salt, and place in a roasting pan. Roast the carrot until completely soft and dark brown, almost black, about 30 minutes. After the carrot has cooked for 15 minutes, toss the peppers with the remaining 1 teaspoon of oil and a pinch of salt, then add the peppers to the roasting pan to cook for the remaining 15 minutes, or until the peppers are completely soft.

○ Meanwhile, warm a small frying pan over low heat. Add the cumin, coriander, and caraway and lightly toast the seeds, stirring occasionally, until they are fragrant, about 2 minutes. Grind the seeds to a powder using a spice grinder or a mortar and pestle.

○ Once cool enough to handle, chop the carrot and put it in a mixing bowl. Add the roasted bell peppers, Fresno chilis, lemon juice, and spice mixture, then pass through a food mill fitted with a medium (3mm) disk or a stand mixer fitted with the meat grinder attachment and the fine meat-grinding plate to make a thick, slightly saucy paste. (You can also pulse in a food processor: pulse the carrots until finely minced, then add the remaining ingredients and pulse to make a paste.) Stir to make sure the harissa is well mixed, then season to taste with salt.

○ Refrigerate in a tightly sealed glass jar for up to 2 weeks.

GARLICKY POTATO SPREAD
SKORDALIA

Greeks have been making skordalia for centuries. Since the earliest days of Greek civilization, "skordo," the word for garlic, has been found in ancient texts. This thick, garlicky spread is beloved across the country and in Greek homes across the world. Many traditional recipes include almonds and bread, like the one Aglaia makes. But as she will tell you, there are as many variations of skordalia as there are cooks. The most important element is that there is always plenty of firm, fresh garlic. We like a simple mash of potato and garlic, but as the seasons change we'll add other vegetables (see below). Skordalia is traditionally paired with fried fish, but we also like to layer it with smoked salmon (page 236).

Makes 3 cups

1 pound russet potatoes, scrubbed

Kosher salt

3 large garlic cloves, peeled

4 tablespoons white wine vinegar

4 tablespoons extra-virgin olive oil

Freshly ground white pepper

○ Put the whole potatoes in a large pot, cover with water by a few inches, season generously with salt, and bring to a boil over medium-high heat. Reduce the heat to medium-low and simmer, uncovered, until tender, about 30 minutes. Drain the potatoes, reserving ½ cup of the cooking liquid, and when slightly cooled, use a kitchen towel to carefully hold the potatoes and peel with a sharp kitchen knife. Pass the warm potatoes through a ricer or food mill into a large mixing bowl or use your preferred potato-mashing method.

○ Grate the garlic using a Microplane or crush with the flat side of a chef's knife, using a pinch of salt to help mash it into a paste. Whisk the garlic and vinegar together in a small bowl, then stir into the potatoes until smooth. Continue stirring and drizzle in the olive oil, adding some of the reserved cooking liquid if needed to make a smooth, silky puree. Season to taste with salt and pepper.

○ Keep the sauce refrigerated in an airtight container for up to a week.

FOR CELERY ROOT SKORDALIA:
Peel and chop a 1-pound celery root (you want 1½ cups chopped celery root). Put the celery root and 1 small russet potato in a pot of salted boiling water and cook until everything is tender, about 20 minutes. Set the potato aside and drain the celery root. Peel the potato once cool enough to handle and put in a food processor. Add the celery root and the garlic-vinegar mixture and puree until well combined, scraping down the sides as needed.

FOR YELLOW SQUASH SKORDALIA:
Wash 2 pounds yellow squash and slice into ½-inch rounds. Sprinkle both sides with salt and place on a parchment-lined rimmed baking sheet. Roast at 300°F until soft, about 15 minutes. Transfer the roasted squash to a food processor along with ¾ cup of canned chickpeas (about 4 ounces). Whisk the garlic with 2 tablespoons of fresh lemon juice instead of vinegar, then whisk in the oil. Add the garlic mixture to the food processor and puree until smooth, scraping down the sides as needed.

SUN-DRIED TOMATO SAUCE

This rich, spreadable sauce (pictured on page 20), packed with intense sun-dried tomato flavor, adds a layer of complexity to buttery baked pide. Turkish pide, or flatbreads, are traditionally made without any sauce, but we think this rich puree helps to not only hold halloumi (page 135) and briami (page 137) in place, but gives a comforting warmth to each bite. This could become your new go-to pizza sauce, or blend it with a little more water and try it on your favorite pasta.

Makes about 3 cups

1½ pounds ripe tomatoes • 8 ounces dry-packed sun-dried tomatoes, preferably Turkish • ¼ teaspoon ground cinnamon • ¼ teaspoon ground allspice • ¾ teaspoon kosher salt • 2 tablespoons extra-virgin olive oil

o Slice the tomatoes in half. Grate the cut side of the tomatoes on the large holes of a flat or box grater set over a medium pot. Discard the skins. Coarsely chop the sun-dried tomatoes, then add to the pot. Add the cinnamon, allspice, and salt and bring to a simmer over medium-low heat, then turn off the heat and let sit for an hour; the sun-dried tomatoes will rehydrate in the tomato juice.

o Drizzle in the olive oil, then puree with an immersion blender until smooth. Depending on the ripeness of the tomatoes, the sauce may be quite thick. Blend in some water, a few tablespoons at a time, if the sauce is like a paste. You want it to be a thick, spreadable sauce.

o Keep the sauce refrigerated in an airtight container for up to a week.

SPICED TOMATO SAUCE

A versatile tomato sauce is an essential ingredient in every kitchen. At Zaytinya, it's no different. Our uniquely spiced sauce (*right*) is a key ingredient in many of our dishes, from vegetables to meats to seafood. The aromatic flavors of this sauce—cinnamon, bay leaf, and dried Greek oregano—are rooted firmly in the Eastern Mediterranean. Combining ripe fresh tomatoes and canned tomatoes will help guarantee a consistent tomato flavor, especially when good ripe tomatoes are harder to find.

Makes about 3 cups

¾ cup extra-virgin olive oil, divided • ½ medium yellow onion, thinly sliced • 2 garlic cloves, thinly sliced • 1 cinnamon stick • 1 bay leaf • 1½ pounds ripe tomatoes, cored and cut in large dice • 1 cup good-quality canned or boxed chopped tomatoes • 1 teaspoon kosher salt • ½ teaspoon freshly ground black pepper • ½ teaspoon dried Greek oregano

o Warm ¼ cup of the olive oil in a large pot set over medium heat, then add the onions and garlic and cook until lightly golden, about 12 minutes. Add the cinnamon stick and bay leaf and continue cooking until aromatic, about 1 minute.

o Stir in the fresh and canned tomatoes, salt, pepper, and oregano and bring to a simmer. Cook over medium heat until reduced by about a quarter, stirring occasionally, about 20 minutes.

o Remove from the heat and take out the cinnamon stick and bay leaf, then use an immersion blender to pulse the sauce while drizzling in the remaining ½ cup of olive oil.

o Keep the sauce refrigerated in an airtight container for up to a week.

FOOD IS ABOUT INTERACTING WITH INGREDIENTS. IF YOU TALK TO THEM, THEY WILL ALWAYS TELL YOU A STORY.

Cheese, like wine (page 330), can tell stories of history, geography, and tradition. I believe that cheese makers are true artists—they share their passion through the cheeses they craft. From the simple milk of the sheep, goats, and cows that graze on hillsides and valleys, cheese makers transform soil, sun, craftsmanship, and love into the true flavor of a place. Tasting your way through a selection of cheeses immediately transports you to a region of the world without leaving your home.

To better understand and celebrate the unique flavors of the Eastern Mediterranean, I love to make a cheese plate with the many beautiful cheeses we can now find from Greece, Turkey, and Cyprus. You are probably familiar with the very famous feta, traditionally made with sheep's-milk cheese in Greece. It's so famous that some consider it to be the cheese mentioned in *The Odyssey*—the cyclops made a simple white cheese in his cave from the milk of his sheep! But there are so many other cheeses in these ancient dairy regions. Most Greek cheeses are made from sheep's or goat's milk, though there are some cow's-milk cheeses being made today. In Greek tavernas, you can get little dishes of cheese and vegetables called pikilia, which means "variety," served alongside ouzo. We serve pikilia at the restaurant: a platter of cheeses with sweet and salty accompaniments, perfect with a drink before or after your meal.

In Turkey, as in Lebanon, cheeses are an essential part of breakfast, convincing me that no matter what time of day, cheese is king! Many of the cheeses made throughout Turkey are salty white cheeses that might make you think of feta, but when you start to taste each one, you will see they each have their own characteristics resulting from an unpredictable combination of factors: the land, the air, the animals, the cheese makers. Some cheeses are unique, like Obruk Tulum, which is made in the Taurus Mountains of southern Turkey. It's aged in caves and wrapped in goat skin (sometimes with the fur still attached!), an incredible expression of the place where it comes from.

Making a great cheese plate is all about variety in flavor and texture. Choose cheeses that give you something creamy, something pungent, something salty. The accompaniments can be just as important: you want sweet, sour, crunchy bits. Be sure to let the cheeses come to room temperature before serving so their flavors can really come through. When planning for a party, big or small, think about serving 3 to 4 cheeses, keeping to about 2 ounces of cheese per person. Look for cheeses from Greece, Turkey, and Cyprus (like the island's renowned halloumi; check out our recipe on page 80) at specialty grocers, at Mediterranean and Middle Eastern markets, and online. Here are some ideas to inspire you.

CHEESES:

LADOTYRI	Traditional Greek sheep's-milk cheese aged in olive oil
VLAHOTIRI	Firm aged sheep's-milk cheese
FETA	Soft and crumbly sheep's- and goat's-milk cheese
İZMIR TULUM	Firm aged sheep's- or goat's-milk cheese from Turkey
OBRUK TULUM	Turkish cheese from the Taurus Mountains, cave-aged wrapped in goat skin
MANOURI	Semisoft fresh cheese made from whey
SHANKLISH	Dried curdled yogurt with herbs
KASSERI	Mild, semi-hard sheep's-milk cheese

ACCOMPANIMENTS:

Smoked walnuts
(page 38)

Turmeric pickled vegetables
(page 36)

Cypriot olive mix
(page 38)

Chopped olives and sour cherries

Honeycomb

Roasted and candied pistachios

Spiced candied walnuts
(page 38)

Dates and date molasses

Cardamom apricots
(page 36)

Greek spoon sweets: quince, fig, and green walnut

SEARED HALLOUMI WITH CITRUS AND DATES

After feta, halloumi is one of the most popular cheeses from the Eastern Mediterranean. A firm white cheese originating in Cyprus, its texture is similar to that of dry mozzarella, but with a strong, salty flavor, because it has been stored in brine. Serving it alongside sweet citrus and dates helps balance out the saltiness. Halloumi doesn't crumble when sliced, so it's often found grilled or pan-seared. It also melts perfectly on pide (page 135). For this simple dish, we love the slightly pink color and sweet flavor of Cara Cara oranges, but any navel orange can work well.

Serves 2 to 4

1 orange, preferably Cara Cara

1 tablespoon extra-virgin olive oil

4 ounces halloumi cheese, sliced into ½-inch pieces

1 tablespoon pomegranate molasses

2 teaspoons Green Mint Oil (page 31)

3 pitted dates, sliced in ¼-inch rings

2 tablespoons pomegranate seeds

2 tablespoons roasted pistachios

O Cut off the top and bottom of the orange, exposing the flesh. Stand the orange on a cut side and remove the skin using a sharp knife, cutting from the top to the bottom in small strips all around the orange and making sure to remove all the bitter pith. Hold the orange in your hand, over a bowl, and carefully cut down to the center along each membrane to release each segment, dropping the segments into the bowl as you go. Make sure that no membrane remains on the segments.

O Warm the olive oil in a sauté pan over medium-high heat. Pat the halloumi dry with paper towel. Once the oil just begins to smoke, lay the halloumi slices in the pan, working in batches if needed so as not to crowd the pan. Sear on one side, then flip with a spatula to sear the other side and warm the cheese through, about 45 seconds per side. Transfer to a plate lined with a paper towel, and continue with the remaining slices of halloumi until they are all nicely browned. You'll want to serve this immediately after searing, while the cheese is still warm and soft.

O To serve, drizzle pomegranate molasses and Green Mint Oil on a serving plate. Lay the slices of halloumi in the center of the plate and arrange the orange segments, date slices, pomegranate seeds, and pistachios around the cheese.

MANOURI CREAM WITH BEETS AND WALNUTS

Chef Costa came upon the brilliant idea of manouri cream on a visit to Kyma in Atlanta. The celebrated modern Greek restaurant of Chef Pano Karatassos features this savory, fluffy creamed cheese in a roasted beet salad topped with beet sorbet. We've simplified the techniques while celebrating the same flavor combination of creamy, slightly sweet cheese, beets, and walnuts. Manouri may not be easy to find in your grocery store's cheese section, but it's worth seeking out online or in specialty shops. A semisoft, fresh style of sheep's- and goat's-milk cheese made with the whey produced in making feta, manouri is great for sweet and savory dishes, or just sliced and served on a cheese platter with a bit of honey. We like to use smoked beets (page 205) in the restaurant, but roasted beets, or even store-bought vacuum-packed beets, will work fine too.

Serves 2 to 4

Kosher salt

1 small beet

2 tablespoons honey, preferably Greek, divided

½ cup walnut pieces, toasted

8 ounces manouri cheese

¼ cup whole milk

1 tablespoon extra-virgin olive oil

Flaky sea salt

○ Preheat the oven to 350°F and pour a ¼-inch layer of salt in the bottom of a small rimmed baking sheet or roasting pan. Wrap the beet in aluminum foil and place on the salt, then roast for 1 hour, or until the beet is tender and easily pierced with a knife. Once cool enough to handle, gently rub off the skin. Set aside to completely cool, then cut into ¼-inch dice and toss with 1 tablespoon of the honey.

○ Combine the walnuts and remaining tablespoon of honey in a small bowl, and stir together with a pinch of salt.

○ Crumble the manouri into a blender. Warm the milk in a small pot over medium heat until it boils, then pour half the milk into the blender. Blend on the lowest setting to combine the cheese and milk, then drizzle in the remaining milk and continue blending until a thick, smooth cream forms. (You want it to look like whipped cream. Use a handheld immersion blender if your blender is large.)

○ To serve, spoon the manouri cream in large dollops onto a plate. Spoon the beets and walnuts around the cream. Drizzle with the olive oil and season generously with salt.

FRESH GOAT CHEESE SHANKLISH

I love how recipes not only inspire us but connect us across continents. In Lebanon and other parts of the Middle East, shanklish is traditionally made from salted, dried yogurt that is shaped and rolled in herbs, often kept in jars of olive oil, with styles that range from very dry and pungent to slightly soft and creamy. We wanted to bring some of that tradition and technique home with us, but give it a more familiar flavor by combining beautiful fresh local goat cheese with rustic za'atar. Spicing and storing the cheese in olive oil, as has been done for generations, makes it all the more special. Bonus: the oil the cheese steeps in makes a fantastic dressing with the addition of fresh lemon juice.

Makes 16 pieces

8 ounces fresh goat cheese

½ teaspoon kosher salt, plus more to taste

½ to ⅔ cup za'atar

1 cup extra-virgin olive oil

1 lemon

2 sprigs fresh thyme

○ Line a rimmed baking sheet with parchment paper. Mix the goat cheese and salt together in a mixing bowl with a spatula. Take ½-ounce spoonfuls of cheese and, with wet hands, shape the cheese into balls. Set the balls on the baking sheet.

○ Take a ball of cheese and place in a bowl with the za'atar. Toss the za'atar over the ball to completely cover, then place back on the baking sheet. Repeat with remaining cheese balls. Add more za'atar to the bowl if needed. Refrigerate uncovered for at least 8 hours, to let the cheese dry.

○ Once the cheese has dried, pour half of the olive oil into at least a quart-size jar and place several of the balls in a layer on the bottom. Tear the thyme sprigs into 1-inch pieces and tuck them between the cheese pieces. Remove a strip of zest from the lemon and lay over cheese pieces. Continue layering the cheese balls, thyme, strips of lemon zest, and oil until the jar is filled, then cover and refrigerate. The drier the goat cheese is, the longer it will keep, but try to use it within a week.

○ When ready to serve, remove the cheese from the oil and place on a serving plate or in a bowl, then drizzle with some of the oil. Allow the cheese to come to room temperature before serving.

03

SALADS & SOUPS

For centuries, women and men have walked the mountains and valleys of Greece gathering wild greens. Families pass down, from generation to generation, the secrets to knowing what is edible and aromatic and how to find the most flavorful amaranth, chicory, and nettles. With hundreds of varieties of wild plants growing across Greece and its many islands, it's no surprise that horta (which means "grasses" or "wild greens") is a common dish found in local tavernas all over the country. It is a humble dish that tastes of the land.

Foraging wild herbs, roots, fruits, and mushrooms is not unique to Greece, however. Spain, Italy, and many other parts of Europe and the Middle East also have traditions, reaching back centuries, of gathering the earth's goodness found tucked between rocks and bushes. But nowhere does it seem to me that the urge to gather wild greens is more a part of a people's DNA than in Greece. You might call it a national obsession . . . or maybe it's a national sport!

Now, I have been known to walk off a golf course, right in the middle of a game, to search for mushrooms in the surrounding trees. I love to make the pilgrimage across the north of Spain known as the Camino de Santiago (or the "Way of Saint James") with my family, and my wife, Patricia, often has to shout out to find me, as I wander far off the trail to find wild strawberries, nasturtiums, or wild fennel. So I knew I found a kindred spirit when my friend Aglaia Kremezi told me stories of pulling off on the side of the road to climb a hill with her wonderful husband, Costas, in order to pick wild greens they spotted on the drive to the port of Korissia on their home island of Kea.

Aglaia and Costas, like many Greeks, keep an old knife and a basket in their car for these opportunities, always on the lookout for what might be growing during the rainy winter months through the early spring. These wild greens might be foraged in the mountains or picked as weeds in fields of cultivated crops. Aglaia remembers learning how to tell between poisonous and healthy greens from her grandfather.

It was the mothers of Greece, however, who taught us all which greens to cook simply with olive oil and lemon (page 93), which ones to combine to fill pies (page 147) or omeletas (page 171), and which ones to add to simple salads (page 99), Aglaia explains.

When I last visited Aglaia, meeting in Athens for a few days, it was no surprise that she would lead us to a woman

who had come down from the surrounding hills to sell her harvested greens. Laid out on boxes along a side street not far from Athens Central Market, the greens were easy for Aglaia to identify. There were nettles, chicory, sorrel, and wild arugula, and a few others that I didn't recognize, such as a variety of mallow and vrouves, tender shoots of white mustard. At markets across Greece, Aglaia tells us, farmers will often have piles of the seasonal wild greens they picked growing between the rows of carrots, potatoes, and peppers on their farm.

Finding a variety of greens here in the United States is easy if you know where to look. Start at your farmers' markets and ask what's in season. Look for different colors, textures, and flavors. Along with kale, Swiss chard, and arugula, available at most grocery stores today, you can often find an assortment of leafy greens, such as mustard and amaranth, at Asian markets and specialty grocers. I believe in using every part of the vegetable, so try adding turnip and beet greens or carrot tops to your recipes. And don't forget the herbs! At Zaytinya, when putting salads together, we like to think of dill, parsley, and mint as being more like hearty greens than a simple garnish.

LEMONY GREENS SALAD
HORTA SALATA

One of the most common salads found in Greece, horta is simmered greens served at room temperature topped with flavorful olive oil and lemon. Easy-to-find kale will always deliver fantastic flavor when making horta, but spinach, Swiss chard, and escarole also work very well; adjust the cooking time to make sure the greens are tender. Look for other seasonal greens, like nettles, dandelion, purslane, and mustard greens, at your farmers' market and try adding them to the kale or create your own favorite combination. To serve these simply boiled greens, we like to combine color, texture, and flavor by starting with a generous layer of vibrant yellow and creamy fava Santorini and topping with smoky Kalamata olives.

Serves 4 to 6

2 large bunches curly kale

Kosher salt

¼ cup thinly sliced red onion

3 sprigs dill

¼ cup ladolemono (page 60)

1 cup fava Santorini (page 61)

1 to 2 tablespoons salted roasted pistachios, roughly chopped

8 to 10 pitted Kalamata olives, halved and smoked (page 205)

1 tablespoon extra-virgin olive oil

¼ teaspoon lemon zest

¼ teaspoon Aleppo pepper

○ Trim the stems from the kale and discard (or save for another use), and tear the leaves into pieces. Bring a large pot of salted water to a boil and fill a large bowl with ice water. Add the kale to the boiling water and blanch for about 2 minutes. Immediately drain in a colander and transfer kale to the ice water. Once cooled, drain the kale and squeeze out any remaining water with a clean towel.

○ Put the kale and onions in a mixing bowl. Tear the dill into the bowl, discarding the large stems. Add the ladolemono and toss until coated.

○ Use the back of a spoon to spread the fava Santorini on the bottom of a serving dish. Lay the kale on top, then scatter the pistachios and olives over the greens. Drizzle with the olive oil, season to taste with salt, and top with the lemon zest and Aleppo pepper.

FATTOUSH

Without a doubt, this bright, tart, crunchy salad is one
of our most popular dishes; it goes with everything.
The original chopped salad, it comes from a class of dishes
known in the Middle East as "fattat," built using scraps of
old pita bread. It's said to have originated with farmers in
the fields in Lebanon who would fry bits of leftover bread
in olive oil to mix together with whatever vegetables they
had on hand. While many recipes for fattoush will call for
lettuce, like romaine, we prefer loading up on fresh parsley
and mint. Rip off the leaves from a bunch with your hands
and toss over the vegetables. If you have leftover pita bread,
this is a great way to revive it with a quick fry in olive oil.
But store-bought pita chips work just as well.

Serves 4

For the vinaigrette:

1½ tablespoons pomegranate
    molasses

1 tablespoon red wine vinegar

1 teaspoon fresh lemon juice

1 teaspoon sumac

¼ cup extra-virgin
    olive oil

Kosher salt

Freshly ground black pepper

For the salad:

12 cherry tomatoes, halved

1 seedless (English) cucumber,
    peeled and diced

1 green bell pepper, cored,
    seeded, and diced

3 radishes, trimmed
    and thinly sliced

½ medium red onion, diced

½ bunch fresh flat-leaf
    parsley, leaves only,
    torn (about ⅓ cup)

½ bunch mint, leaves only,
    torn (about ⅓ cup)

1 cup broken pita chips

2 tablespoons fresh
    pomegranate seeds

1 teaspoon sumac

Kosher salt

○ Whisk the pomegranate molasses,
vinegar, lemon juice, and sumac
in a small bowl. Stream in the olive oil,
whisking until emulsified. Season to
taste with salt and pepper. You'll have
about ⅓ cup vinaigrette.

○ Put the tomatoes, cucumber,
peppers, radishes, onions, parsley, and
mint in a large mixing bowl, then toss
with enough of the vinaigrette to coat
the vegetables and herbs. Stir in the pita
chips and top with the pomegranate
seeds and sumac. Season to taste with
salt and serve. Refrigerate any leftover
vinaigrette for up to a week.

TABBOULEH

In Beirut, it's not surprising to find tabbouleh on every menu. It is the classic mezze of Lebanon. On a recent trip, my team noticed that everywhere we ate, the tabbouleh served on the table looked different than the place before. Dany Abi-Najm (page 42), who was traveling with us, explained that tabbouleh can vary from town to town and from house to house. You'll find varieties loaded with bulgur or cucumbers, or some with no tomatoes or mint. I have to agree with Clifford A. Wright, the great Mediterranean cookbook author, who describes a proper tabbouleh as "a Lebanese herb salad with bulgur, not a bulgur salad with herbs." Freshly chopped parsley and mint, a bright squeeze of lemon, a generous dose of olive oil, and just enough bulgur and tomato to hold it together is a perfect combination.

Serves 4

2 tablespoons fine bulgur

Kosher salt

⅓ cup extra-virgin olive oil, divided

2 bunches flat-leaf parsley, leaves and tender stems only

½ bunch mint, leaves and tender stems only

3 scallions, trimmed and thinly sliced

¼ cup finely diced red onion

1 large ripe tomato, seeded and finely diced

1 lemon

1 teaspoon ground allspice

○ Put the bulgur in a large mixing bowl. Heat ¼ cup of lightly salted water in a microwave for 30 seconds until very hot, then pour over the bulgur. Cover and let the bulgur steam and absorb all the water, about 10 minutes. Stir 1 teaspoon of the olive oil into the bulgur, fluffing it with a fork, then set aside to cool completely. (You can refrigerate for 15 minutes to cool quickly.)

○ Finely chop the parsley and mint leaves and add to the mixing bowl, then add the scallions, onions, and tomatoes. Stir until ingredients are well combined.

○ Zest half the lemon and set it aside, then squeeze 3 tablespoons of juice into a small bowl. Whisk in ¼ cup of the oil, then pour over the salad. Sprinkle the allspice over the salad and season to taste with salt. Continue to toss the salad until the greens are nicely coated in the dressing.

○ To serve, spoon the salad into a large serving bowl. Drizzle with the remaining olive oil, season with a bit more salt, and top with the lemon zest.

WATERMELON AND FETA SALAD
KARPOUZI ME FETA

Ripe summer watermelons are a thing of beauty. All across the Mediterranean they are found on breakfast tables and passed around after a big meal for a simple dessert. Greece is a major exporter of watermelons, with most coming from the Peloponnese, so it's no surprise that in hot months, this sweet-and-savory salad can be found in taverns and restaurants across the region. Try using a mix of watermelons, if you can find yellow or orange seedless varieties at your farmers' market.

Serves 4

1 small seedless watermelon (about 3 pounds), rind removed and cut into 1-inch cubes, or 4 cups pre-cut watermelon pieces • 1 tablespoon fresh lemon juice • 1 teaspoon honey, preferably Greek • ¼ cup extra-virgin olive oil, divided • 6 pitted Kalamata olives, thinly sliced • 8 mint leaves, thinly sliced • 1 scallion, trimmed and thinly sliced • 1 cup red watercress or baby arugula • ½ cup crumbled feta • Flaky sea salt

○ Chill the watermelon in the refrigerator for about 20 minutes. Whisk the lemon juice, honey, and 3 tablespoons of the olive oil in a large salad bowl until emulsified.

○ Add the watermelon, olives, mint, scallions, and watercress and toss well. Scatter the feta over the salad, drizzle with remaining olive oil, and season to taste with sea salt.

GREEK MIXED LETTUCE SALAD
MAROULOSALATA

I like to think of this salad as a garden greens salad, gathering whichever lettuces from my garden are ready to be picked that day and adding lots of fresh herbs. Just as you might with horta, look for an interesting mix of sweet, bitter, and spicy lettuces, and in colors ranging from pale green to dark red. On many Greek menus, you'll find this dish made of shredded romaine and feta, but we like ours as simple greens and herbs tossed with vinaigrette right before you're ready to serve. A salad of greens like this is considered a winter salad in Greece while summer salads are full of ripe tomatoes. We love it all year long and often serve it with salmon or grilled meat for a perfect lunch.

Serves 4

For the dressing: ¼ teaspoon minced (or grated) garlic • 1 teaspoon minced shallot • 1 tablespoon red wine vinegar • Pinch freshly ground white pepper • ½ teaspoon kosher salt • ¼ cup extra-virgin olive oil

For the salad: 1 small head red or green gem lettuce, trimmed, leaves separated and washed • 1 small head red oak lettuce, trimmed, leaves separated and washed • 1 cup baby arugula • ¼ cup chopped fresh chives • ¼ cup chopped fresh dill fronds • ¼ cup fresh parsley leaves • ¼ cup pickled red onion (page 32) • Flaky sea salt

○ Whisk the garlic, shallots, vinegar, pepper, and salt in a small bowl. Slowly drizzle in the oil, whisking until the dressing is emulsified. You'll have about ⅓ cup dressing.

○ Put the lettuce leaves in a large serving bowl. Add the arugula, chives, dill, and parsley. Toss with enough dressing to coat the greens, and continue tossing until the herbs and lettuces are well combined. Garnish with pickled red onions and season with sea salt. Refrigerate any leftover dressing for up to 3 days.

OLIVE, WALNUT, AND TOMATO SALAD

My friend Aline Kamakian is a force of nature. Not only does she have a growing restaurant empire that stretches from her home in Beirut on to Cairo and Riyadh, but she has a line of food products, a digital cooking show, and a cookbook. What is closest to her heart, however, is the humanitarian work she does in Lebanon, working with students and delivering meals to those in need. I first met Aline in 2020, after the port explosion in Beirut. Aline and her team were caught in the path of destruction. Even with significant damage to her restaurant and her own injuries, she jumped into action and helped guide our World Central Kitchen team on the ground. Now any chance I get to visit Beirut she is right there to greet me and ready to explore and eat! On my last trip, after Aline took us all over Beirut in search of great food (and cocktails!), our team spent time at Mayrig, her flagship restaurant that celebrates both her Armenian heritage and her Lebanese home. We ate nearly everything on the menu and could not get enough of her salads, from a Zaatari one loaded with fresh leaves of Mediterranean oregano to a Vospi made of lentils, cilantro, and pomegranate molasses. But the one that stuck with us was her Zeitoun salad. Arabic for olive, this mix is loaded with walnuts, tomatoes, and flavorful olives. Our recipe is inspired by one found in her book *Armenian Cuisine*. For our version, we like to combine meaty Greek Halkidiki green olives with earthy toasted walnuts and sharp, sweet red and gold cherry tomatoes, plus a dab of pepper paste.

Serves 4 to 6

¼ cup diced white onion

Kosher salt

1 pint cherry tomatoes, halved

1 cup chopped walnut halves, toasted

1 cup green Halkidiki or cerignola olives, pitted and quartered

1 teaspoon pepper paste

2 tablespoons pomegranate molasses

2 tablespoons extra-virgin olive oil

¼ cup chopped fresh parsley leaves

○ Put the onions in a mixing bowl, season with salt, and let rest for 10 minutes. Transfer the onions to a paper towel and wring out any juices.

○ Return the onions to the mixing bowl and add the tomatoes, walnuts, and olives, then season again with salt.

○ Add the pepper paste and drizzle the pomegranate molasses and olive oil over the salad. Toss well to combine, then stir in the parsley.

CHEF MOVE

To pit the olives, first place them on a flat work surface. Cut all the way around the outside of the olive, lengthwise, with a sharp knife. Be sure to insert the knife all the way to the pit. Then, using the flat side of a larger kitchen knife, press down on the olive until you feel the pit touching the work surface. Now you can easily pull out the pit, and slice the olives as needed or add them right into your dish.

ROASTED BEET SALAD
PATZAROSALATA

I have a confession to make . . . I am obsessed with beets. I love them in all forms: beet soup, beet gazpacho, salt-roasted beets, even a beet burger, which I serve at my vegetable restaurant, called Beefsteak. I especially like to mix red and gold beets when I can find them. Traveling through the Eastern Mediterranean, I love to see them on mezze menus, usually in cold salads, like in Turkey, where they are grated and tossed with yogurt. In Lebanon, I have seen spreads of shocking magenta–colored beets blended with tahini or mixed with walnuts and pomegranate molasses, similar to the muhammara dip I love so much. Our version of this classic salad gets an extra hit of earthy flavor with a quick smoking of the beets before they are tossed in ladolemono.

Serves 4

Kosher salt

2 medium red beets, trimmed

2 medium golden beets, trimmed

2 clementines

2 tablespoons ladolemono (page 60), divided

5 ounces baby arugula, (about 5 cups)

½ to ¾ cup Whipped Labneh (page 60)

2 tablespoons pomegranate seeds

2 tablespoons chopped roasted pistachios

1 teaspoon sumac

Flaky sea salt

○ Preheat the oven to 350°F and pour a ¼-inch layer of kosher salt in the bottom of a rimmed baking sheet or roasting pan. Wrap each beet in aluminum foil and place on the salt. Roast for 1 to 1½ hours, or until the beets are tender and easily pierced with a knife. Once cool enough to handle, peel the beets by using a paper towel to gently rub off the skin. (Here you can transfer the beets to a stove-top smoker for 30 to 40 minutes, if you like; see page 205.)

○ Peel the clementines and separate into sections. With a clean, dry towel, rub each section to remove as much of the white pith off the membrane as possible. Cut away the white center seam of each segment with a sharp knife or kitchen shears and remove any seeds.

○ Cut the beets into bite-size pieces, keeping the red and golden beets separated, to avoid having the red beets stain the golden beets. Put the red beets in a bowl and toss with 1 tablespoon of the ladolemono, then season to taste with salt. In another bowl, combine the golden beets, clementines, arugula, and remaining 1 tablespoon of ladolemono.

○ When ready to serve, spread 2 to 3 tablespoons of labneh on each of four plates. Add the red beets to the golden beet mixture and gently stir to combine. Divide the beet mixture among the plates. Sprinkle each salad with pomegranate seeds, pistachios, sumac, and a pinch of flaky sea salt.

CHEF MOVE Roasting the beets on a bed of salt, wrapped in aluminum foil, will keep the beets from coming into contact with the hot pan, which can cause the sugars in the beets to burn on the bottoms.

ASPARAGUS SALAD

While we're lucky to find asparagus in grocery stores nearly all year round, to me asparagus remains the sweet and tender start to spring. First, the green asparagus arrives in late February and March, then the thick stalks of white asparagus follow in April. To mark the season in the restaurant, we feature special salads filled with spring vegetables. One of my favorites is this combination of crisp green spears topping a creamy tzatziki loaded with white asparagus and flavored with mint leaves and mint oil. What about purple asparagus? If you find some in your market, try shaving thin strips from a couple of spears and sprinkle over the salad.

Serves 4 to 6

½ bunch medium green asparagus (6 to 10 stalks), woody ends trimmed

Kosher salt

2½ cups white asparagus tzatziki (page 52), with reserved asparagus tips

4 tablespoons ladolemono (page 60), divided

½ cup loosely packed mint leaves

2 tablespoons chopped roasted pistachios

2 tablespoons fresh dill fronds

2 tablespoons Green Mint Oil (page 31)

1 tablespoon lemon zest

○ Cut the green asparagus into 3-inch pieces. Bring a medium pot of salted water to a boil and prepare an ice bath. Blanch the green asparagus for about 1 minute, until tender but firm depending on the thickness of the asparagus, then quickly transfer to an ice bath.

○ Drain the asparagus and combine it with the reserved white asparagus tips (from the tzatziki recipe) in a mixing bowl and toss with 2 tablespoons of the ladolemono and a pinch of salt.

○ To serve, spread the white asparagus tzatziki down the center of a serving platter. Arrange the green and white asparagus pieces and mint leaves on top of the tzatziki and garnish with pistachios and dill. Dot the Green Mint Oil around the plate and drizzle the remaining 2 tablespoons of the ladolemono over the dish. Season with salt and lemon zest.

CITRUS AND OLIVE SALAD
PORTAKAL SALATASI

The combination of citrus, onions, and olives is loved all around the Mediterranean. This take on the classic Turkish orange-and-onion salad has been a favorite winter offering since our earliest days. We add spicy red watercress here, but any peppery greens, such as baby arugula, work well. If you have leftover dressing, keep it refrigerated for up to a week.

Serves 4

For the dressing:

2 tablespoons orange juice

¼ teaspoon orange blossom water

½ tablespoon white wine vinegar

½ teaspoon kosher salt

Pinch freshly ground white pepper

1 teaspoon minced shallot

1 tablespoon canola oil

1½ tablespoons extra-virgin olive oil

For the salad:

2 oranges

1 grapefruit

2 cups red watercress or baby arugula

¼ red onion, thinly sliced (½ cup)

½ bulb fennel, cored and thinly sliced (1 cup)

Kosher salt

½ cup pomegranate seeds

2 tablespoons pine nuts, toasted

8 Kalamata olives, pitted and thinly sliced

½ cup crumbled feta

○ To make the dressing, whisk the orange juice, orange blossom water, vinegar, salt, pepper, and shallots in a medium bowl. Drizzle in the canola and olive oils while whisking, to make a creamy, emulsified dressing. Taste and season with more salt if needed. You'll have about ¼ cup dressing.

○ For the salad, cut the top and bottoms from oranges and grapefruit, exposing the flesh. Stand the fruit cut side down on a cutting board and remove the skin with a sharp knife, slicing from top to bottom all around the fruit to remove it in small strips; make sure to trim away all the white pith. Working over a mixing bowl, hold each fruit in your hand and carefully cut down along each membrane to release the citrus segments into the bowl. Squeeze the remaining membranes over the fruit to release any juices.

○ Add the watercress, red onions, and fennel, then toss with about half of the dressing and season to taste with salt. Arrange the salad on a serving platter or divide among four salad plates, then garnish with pomegranate seeds, pine nuts, olives, and feta. Drizzle with some of the remaining salad dressing, if you like.

CHEF MOVE Get to the beautiful ruby jewels inside a pomegranate with these simple steps. Score the bottom of a pomegranate with a knife, then use your fingers to pry the fruit in half. Use a wooden spoon to tap the back of each half to release the seeds into a bowl. You'll need to do this several times for both halves of the pomegranate. Remove any bits of pith that fall into the bowl with the seeds.

CIRCASSIAN CHICKEN SALAD
ÇERKEZ TAVUĞU

When we began to research the dishes we wanted to create for Zaytinya's menu, we pored over countless cookbooks by renowned experts on cuisines of the region. I came across this dish of chicken, walnuts, and cilantro in an amazing book, *Classic Turkish Cooking*, by the food journalist Ghillie Başan. Ghillie's book was a fascinating look at the ingredients and foods of Turkey. When we saw this unique version of a chicken salad—a classic dish so widely loved here in America, especially for lunch—we had to learn more. In my early travels to Istanbul more than twenty years ago, I was able to find this salad at a restaurant called Fıccın in the Beyoğlu neighborhood. The owner, Leyla Kılıç Karakaynak, and her family have been serving specialties from a region once known as Circassia, in the North Caucasus on the northeastern shore of the Black Sea. When the area was under Ottoman rule, this dish, along with several other Circassian recipes, made its way into the cooking of Turkey. Fresh coriander—or cilantro as we know it—is a telltale sign of these dishes, so be sure to garnish this salad with plenty of fresh leaves. We also like to add a sweet-and-savory crunch by topping the salad with candied walnuts and pickled raisins.

Serves 4 to 6

½ cup panko bread crumbs

1 cup milk

1 cup chopped walnuts

1 small garlic clove, minced

4 tablespoons cilantro leaves, divided

⅛ teaspoon freshly ground black pepper

1 teaspoon kosher salt

4 cups shredded cooked chicken (page 113 or 262)

1 large head sweet gem lettuce, leaves separated

2 tablespoons Candied Walnuts (page 38)

1 tablespoon turmeric pickled raisins (see box)

Flaky sea salt

Extra-virgin olive oil

○ Soak the bread crumbs in milk in a small bowl for 30 minutes.

○ Meanwhile, preheat the oven to 300°F. Spread the walnuts on a baking sheet and lightly toast for about 10 minutes.

○ Put the soaked bread crumbs, toasted walnuts, garlic, 3 tablespoons of the cilantro leaves, black pepper, and ½ teaspoon of kosher salt in a food processor and blend until very smooth. The creamy sauce should be similar to a thin mayonnaise.

○ Put the chicken in a mixing bowl and season to taste with kosher salt. Scrape the bread-walnut sauce into the bowl and toss with the chicken. Cover the bowl and refrigerate for 1 hour.

○ To serve, place the lettuce leaves on a serving platter and spoon the chicken salad over the root side of the lettuce leaves. Garnish with the candied walnuts, raisins, and remaining cilantro leaves. Season with flaky salt and a drizzle of olive oil.

CHEF MOVE To give golden raisins an extra kick, we like to soak them overnight in the liquid from our Turmeric Pickled Vegetables (page 36).

CHICKEN SOUP AVGOLEMONO

One of the most classic Greek sauces, avgolemono, which means simply "egg and lemon," may have had its start in the Sephardic Jewish communities of Spain as agristada, a lemon-and-egg sauce often served with fish. As it traveled with the Sephardic Jews in the 1500s across the Ottoman Empire, it found a forever home in Greece. Avgolemono is a versatile sauce that is served alongside vegetables, stuffed cabbage leaves, fish, and pork. For many of us, however, avgolemono is known as the ultimate chicken soup; some might say it even has healing powers—my daughters swear by it! Carlota, my oldest, loves to top it with a poached egg, breaking it open in the soup and adding even more creamy comfort.

Serves 4

Kosher salt

½ cup orzo pasta

1 bunch kale, stems removed and leaves chopped

4 teaspoons extra-virgin olive oil, divided, plus more for drizzling

1 medium carrot, peeled and sliced

2 celery stalks, trimmed and sliced

½ small yellow onion, diced

3 cups Chicken Stock (page 113)

Zest and 3 tablespoons fresh lemon juice (from 1 lemon), plus more juice as needed

1 large egg

Freshly ground white pepper to taste

2 cups cooked shredded chicken (page 113 or 262)

2 tablespoons dill fronds

Flaky sea salt

O Bring a pot of salted water to a boil. Add the orzo and cook until tender, 8 to 10 minutes. Drain the orzo, reserving the hot cooking liquid, and set aside.

O Return the cooking liquid to the pot, adding more salted water if necessary, and bring to a boil. Meanwhile, fill a large bowl with ice water. Add the kale to the boiling water and blanch for about 2 minutes. Drain and transfer the kale to the ice water. Once cooled, drain again, squeezing out any remaining water from the kale with a clean towel.

O Warm 2 teaspoons of the olive oil in a medium sauté pan over medium-low heat. Add the carrots, celery, and onions and sauté until vegetables begin to soften but not brown, about 3 minutes. Add 2 tablespoons of water, cover the pan, and let the vegetables steam for 3 to 5 minutes, or until the carrots are tender. Remove the pan from the heat and set aside.

O Warm the chicken stock in a medium pot over medium-low heat to just before boiling. You should see wisps of steam coming off the top of the liquid. Whisk the lemon juice and egg together in a medium bowl until well combined and pale in color.

O Slowly ladle about one cup of the hot stock into the egg mixture, a little bit at a time, and continue to whisk until you have a creamy, rich broth.

O Reduce the heat to low and carefully pour the creamy broth back into the stock, constantly whisking to keep the egg from curdling, until all of the stock becomes creamy. Season to taste with salt and pepper. You want the soup to taste like lemon—stir in an additional 1 to 2 teaspoons of lemon juice if needed. Keep the soup warm over low heat; do not let it boil or the egg may begin to clump together.

O When ready to serve, warm the kale, chicken, orzo, and carrot mixture either separately in a microwave, or together in the pan with the carrot mixture. Return the pan to the stove and warm over low heat. Push the carrot mixture to one edge of the pan and add 2 teaspoons of olive oil to the center of the pan. Place the chicken, kale, and orzo in the pan, then cover and allow the ingredients to warm for a few minutes.

O Divide the chicken, orzo, kale, and carrot mixture between bowls and ladle the soup into the bowls. Garnish with dill and lemon zest. Season to taste with flaky sea salt and drizzle with olive oil.

CHICKEN STOCK

I am a soup man. It is a simple fact. My family knows I am happiest when I have pots of flavorful liquid bubbling on my stove. Making stock is never a chore to me, it's a favorite weekend ritual. My restaurants, like most others, begin their day pulling out huge stockpots, filling them with vegetables, bones, or shells, then firing them up to a boil to create these important building blocks for so many dishes. You can use store-bought stock—it's okay, people—but make some for yourself every once and while and keep it in the freezer. The special ingredient in our incredible chicken stock is chickpeas, added to the cooking broth to give extra body and flavor. We don't add salt to this stock, but season it as you like. Also, consider saving the fat you skim off while simmering the stock. It will add great flavor to other dishes, like vegetables or even eggs. And don't worry if the shredded chicken you end up with is a little dry after boiling; just mix some of that reserved fat with a little of this amazing broth and spoon it over the meat, then season with a little salt and add to dishes like our chicken salad (page 108) and chicken soup (page 110). For a fish and shellfish stock, check out our psarosoupa recipe (page 293).

Serves 4

1 whole chicken (about 3 pounds), giblets discarded or reserved for another use

2 pounds chicken wings (or bones from a roast chicken, page 262)

1¼ cups dry chickpeas

1 large yellow onion, peeled and roughly chopped

4 celery stalks, roughly chopped

1 medium carrot, trimmed and roughly chopped

1 small leek, trimmed, cleaned, and roughly chopped

½ bunch fresh thyme

½ bunch fresh parsley

3 garlic cloves, peeled

1 bay leaf

○ Put the chicken, chicken wings (or any bones), and chickpeas in a stock pot. Add 3 to 4 quarts of water to cover the chicken, then bring to a simmer over medium-high heat. Let cook at a strong simmer (nearly a full boil), partially covered, for 1 hour. Skim any fat or foam that rises to the top.

○ Add the onions, celery, carrots, leeks, thyme, parsley, garlic, and bay leaf, reduce the heat to medium-low, and continue to simmer, uncovered, for 2 hours, skimming any foam from the top. The liquid should reduce by half.

○ Remove the chicken from the pot and set aside to cool. Strain the stock and discard the solids. Set the stock aside to cool.

○ Remove all the meat from the chicken and shred for use in other recipes.

○ After the stock has cooled, skim off any remaining fat, transfer to a container, and cover. Keep refrigerated for up to 1 week or freeze for longer storage.

RED LENTIL SOUP
MERCIMEK ÇORBASI

Soups are an important part of life in Turkey. They are the pride and joy of the country, according to Musa Dağdeviren. As a chef and author, he's made it his life's work to honor the culinary traditions of Turkey. At his restaurant, Çiya Sofrasi, in the Kadıköy market in Istanbul, he shares these traditions, including the classic lentil soup mercimek çorbası. Possibly the most popular soup in Turkey, it's served all day long and in every corner of the country. For our version, we add texture with tender French green lentils and wilted spinach as a topping, but if you're short on time, just add some spinach and a pinch of sumac.

Serves 4 to 6

For the soup:

2 tablespoons unsalted butter

1 medium yellow onion, chopped

2 medium carrots, peeled and chopped

2 stalks celery, trimmed and chopped

1 medium leek, trimmed, washed, and chopped

1½ cups red lentils

¼ cup Garlic Confit (page 29)

1 teaspoon ground cumin, plus more as needed to taste

1 sprig thyme

1 bay leaf

4 cups vegetable broth

Kosher salt

Freshly ground white pepper

For the garnish:

⅓ cup French green lentils

1 garlic clove, peeled

1 bay leaf

2 tablespoons extra-virgin olive oil, divided, plus more for drizzling

3 cups baby spinach

½ cup Greek yogurt

1 tablespoon sumac

Flaky sea salt

To make the soup, melt the butter in a medium pot over medium heat. Add the onions, carrots, celery, and leeks and sauté until soft and golden, about 6 minutes. Add the lentils, garlic, cumin, thyme, and bay leaf, stirring until well combined. Continue to sauté, stirring the lentils and vegetables, for about 2 more minutes.

Add the broth and increase the heat to bring to a boil, then reduce heat and gently simmer, partially covered, until lentils are tender, about 20 minutes.

Meanwhile, to make the garnish, put the green lentils, garlic, bay leaf, and 1 tablespoon of the olive oil in a small pot with 2 cups of water. Bring to a boil, then reduce the heat to maintain a simmer. Cook until the lentils are tender, about 15 minutes. Strain the lentils, discarding the garlic and bay leaf.

Once the red lentils are soft, transfer the soup to a blender and puree until very smooth, then strain the soup through a fine-mesh sieve back into the pot. Season to taste with salt and white pepper and cover.

Finish the garnish by warming the last tablespoon of the olive oil in a sauté pan, add the baby spinach, and toss in the oil. As the spinach begins to wilt, add the green lentils and stir to combine and warm the lentils.

To serve, warm the red lentil soup over medium heat. Place a spoonful of yogurt on the side of four to six soup bowls and place a couple tablespoons of the spinach and green lentil mixture in each bowl. Ladle the red lentil soup around the spinach. Sprinkle a pinch of sumac over the yogurt, season the soup, spinach, and lentils with flaky sea salt, and drizzle with olive oil.

CHEF MOVE Be sure to always rinse your lentils and pick through them to make sure there are no pieces of debris or stones.

TOMATO AND TRAHANA SOUP

Trahana is a truly ancient food, made from transforming soured milk and wheat into tiny pebble-like shapes. Originally a way to preserve milk in winter months, this Eastern Mediterranean "pasta," as our friend Aglaia tells us, is a treasured classic not only in Greece but all around the region. In Turkey, it's known as tarhana, and there—like everywhere else—it's traditionally used in soups, especially in the cold winter months and often with a dash of Marash (or Aleppo) pepper. Sometimes it may be found in a breakfast porridge, in the countryside of Lebanon and other parts of the Middle East where it is known as kishk. For our dish, we took inspiration from one of Aglaia's recipes that combines trahana and tomato soup. We've dressed up this hearty soup with oven-roasted cherry tomatoes, feta, chives, and dakos (barley rusks) to give it even more Greek flavor. Be sure to look for sour trahana, which is made with buttermilk or yogurt, when using it in soups. It adds texture and a bit of tartness. Trahana and dakos can be found online and in some specialty grocers.

Serves 4 to 6

1 tablespoon unsalted butter

½ yellow onion, diced

2 garlic cloves, thinly sliced

2 tablespoons tomato paste

3 cups vegetable or chicken stock, plus more if needed

2 pounds ripe tomatoes, blanched, peeled, cored, and chopped

¼ teaspoon ground cinnamon

½ teaspoon dried oregano

Kosher salt

1 cup sour trahana

Ground black pepper

24 Oven-Roasted Cherry Tomatoes (page 37)

4 dakos or pita chips, broken into ¼-inch pieces

½ cup crumbled feta

2 tablespoons minced chives

Extra-virgin olive oil, for drizzling

○ Melt the butter in a 2-quart pot over medium heat, add the onions, and sauté for 2 minutes. Cover the pot and continue to cook, stirring every few minutes, until softened and browned, about 8 minutes. Add the garlic and continue cooking until the garlic becomes aromatic, about 2 minutes, then add the tomato paste, increase heat to high, and cook until a glaze starts to form on the bottom of the pot.

○ Pour in the stock and deglaze the pan. Add the chopped tomatoes and their juices and scrape up all of the browned bits from the bottom of the pan. Then add the cinnamon, oregano, a big pinch of salt, and the trahana. Bring to a simmer over medium-high heat, scrape the bottom to make sure the trahana isn't sticking, then reduce the heat to medium-low and cook, with the pot partly covered, until the trahana is tender, about 15 minutes. (If the soup becomes too thick, like porridge, thin it with a little more stock.)

○ To serve, divide the soup into serving bowls and garnish each with 4 to 6 roasted tomatoes, the dakos or pita chips, feta, chives, and a drizzle of olive oil. Season to taste with salt and pepper.

CHILLED YOGURT SOUP

Yogurt, in all its forms, is an essential element of Eastern Mediterranean cuisine. Soups made of yogurt are a particular comfort food in Turkey, served hot in the winter months and cold in the summers. While those Turkish soups often add rice and maybe saffron, we love this cool garlicky version. Closer in style to the Persian cold soup called abdoog khiar, with flavors of cucumbers, raisins, and rose petals, it makes a perfect canvas for a variety of ingredients. Use the best garnishes for the season: peas in the spring, corn in the summer, and honeycrisp apples in the fall. Okay, I know it's a lot of slicing and dicing just to create the garnish, but that's what makes it so interesting and versatile. We like to add a kick of salty feta flavor to the soup by stirring in some of the brine that blocks of feta are stored in.

Serves 6

For the soup:

½ cup (1 stick) unsalted butter

1 medium yellow onion

2 garlic cloves, peeled

1½ teaspoons kosher salt

1 quart Greek yogurt

2 tablespoons fresh lime juice

¼ cup feta brine (optional)

For the garnish:

¼ cup peeled and diced green apple

¼ cup peeled and diced Persian (small) cucumber

2 tablespoons barberries, soaked (page 186)

2 tablespoons chopped pistachios

2 tablespoons chopped walnuts

2 tablespoons golden raisins

1 to 2 teaspoons extra-virgin olive oil

2 tablespoons dill fronds

1 tablespoon Sumac Rose Spice (page 27)

○ To make the soup, melt the butter in a medium pot over medium heat. Add the onions, garlic, and salt, and cook until translucent, about 5 minutes. Add ¼ cup water and continue to cook, stirring occasionally, until the vegetables are completely soft, about 5 more minutes.

○ Transfer the hot mixture to a blender and add the yogurt, lime juice, and feta brine (if using), then blend until completely smooth.

○ Strain the soup through a fine-mesh sieve, pushing with the back of a spoon to release as much liquid as possible. Chill in the refrigerator for at least 1 hour or until completely cold.

○ To serve, combine the apple, cucumber, barberries, pistachios, walnuts, and raisins in a small bowl and drizzle with a little olive oil. Divide the apple-nut mixture among bowls or cups by making a small pile on one side of each. Pour the chilled soup alongside the mixture. Top with dill and season with Sumac Rose Spice.

CUCUMBER MELON SOUP

This summer soup is easy to play with and a great way to cool off on hot nights. If you like it more herbaceous and less sweet, add more cucumber and less melon, and maybe blend in some basil or parsley leaves. If you like the puree to be creamier, add more of the yogurt to the blender and use less as a garnish. Keep it cold in your refrigerator and serve it up in chilled glasses. We call this dish Cretan Cucumber Soup on our menu due to a garnish of crushed dakos or paximadia, which are traditional barley rusks from Crete. These dense croutons are found in bakeries all over the island and are often topped with chopped fresh tomatoes and feta, but we love the texture and flavor they add to this sweet, creamy soup. Look for them at specialty grocers and online. But don't worry if you can't find them: pita chips also work very well.

Serves 4

1 English cucumber

1 lime

1 honeydew melon (about 5 pounds)

1 bunch fresh mint, leaves only

½ teaspoon dried mint

1 cup plus 2 tablespoons Greek yogurt, divided

½ cup pita chips or dakos, broken into ½-inch pieces

Pinch Aleppo pepper

Flaky sea salt

Extra-virgin olive oil, for drizzling

○ Peel the cucumber, halve lengthwise, and remove any seeds. Finely dice one half of the cucumber and set the other half aside. You want about 1 cup of diced cucumber. Put the diced cucumber in a bowl and zest the lime over the top with a Microplane.

○ Remove the rind from the melon by first cutting off the top and bottom, exposing the flesh. Stand the melon cut side down on a cutting board and remove the rind with a sharp knife, slicing from top to bottom all around the melon to remove it in strips; make sure to trim away all the rind. Halve the melon, scoop out the seeds, and discard. Finely dice 1 cup of the melon and add to the diced cucumber. Set the remaining melon aside.

○ Divide the mint leaves in half. Thinly slice half the leaves and leave the other half whole. Add the sliced mint leaves to the bowl of diced melon and cucumber. Stir to combine, then cover and refrigerate.

○ Chop the remaining melon and cucumber and put into a blender. Add the mint leaves, dried mint, and 2 tablespoons of the Greek yogurt. Juice the zested lime into the blender, then puree until totally smooth, about 3 minutes. Strain the puree through a fine-mesh sieve into a pitcher or container and refrigerate until cold, about 20 minutes.

○ When ready to serve, spoon ¼ cup of Greek yogurt into four serving bowls, then divide the chilled diced cucumber and melon among the bowls. Remove the chilled soup from the refrigerator. Stir the soup briskly if any separation occurred, then pour the chilled soup into each bowl and top with pita chips or dakos. Sprinkle with Aleppo pepper and flaky sea salt, then drizzle with olive oil.

04

BREADS
&
PHYLLO

The great Greek philosopher and mathematician Pythagoras supposedly wrote that the universe begins with bread. Well, I don't know about that—I wasn't there at the very beginning—but I like where Pythagoras's mind was going. Many cultures around the world start their meals with bread: the dinner table is a miniature universe of good food, drink, and company, always starting with a loaf fresh from the oven. Pythagoras was on to something; he obviously understood the important things in life.

At the restaurant, every meal starts with a basket of freshly baked warm pita bread, served with a dish of peppery Greek olive oil and tart pomegranate molasses. To me, it's an amazing way to start eating, and the pitas keep coming once you've finished the first basket— a perfect transition into the dips and other mezze. My team and I originally learned to make our pita from the Abi-Najm family before we opened, and twenty years later we are using the same recipe and methods, producing thousands of pita breads every single day. The ovens go on at ten a.m. and bake till midnight, the team's hands quickly putting in ovals of dough and, three minutes later, pulling out pillows of warm pita, ready for the table.

Through my travels in Turkey I fell in love with another bread, pide, the boat-shaped flatbreads topped with cheese, meat, vegetables, and eggs. We built a domed brick oven in the restaurant's kitchen to get the same fire as ovens in Turkey—baking the crust to a perfectly crispy finish, with cheese bubbling on top. One of the most incredible moments in a meal at Zaytinya is when the Za'atar Pide (page 130) comes to your table, fresh from the oven, with the top covered in cheese and a sprinkling of tangy za'atar— and the crown, a beautiful golden orb of egg yolk. You drag your fork through the yolk, spreading it over the still-hot flatbread so that it becomes a warm, creamy, sunshine-colored sauce for the pide.

We're also proud to make our own phyllo dough in the restaurant, a directive from Aglaia many years ago. It wouldn't be a proper Eastern Mediterranean restaurant without freshly made phyllo, she told us. Luckily for us, one of our first cooks, Abdelrazzaq Hashhoush (more about him on page 257), is not only an excellent chef but a master phyllo maker as well. He learned from his father, who had made pastries at Lebanon's renowned pastry and

confectionary shop Hallab. Abdelrazzaq, who no longer cooks in restaurants, would come early in the mornings, and a team would gather around to watch him. "Your hand is the measuring cup," he would say, "because when you do it in your hands you never forget." Hilda Mazariegos (*above*) was one of those cooks who learned at his side. Today, she is our executive sous chef, and continues to make phyllo two or three times a week with a few helpers, always early in the morning, before anyone else is taking up space in the kitchen. She rolls out each piece on a cornstarch-coated workbench, getting them thinner and thinner, then billowing them in the air like the sail of a ship. It's amazing to watch a master at work. To me, Hilda is the heart of Zaytinya. For more than twenty years she has been the steady hands with a big smile, a guiding spirit that teaches each generation the secrets of the last.

Pythagoras was smart, of course, but I think he may have forgotten something. If the universe begins with bread, there must be someone in the kitchen, turning on the lights, opening a bag of flour, firing up the ovens, and rolling out the dough.

ONE DOUGH THREE WAYS

This is our recipe for a master dough that transforms into pita, pide (page 130), and lahmacun (page 138). Its most recognizable form, no doubt, is the warm, airy pita that welcomes guests to the restaurant. At the start of every meal, a basket of these steamy golden breads arrives at the table with a dipping bowl of olive oil and pomegranate molasses. There are a few keys to getting the dough right for these recipes. First, it's best to weigh your ingredients anytime you're baking—it's more precise and lets you be more consistent. Also, this dough needs to proof in a warm place. Try a microwave oven—place a cup of just boiled water inside with the dough and shut the door to keep the humidity up.

❋✼❋✼❋✼❋✼❋✼❋

**Makes enough dough for
8 pita, 4 pide, or
2 lahmacun**

½ cup + 1 tablespoon
(130 grams) milk

2¼ teaspoons (10 grams)
sugar

1 teaspoon (4 grams)
active dry yeast

½ cup + ½ tablespoon
(125 grams) warm water

4 cups (488 grams)
all-purpose flour

1 teaspoon (6 grams) sea salt

1 tablespoon (12 grams)
extra-virgin olive oil,
plus more for proofing

Semolina flour, for dusting

○ Combine the milk, sugar, yeast, warm water and 1 cup (139 grams) of the all-purpose flour in the bowl of a stand mixer fitted with a dough hook. Briskly stir with a fork until well combined and let sit for 10 minutes.

○ Meanwhile, mix the remaining 3 cups (349 grams) of all-purpose flour with the salt in another bowl.

○ Turn the stand mixer on low (number 2 on the dial) and slowly add the flour mixture, tablespoon by tablespoon. After all the flour is added, continue to mix for 2 more minutes—your dough will be dense and shaggy—then add the tablespoon of olive oil in a slow drizzle. Keep mixing on low for another 5 to 7 minutes, until the dough is smooth and soft, making sure there are no dry spots or loose flour. If after a few minutes the dough isn't coming together, drizzle in 1 to 2 more tablespoons of warm water.

○ Grease the mixer bowl with olive oil, roll the dough in the oil to cover completely, then cover tightly. Put the dough in a warm spot and allow to rise for 2 hours, until doubled in size.

○ After the dough has risen, punch down the dough in the bowl, then turn it out onto a work surface. (Note: See recipes for pide and lahmacun, on the following pages, for using the dough at this point.)

○ Divide the dough in half, then in half again until you have 8 equal portions of dough, each weighing about 3 ounces (95 grams). Roll each piece of dough into a ball, then add a little olive oil to your hands and roll each ball to cover with a thin layer of oil. Cover with a towel and let rest a few minutes to relax the gluten and make the dough easier to roll.

○ Generously dust a baking sheet with the semolina. Roll a ball of dough into an oval 9 inches long and about ⅛ inch thick (there should be enough oil on the dough to prevent sticking). Carefully transfer the pita dough to the baking sheet and cover with a kitchen towel to prevent drying. Repeat with the remaining balls of dough, overlapping them slightly to fit them on the baking sheet, then let rest in a warm spot for 20 minutes.

○ Meanwhile, place a baking stone on the bottom rack in the oven and preheat to 450°F. Working in batches, carefully place the pita on the hot stone and bake until the bread inflates and lightly colors, 3 to 5 minutes. Do not let it brown or the pita will be too crispy. Wrap in a towel to keep it warm while you bake the remaining pita. Serve warm.

ZA'ATAR PIDE

Pide, which shares an ancient root with the word "pita," is Turkey's answer to pizza. It's usually shaped like a boat and topped with cheese or meat, spices, and sometimes an egg. For this pide, we make a simple za'atar oil, which will soften the texture of the herbs and intensify its aroma. You are going to want to use it everywhere, I promise; spoon it over grilled fish or vegetables. We love to top pide with bright yellow egg yolks to add extra creaminess. At the table, break the egg yolk and let it run into the bubbling cheese—very dramatic!

Makes 4 pide

Semolina flour, for dusting

1 batch dough (page 129), divided into 4 balls

¼ cup za'atar oil (see below)

8 ounces kaşar cheese, shredded

4 large eggs

2 tablespoons unsalted butter, melted

1 tablespoon za'atar

Flaky sea salt

○ Generously dust 2 baking sheets with semolina. On a clean work surface, roll a ball of dough into an oval 13 inches long, 8 inches wide, and about ⅛ inch thick (A). Dust the surface and rolling pin with semolina if needed.

○ Fold over ½ inch of the dough all around the oval, then fold again with another ½ inch, pressing down on the folds (B). Shape the ends into pointed tips. Crimp the edges with the handle of a pizza cutter (C) or your fingertips and pinch the folds together.

○ Carefully transfer the pide to the prepared baking sheet and cover with a kitchen towel to prevent drying. Repeat with the remaining dough. Allow the pide to rest in a warm spot for 20 to 30 minutes, until slightly puffed. Preheat the oven to 475°F and place a baking stone in the oven on the bottom rack.

○ When ready to bake, slide one of the rested ovals from the baking sheet to a lightweight cutting board sprinkled with semolina. Prick the dough all over, including the edges, with a fork. Make sure the ends are still pinched and the edges crimped. Sprinkle a quarter (about 2 ounces) of the shredded cheese down the center of the pide. Spoon 1 tablespoon of the za'atar oil over the top (D).

○ Working with one egg at a time, separate the yolk from the white into two small bowls. Briefly beat the egg white to loosen it (not whip it), then pour the egg white down the center of the pide. Set the egg yolk aside.

○ Carefully transfer the pide to the hot baking stone by pinching the ends and sliding the pide onto the stone. Bake until the edges are evenly browned and the cheese is bubbling, about 10 minutes. Depending on the size of your oven and baking stone, you may be able to bake two at a time.

○ Transfer the pide to the cutting board, brush the edges with melted butter, then place the egg yolk in the center of the pide. Using a fork, break up the egg yolk and spread over the pide. (The heat from the pide will slightly cook the yolk.) Sprinkle with za'atar and sea salt, then cut into quarters to serve. Repeat with the remaining ovals.

FOR ZA'ATAR OIL:

Stir ¼ cup za'atar and ¼ teaspoon kosher salt together in a small mixing bowl. Pour ¼ cup of just-boiled water over the za'atar then let hydrate for 15 minutes. Stir in ¼ cup extra-virgin olive oil and let rest for another 15 minutes before using. Makes a generous ½ cup. Cover and refrigerate leftover za'atar oil for up to a week.

SOUJOUK PIDE

It's believed that pide originated along the Black Sea coast, in northern Turkey, where they were topped with spiced ground meat, onions, and peppers. This Soujouk Pide takes a delicious shortcut to intense meaty flavor by using soujouk, a spicy, fatty, and very savory sausage from Turkey, the Balkans, and the Middle East. This pide is one we tasted in Istanbul at the very popular (and sadly now closed) Şimşek Pide, where Chef Costa first tried it on a research trip. It has everything you want in a rich flatbread: sausage, egg, and cheese, and a light brush of butter after baking. Look for soujouk at specialty grocers or Middle Eastern markets, as well as online. You can find it in mild and spicy varieties; just note—be sure to peel off the synthetic coating it is wrapped in before cutting it up. If you like, a spicy chorizo will also work well.

Makes 4

Semolina flour, for dusting

1 batch dough recipe (page 129), divided into 4 balls

8 ounces spicy soujouk sausage, peeled, halved, and cut into ⅛-inch-thick slices

4 ounces kaşar cheese, diced

4 large eggs

2 tablespoons unsalted butter, melted

1 tablespoon minced chives

1 tablespoon sumac

Kosher salt

○ Generously dust 2 baking sheets with semolina. On a clean work surface, roll a ball of dough into an oval 13 inches long, 7 inches wide, and about ⅛ inch thick. Dust the surface and rolling pin with semolina if needed.

○ Fold over ½ inch of the dough all around the oval, then fold again with another ½ inch, pressing down on the folds. Shape the ends into pointed tips. Crimp the edges with the handle of a pizza cutter or your fingertips and pinch the folds together.

○ Carefully transfer the pide to a prepared baking sheet and cover with a kitchen towel to prevent drying. Repeat with the remaining dough. Allow the pide to rest in a warm spot for 20 to 30 minutes, until slightly puffed. Preheat the oven to 475°F and place a baking stone in the oven on the bottom rack.

○ When ready to bake, slide one of the rested pide ovals from the baking sheet to a lightweight cutting board sprinkled with semolina. Prick the dough all over, including the edges, with a fork. Make sure the ends are still pinched and edges crimped. Lay 2 ounces of sliced soujouk (about ¼ cup) and 1 ounce of diced cheese over the pide.

○ Working with one egg at a time, separate the yolk from the white into two small bowls. Briefly beat the egg white to loosen it (not whip it), then pour the egg white down the center of the pide. Set the egg yolk aside.

○ Carefully transfer the pide to the hot baking stone by pinching the ends and sliding the pide onto the stone. Bake until the edges are evenly browned and the cheese is bubbling, about 10 minutes. Depending on the size of your oven and baking stone, you may be able to bake two at a time.

○ Transfer the pide to the cutting board, brush the edges with melted butter, then place the egg yolk in the center of the pide. Using a fork, break up the egg yolk and spread over the pide. (The heat from the pide will slightly cook the yolk.) Sprinkle chives and sumac over each pide, season with a little salt, and cut into quarters to serve. Repeat with the remaining ovals.

HALLOUMI PIDE

The very famous Cypriot cheese, halloumi, makes for a great pide topping. In fact, this was one of my daughters' favorite dishes at the restaurant when they were little. It maybe looks a bit like a traditional Italian pizza, since we use tomato sauce and mozzarella, but the flavors of it, and the satisfying texture of the soft, chewy halloumi, keep it in the world of pide. It's so simple and warming. I know the little ones in your life are going to love it—and I bet you will too!

❋✲❋✲❋✲❋✲❋✲❋✲❋

Makes 4

Semolina flour, for dusting

1 batch dough (page 129), divided into 4 balls

¼ cup sun-dried tomato sauce (page 74)

2 cups shredded mozzarella

4 ounces halloumi cheese, diced

2 tablespoons unsalted butter, melted

1 tablespoon minced chives

Kosher salt

○ Generously dust 2 baking sheets with semolina. On a clean work surface, roll a ball of dough into an oval 13 inches long, 8 inches wide, and about ⅛ inch thick. Dust the surface and rolling pin with semolina if needed.

○ Fold over ½ inch of the dough all around the oval, then fold again with another ½ inch, pressing down on the folds. Shape the ends into pointed tips. Crimp the edges with the handle of a pizza cutter or your fingertips and pinch the folds together.

○ Carefully transfer the pide to a prepared baking sheet and cover with a kitchen towel to prevent drying. Repeat with the remaining dough. Allow the pide to rest in a warm spot for 20 to 30 minutes, until slightly puffed. Preheat the oven to 475°F and place a baking stone in the oven on the bottom rack.

○ When ready to bake, slide one of the rested pide ovals from the baking sheet to a lightweight cutting board sprinkled with semolina. Prick the dough all over, including the edges, with a fork. Make

sure the ends are still pinched and the edges crimped. Spread 1 tablespoon of the tomato sauce over the pide, sprinkle ½ cup of the mozzarella over the sauce, and top with 1 ounce of the diced halloumi.

○ Carefully transfer the pide to the hot baking stone by pinching the ends and sliding the pide onto the stone. Bake until the edges are evenly browned and the cheese is bubbling, about 10 minutes. (The halloumi will soften but may not completely melt.) Depending on the size of your oven and baking stone, you may be able to bake two at a time.

○ Transfer the pide to the cutting board, then brush the edges with melted butter and garnish with chives. Season with a little salt and cut the pide into quarters to serve. Repeat with the remaining ovals.

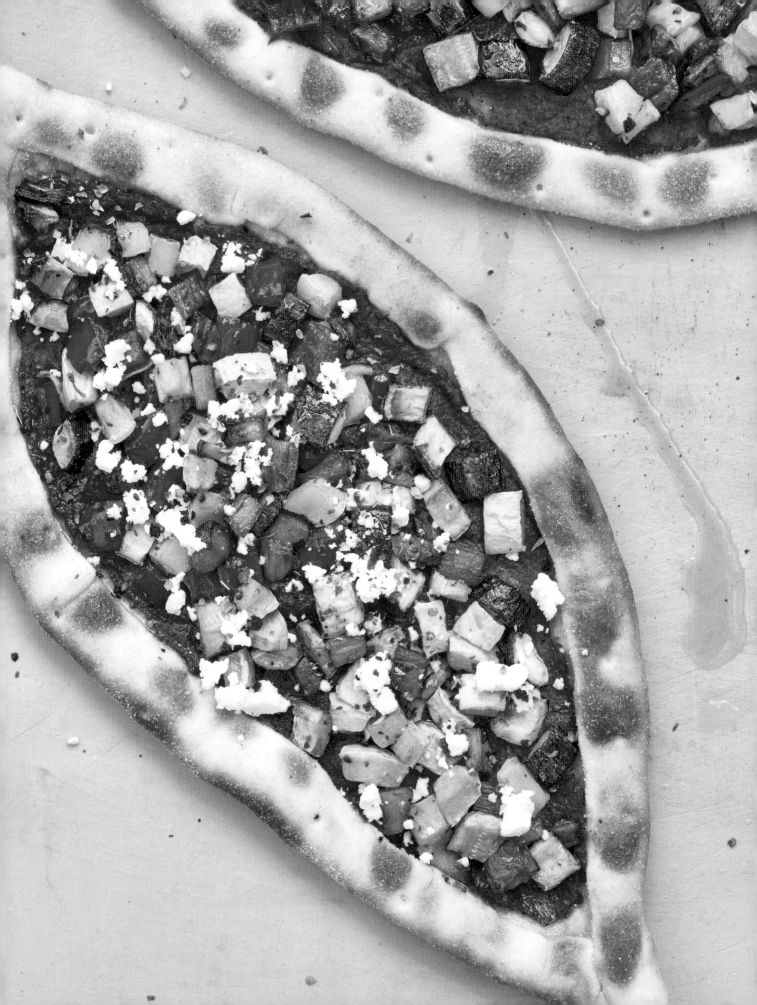

BRIAMI PIDE

"Briami," a Turkish word borrowed by Greek cooks to describe a dish of olive oil–roasted summer vegetables, makes a perfect topping for pide. It's summer at its best; tomatoes, zucchini, eggplants, peppers, and onions, roasted with garlic and spices until they're sweet and aromatic. Just make sure to cut the vegetables to generally the same size so they roast evenly. You'll have more roasted vegetables than you need for the pide, but you can keep them in the refrigerator for a few days and serve as a side dish for meat or fish, or fry an egg and serve it for breakfast.

Makes 4

1 pound ripe tomatoes, blanched, peeled, and diced

1 medium yellow onion, cut in ½-inch dice

1 medium red onion, cut in ½-inch dice

2 medium zucchini, trimmed and cut in ½-inch dice

2 small eggplants (about 1 pound), trimmed and cut in ½-inch dice

2 medium bell peppers, seeded, stemmed, and cut in 1-inch dice

3 garlic cloves, minced

¼ cup extra-virgin olive oil, plus more for drizzling

Kosher salt

1 tablespoon dried oregano

1 teaspoon Aleppo pepper

½ teaspoon ground cumin

½ cup chopped fresh parsley

Semolina flour, for dusting

1 batch dough (page 129), divided into 4 balls

½ cup sun-dried tomato sauce (page 74)

2 tablespoons unsalted butter, melted

½ cup crumbled feta

○ Preheat the oven to 400°F.

○ Put the tomatoes, onions, zucchini, eggplants, peppers, and garlic in a 9-by-13-inch baking dish. Add the olive oil, 2 teaspoons of salt, oregano, Aleppo pepper, cumin, and parsley and toss well with your fingers. Spread the vegetables into an even layer, drizzle with ¼ cup of water, then press down to pack tightly. Roast for 30 minutes.

○ Remove vegetables from the oven and stir to mix in the juices and vegetables that have started to brown on top. Roast for another 30 minutes and stir again, and if needed, roast for another 15 to 20 minutes, or until the vegetables are completely soft and have begun to caramelize. Remove from the oven and let cool completely.

○ Generously dust two baking sheets with semolina. On a clean work surface, roll a ball of dough into an oval 13 inches long, 8 inches wide, and about ⅛ inch thick. Dust the surface and rolling pin with semolina if needed.

○ Fold over ½ inch of the dough all around the oval, then fold again with another ½ inch, pressing down on the folds. Shape the ends into pointed tips. Crimp the edges with the handle of a pizza cutter or your fingertips and pinch the folds together.

○ Carefully transfer the pide to a prepared baking sheet and cover with a kitchen towel to prevent drying. Repeat with the remaining dough. Allow the pide to rest in a warm spot for 20 to 30 minutes, until slightly puffed. Preheat the oven to 475°F and place a baking stone in the oven on the bottom rack.

○ When ready to bake, slide one of the rested pide ovals from the baking sheet to a lightweight cutting board sprinkled with semolina. Prick the dough all over, including the edges, with a fork. Make sure the ends are still pinched and the edges crimped, then spread 2 tablespoons of the sun-dried tomato sauce on the pide and spoon a generous ⅓ cup of vegetable mixture across the center of each pide.

○ Carefully transfer the pide to the hot baking stone by pinching the ends and sliding the pide onto the stone. Bake until the edges are evenly browned, about 12 minutes. Depending on the size of your oven and baking stone, you may be able to bake two at a time.

○ Transfer the pide to the cutting board, brush the edges with melted butter, then top each with crumbled feta. Drizzle some of the remaining olive oil over the top and season with salt, then cut into quarters. Repeat with the remaining ovals.

MUSHROOM FLATBREAD
LAHMACUN

Exploring the Kadıköy Market in Istanbul not long ago, Chef Costa and I came upon the famous shops selling lahmacun—meat-topped flatbreads with a long history in Turkey, Armenia, and the Middle East. It's a first cousin of manoushe, the flatbreads of Lebanon and beyond. I had some of the best manoushe of my life in Beirut, where I tried the famous elongated pies of Abu Shadi. This lahmacun-inspired dish is stretched oblong like Abu Shadi's, but made with a spiced mushroom instead of meat. Enjoy it the traditional way: roll it up and take a bite!

❋✶❋✶❋✶❋✶❋✶❋✶❋

Makes 2

3 tablespoons extra-virgin olive oil, plus more for drizzling

1 pound cremini mushrooms, cleaned and quartered

¼ yellow onion, diced (about ⅓ cup)

2 garlic cloves, thinly sliced

½ tablespoon tomato paste

1 small plum tomato, blanched, peeled, and diced

1 teaspoon Mushroom Garlic Salt (page 28)

¼ teaspoon ground cumin, plus more for garnish

¼ teaspoon Urfa pepper, plus more for garnish

⅛ teaspoon freshly ground black pepper

¼ teaspoon Aleppo pepper, plus more for garnish

Semolina flour, for dusting

1 batch dough (page 129), divided into 2 balls

2 tablespoons pomegranate molasses

Flaky sea salt

Leaves from 1 bunch flat-leaf parsley

1 lemon, cut into wedges

○ Put a baking stone on the middle rack of an oven and preheat to 400°F, letting the oven get hot, about 30 minutes.

○ Meanwhile, warm the olive oil in a wide, shallow pan set over high heat. When the oil begins to smoke, add the mushrooms and cook until browned, tossing occasionally, about 5 minutes. Reduce the heat to medium-high, add the onions, and cook until soft, about 7 minutes. Then add the garlic and cook until lightly browned, 2 more minutes. If needed, do this in batches, working with half the mushrooms, onions, and garlic at a time and transferring the cooked mushrooms to a bowl.

○ If cooking in batches, return all the cooked mushrooms to the pan. Stir in the tomato paste and cook until it glazes the bottom of the pan. Add the chopped tomatoes, mushroom salt, cumin, Urfa pepper, black pepper, and Aleppo pepper and cook, scraping up any browned bits with a wooden spoon, until the tomatoes are very soft and the liquid has cooked down, about 3 minutes. The pan should be nearly dry. If any dry bits remain stuck to the bottom of the pan, add a little water to soften, then scrape up, stir into the mixture, and cook until the liquid evaporates. Remove the pan from the heat and let cool slightly. Spoon the mushroom mixture into a food processor and pulse 2 or 3 times until finely minced but not pureed.

○ Lightly dust a work surface with semolina. Roll out one ball of dough into a long oval, about 18 inches long and 6 inches wide. Stretch the dough with your hands, if necessary, to spread out to an oval shape, then prick the dough all over with a fork.

○ Spread half the mushroom mixture over the dough in a thin layer, leaving about a ½-inch edge around the oval.

○ Carefully remove the hot baking stone from the oven and place on trivets or stove grates. Sprinkle the stone with some semolina, then slide the mushroom-topped dough onto the stone. Return the hot stone to the oven and bake for 10 minutes, or until nicely browned around the edges.

○ Transfer the lahmacun to a serving board and drizzle with half the pomegranate molasses. Sprinkle with a pinch of cumin, Urfa pepper, and Aleppo pepper, and season to taste with flaky sea salt. Top with half the parsley, a squeeze of fresh lemon, and a drizzle of olive oil. Repeat with the remaining dough and mushroom mixture.

PHYLLO

First things first: don't be intimidated about making your own phyllo. I think you can do it. There was a time in my life I hadn't ever made phyllo, and then I learned (along with the rest of our team) from the amazing Abdelrazzaq Hashhoush. He learned from his own father, a baker from Palestine who moved to Jordan and then to Lebanon, where Abdelrazzaq and his siblings grew up. He taught me and, of course, Hilda (*below*), who is the master of phyllo these days. We make paper-thin phyllo in the morning, two or three times a week, using a rolling pin and a long dowel, as Abdelrazzaq taught us. At home, you might find it easier to use a pasta machine. Start with the thickest setting and run the dough through a few times until you get to super thin sheets. Or find a good work surface and give hand rolling a try. Homemade phyllo might be a bit thicker than store-bought, but it will be flexible and easier to work with. If a sheet tears, don't worry, just place another layer on top!

**Makes 8 large
(14 by 20 inch) sheets**

⅓ cup (85 grams) whole milk

1 large egg

1½ tablespoons (17 grams)
extra-virgin olive oil, plus
more for greasing

3½ tablespoons (43 grams)
sugar

¾ tablespoon (7 grams)
kosher salt

3⅓ cups (456 grams) bread
flour, plus more for dusting

3 or more cups cornstarch,
for dusting

O Lightly whisk together the milk, egg, oil, sugar, salt, and 1 cup (222 grams) of water in a bowl.

O Put the flour in the bowl of a stand mixer fitted with a dough hook. Pour ¾ of the liquid mixture into the bowl and mix on the lowest speed for 2 minutes, or until the dough begins to wrap around the hook. Add the remaining liquid, increase the mixer to medium speed, and continue to mix the dough for 15 minutes, until the dough is smooth and elastic. It will be quite soft, but do not add more flour.

O Lay plastic wrap on a work surface and grease with olive oil. Remove the dough from the mixer and place on the oiled plastic wrap. Rub the dough with olive oil and cover completely with the plastic wrap. Let the dough rest, covered, for 15 minutes.

O Dust a work surface with bread flour, remove the dough from the plastic, and shape into a rectangle about the size of a sheet of paper (8½ by 11 inches). Using a pastry cutter or sharp knife, divide the dough into 8 equal pieces, about 4 ounces each. Roll each piece into a ball, grease with olive oil, and wrap in plastic. Refrigerate overnight or for up to 3 days, or freeze for up to one month.

O Remove dough balls from the refrigerator, depending on how many pieces you will need, and set aside, still wrapped in plastic, to come to room temperature, about 1 hour. The dough will become sticky.

O Generously dust a work surface with cornstarch, unwrap 1 ball, and place on the surface. Pat down and stretch the dough into a rectangle, using your hands and a rolling pin, dusting with more cornstarch if the dough starts to stick to your surface.

O Roll out the dough a few times with a rolling pin, then rotate the dough about 90 degrees on the work surface, dust with more cornstarch, and continue to roll and stretch the dough.

O As the dough gets larger and thinner, gently roll up the dough around the rolling pin (or a wooden dowel) and dust the work surface with more cornstarch. Unroll the dough, rotating it again, and continue to use a rolling pin to stretch the dough into a paper thin rectangle, about 14 by 20 inches.

O Generously grease several pieces of parchment paper with olive oil. Carefully drape the phyllo over the rolling pin and brush off the excess cornstarch, then lay dough flat on the greased parchment. Using a spray bottle filled with olive oil, cover the dough completely with more oil. Lay more greased parchment paper over the dough and flatten out to completely seal the dough. Fold the enclosed phyllo in thirds like a letter, then in half, widthwise, and place inside a large plastic sealable bag.

O Repeat with the remaining dough. Refrigerate the sheets, sealed in the bag, for up to 5 days, or freeze for up to 1 month.

CHEF MOVE Don't be afraid to be generous with your cornstarch! Use more than you think you will need when rolling out sheets of phyllo. It keeps them from sticking to the work surface and to each other. We stack sheets of phyllo—with lots of cornstarch between the layers—and roll them out together on our work surface (*left*). Cornstarch is also slow to absorb into the dough so it won't alter the flavor of the phyllo. Just be sure to shake off any excess cornstarch from the sheets before you spray them with olive oil.

SPANAKOPITA

Ours might not look like the spanakopita you've had before—as a pie, a triangle, or a spiral. Ours is shaped more like a classic Chinese egg roll. Why, you ask? I think it's the best way to get it super crispy, and it also uses less phyllo than the other shapes. And when you've made your own phyllo dough from scratch, you probably want to get the most out of it! This is a great dish to bring to a party—it hits all the classic flavors, and everyone will be impressed when you tell them the phyllo is homemade.

Makes 12 rolls

Kosher salt

1 pound spinach,
    stems removed

Extra-virgin olive oil

1 leek, white and light green
    parts only, cleaned and
    thinly sliced

2 scallions, trimmed and
    thinly sliced

1 tablespoon finely chopped
    fresh parsley

1 teaspoon finely chopped
    fresh dill

⅔ cup crumbled feta

Freshly ground white pepper

6 to 8 phyllo sheets
    (page 141)

○ Bring a pot of salted water to a boil, add the spinach, and blanch for 1 minute (30 seconds if using baby spinach). Drain and transfer to a bowl of ice water. Once cool, drain again and squeeze out excess water with paper towels. Chop the spinach and put it into a large mixing bowl.

○ Warm 3 tablespoons of olive oil in a skillet over medium-low heat. Add the leeks and cook until soft but not browned, about 8 minutes. Stir in the scallions and continue to sauté until soft. Transfer the leeks and scallions to the spinach bowl and stir in the parsley and dill. Fold in the feta and season with pepper.

○ Preheat the oven to 400°F. Place a sheet of phyllo, still on its oiled parchment, on a work surface. Trim the phyllo into two long rectangular shapes, roughly 5 inches wide by 8 inches long. Spray or brush the phyllo with olive oil. Place a tightly packed ¼ cup of the spinach mixture along the shorter side of the phyllo, about 1 inch from the edges. Pull the

end of the phyllo over the mixture and begin to roll the phyllo around the spinach mixture. Halfway through rolling, tuck in the sides of the phyllo around the mixture (like an egg roll) and continue rolling until sealed. Discard the oiled parchment and reserve any phyllo trimmings for another use. Place the spanakopita on a parchment-lined baking sheet and repeat with the remaining filling and dough.

○ Brush or spray each spanakopita with olive oil, then bake until golden and crispy, 20 to 25 minutes. Flip the spanakopita over after 10 minutes to ensure even browning. Serve warm.

LAMB KLEFTIKO

This dish has a great background story to it, like something out of an adventure novel. The Klephts were a group of Greek mountain rebels who fought back against the Ottoman Empire during the fifteenth century and later, raiding farms and passing travelers for food. When they would steal a sheep (or anything else), they would have to cook it underground so that no aromas or steam could escape, keeping themselves hidden. The dish kleftiko—named for the Klephts—is traditionally wrapped in foil or parchment and baked in an airtight oven. Our version "hides" lamb in phyllo triangles—leftover roast lamb from page 280 works well, or even roast chicken (page 262). If you're using store-bought phyllo, trim the sheets into 5-by-10-inch rectangles. You can stack two oiled rectangles, placed on top of each other, if you find one sheet of phyllo tears too easily. I can't promise that the aromas will stay inside your phyllo packets—but hopefully you won't get into trouble for stealing a lamb!

Makes 12

Extra-virgin olive oil

1 medium yellow onion, thinly sliced (1½ cups)

Kosher salt

5 garlic cloves; 4 thinly sliced and 1 minced

1 pound lamb shoulder (page 280), chopped

3 tablespoons Chicken Stock (page 113)

1 tablespoon finely chopped thyme leaves

1 tablespoon dried Greek oregano

½ teaspoon freshly ground black pepper

⅓ cup shredded Kefalograviera cheese

6 to 8 phyllo sheets (page 141)

1 cup baby arugula

1 tablespoon ladolemono (page 60)

½ cup Greek yogurt

2 teaspoons chopped fresh dill

⅛ teaspoon ground white pepper

2 tablespoons crumbled feta

○ Warm 1 tablespoon of oil in a large sauté pan over medium-high heat, until just starting to smoke. Add the onions, sprinkle with salt, and cook, stirring often, until the onions begin to brown, about 3 minutes. Stir in a tablespoon of water and deglaze the pan, then continue cooking until the onions begin to caramelize, about 15 minutes.

○ Add the sliced garlic and cook until soft and golden brown, 5 more minutes. Stir in the lamb, chicken stock, thyme, oregano, and pepper, then remove from the heat and fold in the cheese. Season lightly with salt, if needed; remember, Kefalograviera is salty. Let the lamb mixture cool completely.

○ Preheat the oven to 400°F. Place a sheet of phyllo, still on its oiled parchment, on a work surface. Trim the phyllo into two long rectangular shapes, roughly 5 inches wide by 8 inches long. Spray or brush the phyllo with olive oil. Spoon ⅓ cup of the lamb mixture on the bottom center of the shorter side of the phyllo, about 1 inch

from the edges. Fold into a triangle by first taking one corner of the phyllo close to the filling and fold across to the opposite side, then lifting the bottom corner and folding straight over. Continue folding the dough, maintaining the triangle shape. Discard the oiled parchment and reserve any phyllo trimmings for another use.

○ Spray or brush the triangle package with olive oil, then place on a parchment-lined baking sheet. Continue with the remaining lamb mixture and phyllo dough. Bake the triangles until golden brown and crispy, about 20 minutes, flipping after 10 minutes to ensure even browning.

○ Toss the arugula with ladolemono in a mixing bowl. Mix the yogurt, dill, minced garlic, white pepper, and ¼ teaspoon of salt together in another bowl. Spread spoonfuls of the herbed yogurt on a serving plate, then top with 2 crispy triangles. Garnish with the arugula and a sprinkle of feta.

GREENS PHYLLO PIE

HORTOPITA

In Greece, there's a long tradition of dishes celebrating the wild greens of springtime. In our hortopita—literally "greens pie"—we cook down more than four pounds of bitter, spicy, and sweet greens into a rich, savory pie. They're baked under a layer of phyllo (homemade is best, but store-bought will work) until crispy, then usually served at room temperature. When working with phyllo, I like to fill a spray bottle with olive oil, which I use to spray the layers as I build them. If you are using store-bought phyllo, don't worry if it cracks while you're working with it—a couple more sprays of oil and an extra sheet or two of phyllo should help it look, and taste, just fine.

Serves 6 to 8

3 bunches mustard greens (about 2 pounds)

3 bunches Swiss chard (about 1 ½ pounds)

2 bunches lacinato kale (about 1 pound)

Extra-virgin olive oil

1 fennel bulb, thinly sliced

1 yellow onion, thinly sliced

1 bunch scallions, ends trimmed and thinly sliced

2 star anise

Kosher salt

1 bunch fresh dill, fronds removed and chopped

1 bunch fresh parsley, leaves removed and chopped

1 teaspoon ground cumin

½ teaspoon freshly ground black pepper

½ teaspoon Aleppo pepper

½ cup pine nuts, toasted

½ cup golden raisins, coarsely chopped

¼ cup capers, drained and rinsed

2 large eggs

6 sheets phyllo dough (page 141)

○ Separate the stems from the mustard greens, Swiss chard, and kale. Wash well, then coarsely chop the leaves and finely slice the stems. Spin the leaves dry with a salad spinner or blot dry with paper towels.

○ Warm ½ cup of olive oil over high heat in a large, wide pot. Add the stems from the greens, along with the fennel, onions, scallions, and star anise, and cook until softened, about 7 minutes. Add the greens and a large pinch of salt and cook, stirring occasionally, until the greens wilt, about 10 minutes. Depending on the size of your pot, add the leaves in batches, stirring more in as they cook down. Stir in the dill, parsley, cumin, black pepper, and Aleppo pepper, then remove from the heat and let cool.

○ Once the greens have cooled, remove the star anise and stir in the pine nuts, raisins, and capers, then season to taste with salt and additional black pepper if needed. Add the eggs and mix until well combined. (Be sure the greens have completely cooled so you don't get scrambled eggs.)

○ Preheat the oven to 375°F. Brush or spray a 9-by-13 inch (or similar sized) baking dish generously with olive oil. Lay the first sheet of phyllo in the pan, lifting the edges of the phyllo so it falls into the sides and 1 to 2 inches hang over the edges. Gently push the phyllo down into the corners, being careful not to stretch or tear it. Spray the dough with olive oil, then repeat with another layer of phyllo and make sure the whole pan is covered. Spray the dough again with olive oil, then place the third phyllo sheet in the pan, making sure to press the it into the corners and edges. You may need to add another piece of phyllo, spraying first with olive oil, to overlap the other sheets and completely cover the bottom of the pan. Make sure there is some dough hanging over the edges.

○ Spoon the greens mixture into the pan and spread evenly across the pan, then drizzle with a little olive oil.

Fold the overhanging edges of phyllo back over the greens mixture. Add another sheet or two of phyllo over the top to cover the greens and tuck any extra dough down the edges of the pan. Spray with olive oil.

○ Bake for about 1 hour; the crust should be golden brown and have slightly pulled away from the edges of the pan. Let cool for about 20 minutes, to room temperature, then slice and serve.

LAVASH

Lavash has thousands of years of history in the Middle East, Caucasus, and Turkey. In fact, it's so important to many of the countries of the region that it's been recognized as intangible cultural heritage by the United Nations. The process of making lavash is deeply respected in many communities, and traditionally relies on a wood-fired clay oven. Our lavash is simpler than the traditional version and uses a flat cooktop instead of a clay oven. But it's still a delicious bread to go with our dishes. I love putting lavash down underneath grilled kebabs, so they soak up the juices—perfect with a simple spread of spicy harissa. We also use them in the style of Turkish dürüm, or rolls, by wrapping them around chicken, salmon, or falafel. Join in the history and make some lavash!

Makes 6

1 teaspoon (4 grams) active dry yeast

1½ tablespoons (18 grams) granulated sugar

¾ tablespoon tablespoons (6 grams) kosher salt

¾ cup (96 grams) whole-wheat flour

2¼ cups (313 grams) all-purpose flour

¼ cup (48 grams) extra-virgin olive oil

Semolina flour, for dusting

○ Stir together the yeast, sugar, and 1 cup warm water in a bowl. Let sit for 10 minutes to allow bubbles to form.

○ Put the salt and flours in the bowl of a stand mixer fitted with a dough hook. Turn the stand mixer on low and slowly add the water-yeast mixture, then drizzle in the olive oil. Knead the dough for 5 to 7 minutes, until the dough is well incorporated, making sure there are no dry spots or loose flour.

○ Remove the bowl from the mixer and cover tightly. Set the dough aside to rise for 1 hour, or until roughly doubled in size.

○ After the dough has risen, punch it down in the bowl, then turn it out onto a work surface dusted with semolina. Flatten the dough into a disk, then divide into 6 equal pieces.

○ Generously flour a rolling pin and roll each dough ball into a sheet about 9-by-11 inches—trim the edges to be precise if you like. Place each sheet of dough on a floured baking sheet, sprinkling with a little semolina and separating each with parchment paper as you roll and stack the remaining dough.

○ Warm a flat cooktop, griddle, or extra-large sauté pan over medium-high heat. (Do not add any oil to the cooktop—it should be dry.)

○ If the sheets have shrunk, roll them thin again, then cook the sheets of dough until lightly browned, about 1 minute per side (if it takes longer, your cooktop isn't hot enough). As each lavash finishes, stack them under a damp towel so they briefly steam.

○ Lavash are best eaten fresh. However, they can be refrigerated, sealed in plastic, for up to 2 days. Warm them in a low oven for about 3 minutes before using.

05

RICE, BEANS, GRAINS & EGGS

Rice is the great unifier. In cooking across the globe, people share bowls, platters, and paella pans (of course!), filled with steaming seasoned rice. We find it stuffed inside vegetables and meats; rolled in leaves, greens, and seaweed; sautéed, fried, baked, and flavored with countless herbs and spices. Through conquests and commerce, rice traveled from China, India, and Persia to the Middle East, and then took hold in the Mediterranean. Initially expensive and rare, rice was a specialty reserved for royalty and the wealthy, while wheat remained the grain of the common people, especially in Turkey and Lebanon, often eaten as bulgur (cracked wheat) or baked into breads. Dishes of roasted young green wheat, known as freekeh, or whole wheat kernels called wheat berries were simmered with herbs, greens, and vegetables, and sometimes seasoned with bits of meat, for hearty meals.

Under the rule of the Ottomans, extravagant rice dishes were crafted by the cooks of the Topkapi Palace in Istanbul and served at celebrations and feasts, inspired by the jeweled rice of Persia, colored golden with saffron. Rich with butter or olive oil, nuts, and dried fruits, these rice pilafs, primarily made today with aromatic long-grain rice like basmati, became an important part of the Ottoman table. These fluffy rices were served alongside roasts of lamb or seafood, or as the main dish, baked in dough as a "veiled pilaf" for special occasions. Over the following centuries, regional variations of pilaf would include different legumes, grains, bulgur, and small pieces of pasta such as orzo. Mujadara, made with rice, lentils, caramelized onions, and spices and served with cooling yogurt, would become a popular dish throughout the Middle East and particularly in Lebanon.

As sophisticated as pilafs can be, I am a believer in the greatness of flavorful rice stuffed inside tender leaves and vegetables. For these dishes, a short-grain variety of rice is important. To make paella in Spain, we cook with short-grain rice from Valencia because it easily absorbs the flavors of stock and other liquids while keeping its shape and bite. My friends in Turkey and Greece also prefer short-grain rice for dolmas, as it makes for a perfect savory, sticky, pillowy filling when mixed with herbs, vegetables, and toasted pine nuts. When you think "dolma" (the Turkish word for "stuffed"), you probably think of stuffed grape leaves—the most classic of mezze in the Eastern Mediterranean—but in reality, any stuffed vegetable, like a bell pepper, a tomato, a zucchini, even seafood can be called

dolma! One of my favorite street foods in Istanbul is stuffed mussels, midye dolmasi. Walking through the Beyoğlu neighborhood on the way to one of my favorite bars in Istanbul, Flekk, I came upon a man on a street corner with an enormous tray of rice-filled mussels flavored with fresh lemon. Before I knew it, I had devoured nearly a dozen.

Stuffed grape (or vine) leaves, known as dolmades in Greece and sarma in Turkey and found all over the region on tables of mezze, traditionally come in two styles: with or without meat. Those with meat are usually served warm, even grilled, while those filled with only rice and herbs are a cold or room-temperature dish, flavored with plenty of olive oil and served alongside rich yogurt. In fact, dolma made without meat are considered Lenten food in Greece, when people refrain from eating meat in the run-up to Orthodox Easter. While in Turkey, you may see them called "yalancı" (or fake) sarma or dolmades. Let me assure you people, the grape leaves we make every day at the restaurant are anything but fake: we fill them with a savory fennel-scented rice, then roll them up into little cigar shapes. Aglaia Kremezi taught us how to make these iconic rolls, and for the past twenty years she has been making sure that we keep just the right balance of flavors and texture. No wonder they remain one of our most popular dishes.

RICE AND TOMATO STUFFED GRAPE LEAVES

DOLMADES

Aglaia, who makes some of the best stuffed grape leaves I've ever had, taught me that for the best flavor, you should make these dolmades—an iconic mezze throughout the Mediterranean and Middle East—the day before you want to serve them, and let them chill overnight. She also showed us the technique of placing the stuffed grape leaves between layers of slices of potatoes. The bottom layer of potatoes creates a protective barrier from the hot pan, to keep the grape leaves from burning, and the top layer helps to cover and weigh down the rolls so they stay tightly packed while they cook.

Makes about 40

2 medium ripe tomatoes, finely diced (about 1¼ cups)

1 small fennel bulb, trimmed, cored and finely diced (about ⅔ cup)

½ cup pine nuts, toasted

½ cup golden raisins

1 cup Valencia rice (or other short-grain rice such as arborio)

½ cup chopped mint leaves

1 cup chopped parsley leaves

1¼ teaspoons ground allspice

2 tablespoons kosher salt

½ tablespoon freshly ground black pepper

2¾ cups (26 ounces) boxed chopped tomatoes

¾ cup fresh lemon juice (from 4 to 5 lemons)

2 tablespoons pomegranate molasses

½ cup extra-virgin olive oil, plus more for drizzling

1 to 2 medium potatoes, cut into ½-inch slices

40 to 50 brine-packed grape leaves (from one 16-ounce jar), rinsed with hot water

½ cup Whipped Labneh (page 60)

1 teaspoon sumac

○ Combine the diced fresh tomatoes, fennel, pine nuts, raisins, rice, mint, parsley, allspice, salt, and pepper in a large mixing bowl. Stir in the boxed tomatoes, lemon juice, pomegranate molasses, and olive oil. Cover and refrigerate for ½ hour, then transfer the mixture to a fine-mesh sieve (or large colander lined with cheesecloth) set over a mixing bowl. Let the mixture drain for ½ hour, occasionally pressing on it with the back of a ladle, and reserve the liquid. (You should end up with 3 to 4 cups of liquid.)

○ Line the bottom of a 2-quart Dutch oven with a layer of potato slices, making sure to completely cover the bottom. Make a single layer of grape leaves over the potatoes (use any torn or misshapen leaves for layering). Return the rice mixture to a mixing bowl and stir until well combined. Lay a few grape leaves out flat on a work surface, vein side up, and trim off any stems. Take 1 tablespoon of the rice and place it in the center of the leaf. Fold the stem end over the top of the rice, then fold the two sides into the middle over the rice. Roll the leaf up tightly like a cigar. Place the stuffed leaf in the pot, seam side down so it doesn't unravel. Repeat with the remaining leaves and rice mixture, placing the stuffed leaves tightly together in a single layer in the pot. Once the bottom layer is full, start a second layer of stuffed leaves, seam side down.

○ Pour the reserved liquid over the stuffed grape leaves and add enough water to just cover them. Lay a few grape leaves flat over the top and cover with a layer of the remaining potato slices. Place a heatproof plate on top to weigh down the stuffed leaves. Cook, uncovered, at a low simmer until the rice is tender, the liquid has nearly evaporated, and the grape leaves have tightened, about 1 hour. If the liquid evaporates too quickly, before the rice has cooked, add a little more water.

○ Take the pot off the heat and allow the dolmades to cool in the pot, then transfer to a container, stacking them in layers. Discard the potatoes (or do what Aglaia does and save for a snack!) and extra grape leaves. Cover and refrigerate until ready to serve, or overnight.

○ To serve, allow the stuffed grape leaves to come to room temperature. Spread the Whipped Labneh on a serving platter and sprinkle with sumac. Arrange the stuffed grape leaves on the platter and drizzle with olive oil.

SAFFRON PILAF

This dish is a tribute to the Ottoman pilaf tradition. In Istanbul, the addition of nuts, fruits, and warm spices in pilafs started with cooks in the Topkapi Palace, influenced obviously by the neighboring Persians, whose pilafs were the center of every celebration. With a golden yellow color, thanks to saffron and turmeric, our version is laced with a cut vermicelli-style pasta, easily found in grocery stores as fideo noodles. The crispy shallot topping adds extra flavor and a little extra glamour.

Serves 4 to 6

6 tablespoons unsalted butter, divided

1 large shallot, thinly sliced

½ cup fideo, or chopped fine egg noodles

1 bay leaf

½ teaspoon saffron threads

1 cardamom pod

¼ teaspoon ground nutmeg

1 teaspoon ground cumin

½ teaspoon ground coriander seeds

1 teaspoon ground turmeric

2 cups basmati rice

3 cups vegetable stock

1 tablespoon kosher salt

¼ cup crushed roasted pistachios

¼ cup slivered almonds

½ cup dates, diced

½ cup dried apricots, diced

¼ cup crispy shallots (see right)

1 tablespoon thinly sliced flat-leaf parsley leaves

○ Melt 4 tablespoons of the butter in a large pot over medium heat. Add the shallots and cook until translucent but not browned, about 5 minutes. Add the pasta and toast, stirring, about 2 minutes. Add the bay leaf, saffron, cardamom, nutmeg, cumin, coriander, and turmeric and continue to toast for 1 minute. Stir in the rice and continue to toast for 2 more minutes.

○ Meanwhile, heat the stock in a small saucepan until just boiling. Pour the hot stock over the toasted rice mixture and add the salt; the stock should cover the rice by ½ inch. (Add hot water if more is needed to fully cover the rice.)

○ Cover the pot and reduce the heat to low. Cook for 15 minutes, until the rice is tender and cooked through. Remove the pot from the heat and let the rice steam for another 5 minutes.

○ To serve, remove the cardamom pod and fold in the pistachios, almonds, dates, and apricots and the remaining 2 tablespoons of butter. Stir until the butter has melted and is thoroughly combined. Spoon the rice onto a serving plate and top with crispy shallots and parsley.

FOR CRISPY SHALLOTS:
Peel and trim the ends from 3 medium shallots, then thinly slice them widthwise and separate into rings. (You should have about ⅔ cup of sliced shallots.) Heat 2 to 3 inches of canola oil in a medium pot to 350°F. Combine the shallots and 1 cup of all-purpose flour in a mixing bowl and toss until evenly coated. Shake off excess flour and fry the shallots, working in batches, until golden brown and crispy, about 2 minutes. Transfer them to paper-towel-lined plate to drain and season with fine sea salt.

SPICED LENTILS AND RICE
MUJADARA

Serves 4 to 6

For the rice:

2 teaspoons extra-virgin olive oil

1 tablespoon minced onion

1 teaspoon minced garlic

1 bay leaf

2 cardamom pods

1 stick cinnamon

1 cup basmati rice

2 teaspoons kosher salt

For the lentils:

2 tablespoons extra-virgin olive oil, divided

1 medium yellow onion, thinly sliced

1 bay leaf

Kosher salt

3 large cremini mushrooms, destemmed and finely diced

½ teaspoon minced garlic

1 cup French green lentils, rinsed and debris removed

¾ teaspoon tomato paste

½ tablespoon Golden Baharat (page 27)

2 to 3 cups vegetable stock

1 small carrot, peeled and finely diced

For serving:

2 teaspoons Lebanese Seven Spice (page 27)

1 to 2 tablespoons extra-virgin olive oil

1 cup crispy shallots (page 156) or store-bought fried onions

1 tablespoon minced chives

Flaky sea salt

½ cup Greek yogurt

In the Middle East, there's a saying that "a hungry man would be willing to sell his soul for a dish of mujadara." Once you taste it, you'll know why. Mujadara is a popular dish throughout the Middle East, with the first recipe recorded in 1226 in the *Kitab al-Tabikh*, one of the first published cookbooks in the world. Our mujadara is a bit more modern, with extra texture coming from French Puy lentils. It's the onions, though, that make this dish memorable; deeply caramelized onions are stirred into the rice, and crispy fried onions (or shallots) are piled on top.

O To make the rice, warm the olive oil in a medium pot over medium heat. Cook the onions and garlic until translucent but not browned, about 2 minutes. Add the bay leaf, cardamom, and cinnamon and briefly toast, then add the rice and stir until well coated.

O Increase the heat to medium-high, add 1½ cups of water and the salt, and bring to a boil. Cover and reduce heat to low and simmer, stirring occasionally, until the rice is tender and the water is absorbed, about 20 minutes. Remove from heat and discard the bay leaf, cinnamon stick, and cardamom pods. Keep the pot covered.

O Meanwhile, to make the lentils, warm a large sauté pan over medium-high heat. Add 1 tablespoon of the olive oil, then the onions, bay leaf, and 1 teaspoon of kosher salt. Cook, stirring occasionally, until the onions have completely softened and caramelized, about 15 minutes. If the onions begin to darken and stick to the pan, add a little water to deglaze the pan and scrape up any browned bits.

O Push the onions to one side of the pan. Add 1 tablespoon of the olive oil to the other side of the pan, and add the mushrooms and garlic. Cook until the mushrooms have browned and the garlic is golden, about 3 minutes.

O Add the lentils and tomato paste and stir to coat. Sprinkle the Golden Baharat over the lentils and continue to stir, lightly toasting the mixture, about 20 seconds. Add 2 cups of the vegetable stock to deglaze the pan, scraping up any browned bits. Bring to a boil, add the carrots, then reduce the heat to maintain a simmer and cover. Cook the lentils and carrots until tender but still holding their shape, 10 to 15 minutes. Add additional stock if needed, but nearly all of the liquid should be absorbed once the lentils are cooked through.

O To serve, add the rice to the lentils in the pan. Sprinkle with the seven spice and stir to combine. Add a few tablespoons of the vegetable stock if needed to coat the rice and lentils. Season to taste with salt.

O Spoon into a serving bowl and drizzle with olive oil, then top with crispy shallots, chives, and flaky sea salt. Serve with some Greek yogurt drizzled with olive oil and seasoned with sea salt, if you like.

FALAFEL

I've tried falafel a hundred different ways. Large and fluffy, small and crispy, bright green with herbs or blond with chickpeas. During a recent trip to Beirut, I visited the shops of two brothers next door to each other whose father used to run a falafel shop called Falafel Sahyoun on Damascus Street, the border between east and west Beirut. It was once a place for people to break bread and eat a meal together during the war—now the two brothers are notorious rivals themselves! Just steps away from each other, two pots of oil bubble away, as cooks drop in a nearly identical chickpea mixture from their traditional falafel scoops, with patrons lining up outside both shops, waiting for sandwiches to eat on the sidewalk or to take back to cars idling nearby. The falafel we make are small, crunchy two-bite fritters. I love smaller ones because the outside gets nice and crispy while the inside is packed with herbs and spices. Serve them piled on a platter or stuffed into pita.

Makes 24 balls

¼ teaspoon plus ½ teaspoon baking soda

2 cups dried chickpeas

Leaves from 1 bunch fresh cilantro

Leaves from 1 bunch fresh parsley, 1 tablespoon reserved

1 stalk celery, chopped

1 small onion, chopped

½ leek, halved, washed and chopped

2 garlic cloves, peeled

½ cup chickpea flour

1 teaspoon baking powder

2½ teaspoons kosher salt

¾ teaspoon ground coriander

¾ teaspoon ground cumin

½ teaspoon freshly ground black pepper

¼ teaspoon ground allspice

Canola oil

Fine sea salt

½ cup Tahini Sauce (page 67)

¼ cup turmeric pickled summer vegetables (page 36)

1 tablespoon fresh mint leaves

○ Dissolve the ¼ teaspoon of baking soda in 1 cup room-temperature water in a medium mixing bowl, then add the chickpeas and cover with water by 2 inches. Cover and let soak overnight, or for at least 8 hours. The next day, drain and rinse the chickpeas.

○ Roughly chop the cilantro and parsley and combine with the chickpeas in a mixing bowl. Add the celery, onions, leeks, and garlic.

○ Position a meat-grinder attachment, fitted with the smallest die, on a stand mixer, then pass the chickpea mixture through the grinder into a large mixing bowl. Once all the mixture is ground, pass it through the grinder a second time. (You can also use a food processor: work in 2 batches to not crowd the processor bowl, pulse the ingredients until they are finely minced but not pureed, then transfer to a large mixing bowl.)

○ Whisk together the chickpea flour, baking powder, remaining ½ teaspoon baking soda, salt, coriander, cumin, pepper, and allspice in a small bowl, then sprinkle over the ground chickpeas

and mix together until well combined. Don't overwork the mixture; you want it to remain a little loose.

○ Line a rimmed baking sheet with parchment paper. Scoop 1 tablespoon-size balls of the chickpea mixture (a number 70 squeeze-handle cookie scoop works great here) and set on the baking sheet. Do not crowd them.

○ Heat 3 inches of oil to 350°F in a large, deep saucepan. Working in batches, fry the balls until they are brown and crunchy, about 3 minutes. Transfer to a paper-towel-lined tray to drain and season to taste with sea salt. Repeat with the remaining falafel, letting the oil return to 350°F before frying the next batch.

○ To serve, spoon some of the tahini sauce onto serving plates, add pickled vegetables, and drizzle with olive oil. Top each with falafel, then garnish with mint and the reserved parsley leaves.

WHITE BEAN STEW

PIYAZ

This warm bean stew, made with kale, sun-dried tomatoes, and a lemon–olive oil sauce, is worth going out of your way to find the right ingredients. Greek gigantes beans are so good: big, creamy white beans that hold their shape, with an almost meaty texture to them. You can use large lima beans, but the texture won't be quite the same. Piyaz is traditionally a Turkish bean-and-onion salad, but we've given it a bit of a Greek twist with the addition of bright ladolemono and dill—and, of course, those beautiful beans, which you can find in Greek markets or online. I'm telling you, it's worth it!

Serves 4

2 cups dried Greek gigantes beans, or large dried lima beans

1 small yellow onion, quartered

1 Yukon gold potato, peeled and quartered

Kosher salt

½ tablespoon canola oil

1 large garlic clove, thinly sliced

½ small red onion, thinly sliced

3 large leaves kale, stemmed and chopped

12 dry-packed, sun-dried tomatoes, preferably Turkish, diced

½ cup ladolemono (page 60)

½ bunch fresh dill, chopped

Extra-virgin olive oil, for drizzling

○ The day before you want to prepare the dish, rinse the beans, then put them in a pot and cover with double the amount of water. Set aside to soak overnight, or for at least 8 hours.

○ When ready to cook, add the quartered onion and potato to the pot with the beans and soaking liquid, then add enough water to cover by 2 inches. Bring to a boil over medium-high heat, then reduce the heat to low, cover, and gently simmer. Cook the beans until tender, 1½ to 2 hours, occasionally skimming any foam that rises to the top. (Cooking time will depend on how old the beans are.) Using a slotted spoon or tongs, remove the potatoes and onions from the pot and season the beans with salt. Set the beans aside to cool in their cooking liquid.

○ Warm the canola oil over medium heat in the pot, then add the garlic and red onions and cook, stirring, until lightly starting to brown, about 7 minutes. Add the kale and sun-dried tomatoes and cook until the kale just starts to wilt, about 3 minutes. Add the beans and enough of the reserved cooking liquid to make the mixture slightly soupy, about ½ cup. Continue to cook until the kale and

sun-dried tomatoes are soft, about 5 more minutes. Stir in the ladolemono and half the chopped dill, then season to taste with salt. Stir in another tablespoon or two of the reserved cooking liquid to keep the mixture slightly soupy.

○ To serve, divide the piyaz into bowls, drizzle with olive oil, and garnish with the remaining chopped dill.

WHEAT BERRY KISIR

This Turkish salad is an iconic dish that is loved across the country and traditionally made with bulgur, tomatoes, and pepper paste. It may be a distant cousin of Tabbouleh (page 97). But while tabbouleh is an herb salad with some bulgur in it, kisir is most definitely a bulgur salad with some herbs mixed in—and some spice! We like to add whole wheat berries to our kisir along with the coarse bulgur for extra texture—the wheat berries give a nice chewiness to the salad. Try this with einkorn wheat berries, if you can find them. Considered one of the oldest cultivated grains, einkorn adds a nutty, rich flavor. Some people like their kisir a bit punchier; some like it milder. Play with the amount of pepper paste and lemon juice to suit your tastes. We love the sweet-sour flavor from the pomegranate molasses and fresh pomegranate seeds.

Serves 4 to 6

½ cup coarse bulgur

1½ teaspoons kosher salt, divided

1 cup wheat berries

1 tomato, cored and diced

½ red onion, minced

1 tablespoon pepper paste

1 teaspoon fresh lemon juice

2 tablespoons pomegranate molasses

¼ cup extra-virgin olive oil

½ bunch flat-leaf parsley, leaves removed and thinly sliced

3 sprigs fresh mint, leaves removed and thinly sliced

1 teaspoon Aleppo pepper

¾ cup pomegranate seeds

½ cup roasted pistachios, chopped

Flaky sea salt

○ Stir the bulgur and ½ teaspoon salt in a medium mixing bowl. Bring 1 cup of water to a boil, then pour over the bulgur. Cover and let sit until the water is absorbed, about 30 minutes.

○ Meanwhile, toast the wheat berries in a small, dry pot set over high heat until aromatic and starting to brown, about 5 minutes. Let cool slightly, then add 3 cups of water and the remaining teaspoon of salt. Bring to a boil over high heat, then reduce to maintain a gentle simmer and cook until the wheat berries are tender, about 35 minutes. Remove from the heat and let cool.

○ Add the tomatoes, onions, and pepper paste to the soaked bulgur. Mix together with a fork, or use your hands to work the vegetables and pepper paste into the bulgur until well combined, about 3 minutes.

○ Drain any excess liquid from the wheat berries and add them to the bulgur mixture. Mix together by lightly fluffing with a fork (a large two-prong meat fork works really well). Add the lemon juice, pomegranate molasses, and olive oil, then continue mixing and add half of the parsley, half of the mint, and half of the Aleppo pepper.

○ Let the mixture cool to room temperature before serving, then spoon into bowls and garnish with pomegranate seeds, pistachios, the remaining herbs and Aleppo pepper, and flaky sea salt.

CHICKEN FREEKEH

Freekeh—underripe green wheat that's harvested, roasted in fire, and rubbed of its chaff—is both ancient and modern. It always feels like what's old is new again. Farmers have been making this nutty, smoky grain for generations, but it's having a moment as chefs and home cooks look back to the old days for inspiration. This dish is based on a classic Anatolian pilaf from Gaziantep in southern Turkey called Firik Pilavı ("firik" is the Turkish word for freekeh). This version uses half freekeh and half bulgur, a trick we learned from the incredible Chef Maksut Aşkar of Michelin-starred Neolokal in Istanbul, who has worked to preserve the traditions of Turkish culinary culture and explore the ingredients—like freekeh—that come to us from ancient times. Be sure to look for coarse bulgur (not fine bulgur used in tabbouleh) for this dish, sometimes seen as number "3" in grocery stores, which will better match the chewiness of the freekeh.

Serves 4

1 cup coarse bulgur

Kosher salt

4 tablespoons olive oil, divided, plus more for finishing

1 pound boneless, skinless chicken thighs, cut into 1-inch cubes

Freshly ground pepper

2 tablespoons tomato paste

½ yellow onion, diced

4 garlic cloves, minced

1 cup freekeh

2 cinnamon sticks

2½ cups Chicken Stock (page 113)

2 cups baby spinach

1½ teaspoons Aleppo pepper

○ Bring 2 cups of water to a boil, then pour over the bulgur in a medium mixing bowl and season with a large pinch of salt. Cover and let sit until all of the water is absorbed, about 30 minutes. Once done, drizzle in 2 tablespoons of the olive oil and fluff with a fork.

○ Meanwhile, warm 2 tablespoons of the olive oil in a large pot over medium-high heat. Season the chicken with salt and pepper to taste, then add to the pan and cook until the chicken lightly browns and a glaze forms on the bottom of the pan.

○ Add the tomato paste and cook just until aromatic, then stir in the onions and garlic with a generous pinch of salt and use the moisture released by the onions to deglaze the bottom of the pan. Cook for a few minutes, then stir in the freekeh and cinnamon sticks.

○ Pour in the chicken stock, season with another large pinch of salt, stir well, and allow to come to a simmer. Reduce heat to medium-low and continue to simmer until the freekeh is al dente, about 20 minutes.

○ Remove from the heat, add the spinach and bulgur, stir, then cover. Let sit for 2 minutes to wilt the spinach.

○ Season to taste with salt and spoon into serving bowls, discarding the cinnamon sticks. Sprinkle each bowl with Aleppo pepper and drizzle with olive oil.

SPICED PEPPERS, TOMATOES, AND EGGS

SHAKSHOUKA

Many, many people love shakshouka, the famous North African dish of eggs poached in tomato-pepper sauce. This version uses one of my favorite preparations for eggs. It's half-fried, half-poached. I fry the eggs in lots of hot olive oil, which makes the whites into a delicate and crispy jacket around a creamy, runny yolk. When you break open the egg, the whole thing melts into the rich, spicy pepper-and-tomato sauce. I'm telling you, you might not go back to poaching eggs in water. Sometimes when I want to make shakshouka into more of a meal for my family, I will add browned chicken thighs and mushrooms to the sauce.

Serves 4

3 large red bell peppers

12 to 14 (about ½ cup) dry-packed, sun-dried tomatoes, preferably Turkish

3 tablespoons extra-virgin olive oil, divided, plus ½ cup for frying

½ yellow onion, thinly sliced

2 garlic cloves, thinly sliced

½ cup tomato paste

1 pound ripe tomatoes, blanched, peeled, and diced

¼ teaspoon ground cinnamon

¼ teaspoon ground allspice

½ teaspoon Urfa pepper, plus a few pinches for garnish

½ teaspoon Aleppo pepper, plus a few pinches for garnish

4 large eggs

Flaky sea salt

Handful parsley leaves, thinly sliced

¼ preserved lemon rind, cut into thin strips

○ Set the peppers directly on the grate of a gas burner set to medium heat. Using tongs, rotate the peppers to char evenly on each side, 30 seconds to 1 minute per side. Transfer the peppers to a mixing bowl and cover tightly. Leave the peppers to steam for about 15 minutes, until cool enough to handle.

○ Meanwhile, put the sun-dried tomatoes in a bowl and cover with boiling water. Allow them to soften for about 15 minutes, then drain, dice, and set aside.

○ Peel away the charred pepper skin, remove the stem and seeds, then slice into long, thin strips.

○ Warm 2 tablespoons of the olive oil in a sauté pan set over medium-high heat. Stir in the onions and garlic and cook for 3 minutes, until they begin to brown. Add the tomato paste and cook, stirring, until it forms a glaze on the bottom of the pan. Mix in the fresh tomatoes, roasted peppers, sun-dried tomatoes, cinnamon, allspice, and Urfa and Aleppo pepper.

○ Reduce heat to medium and scrape up any browned bits from the bottom of the pan, adding a little water if necessary. Simmer until a thick stew forms, about 10 minutes. Season to taste with salt and keep warm.

○ Heat the ½ cup of the olive oil in a small (about 8-inch) sauté pan over medium-high heat. Crack an egg into a small bowl and line a plate with a paper towel. When the oil just begins to smoke, tip the pan to a 45-degree angle so the oil collects on one side to create a hot oil bath. Carefully slide the egg into the hot oil. As the egg begins to sizzle and fry, spoon the oil over the egg 3 to 4 times. The egg will slightly puff up and be ready in about 30 seconds.

○ Lay the pan flat and use a slotted spoon to move the egg to the paper-towel-lined plate, then sprinkle with salt and cover with a bowl to keep warm. Repeat with the remaining eggs.

○ To serve, divide the warm pepper-tomato sauce into 4 bowls. Garnish with parsley and preserved lemon, then top each with a fried egg. Drizzle with the remaining 1 tablespoon of olive oil, then sprinkle Urfa and Aleppo pepper on top.

GREEK-STYLE OMELETA

This Greek-style omelet, inspired by the ones I've seen my friend Aglaia make, is in the family of Southern European egg "pies," which are always more interesting to me than the standard French omelette. I would say it's a cousin of the Spanish tortilla or Italian frittata. Traditionally it would be made with wild foraged greens from the fields on whatever island you live on, but for ours we use good fresh kale—you could try a mix of seasonal greens. It might seem like a lot of kale, I know, but it cooks down perfectly. And remember that it's important to not have the heat too high when cooking the omeleta—you don't want it to brown, just stay a nice light color. It's a great addition to a brunch spread or can even be a simple dinner with some crusty bread and a bottle of crisp white Assyrtiko from Santorini (page 331).

Serves 4

1 large bunch kale, ribs removed

2 tablespoons unsalted butter

1 small sweet onion, such as Vidalia, thinly sliced

1 leek, white and light green parts only, cleaned and thinly sliced

6 large eggs

3 tablespoons crumbled feta

1 teaspoon kosher salt

3 tablespoons extra-virgin olive oil, divided

1 teaspoon dill fronds

1 teaspoon finely chopped chives

Flaky sea salt

○ Fill a bowl with ice water and set aside. Bring a medium pot of water to a boil over medium-high heat. Tear the kale into large pieces, add to the boiling water, and blanch for 2 minutes. Drain and transfer to the ice water to cool, then drain and squeeze out any excess water with a paper towel. Lay the kale pieces flat on a cutting board and thinly slice.

○ Melt the butter in a large sauté pan over low heat. Add the onions and leeks and cook until soft and translucent, about 10 minutes. Stir in the kale and cook for another 10 minutes, until the kale is soft. Transfer to a plate or sheet pan, spread out, and let cool completely.

○ Crack the eggs into a mixing bowl and whisk well, then fold in the cooled greens, 2 tablespoons of the feta, and the salt and stir to combine.

○ Warm 2 tablespoons of the olive oil in a small (8- to 9-inch) nonstick skillet over medium heat. Add the egg mixture and stir quickly a few times with a rubber spatula to prevent it from sticking to the bottom of the pan. Shake the pan in a circular motion a few times to keep the mixture loose as the eggs start to coagulate. Reduce the heat and cook for another minute, until the eggs are set on the bottom but still loose on top.

○ Place a plate over the pan and quickly invert the pan and plate together, then shake the omelet loose onto the plate. Add the remaining tablespoon of olive oil to the pan and slide the omelet back into the pan, raw side down. Continue to cook for another 2 minutes, or until set on the bottom.

○ Slide the omelet from the pan onto a platter. Garnish with the remaining feta, dill, and chives. Season with flaky salt, slice, and serve immediately.

TURKISH TOMATO AND EGG SCRAMBLE
MENEMEN

Menemen, which has its origins in a small town in Turkey's far-west İzmir Province, is a hearty dish of eggs cooked in a spiced tomato sauce with vegetables, usually green peppers. It's easy to make, but can take some practice to get it right. The key to cooking menemen is to be gentle with all your motions. You want different textures and colors as you eat the dish, so you shouldn't mix it too much in the pan. The eggs should be barely soft scrambled, so remove from the stove before they're done, since they'll keep cooking away from the heat. I like my menemen with more rich, red tomato sauce than egg. Find your favorite combination, because it's the perfect weekend breakfast dish.

Serves 2 to 4

¼ cup extra-virgin olive oil, plus more for drizzling

½ cup diced green bell pepper

½ cup diced yellow onion

2 pounds tomatoes, cored and diced

Kosher salt

½ teaspoon Aleppo pepper, plus more for garnish

1 teaspoon smoked sweet paprika

1 teaspoon sumac

4 large eggs

¼ cup crumbled feta

1 tablespoon minced chives

○ Heat the olive oil in a large skillet, preferably nonstick, over high heat. Add peppers and onions and sauté for 2 minutes.

○ Add tomatoes, 1 teaspoon of salt, Aleppo pepper, and paprika. Continue to cook over high heat, stirring frequently, until the tomatoes have broken down into a thick sauce, about 10 minutes.

○ Lower the heat to medium low and add the sumac. Crack the eggs into a small bowl, then pour them into the pan over the tomatoes. Allow the eggs to cook briefly, until the whites start to color, then break the yolks and gently stir them into the sauce. Cook until the eggs are just barely starting to set, about 2 minutes. (The eggs should be loose and slightly undercooked—they will continue to cook in the warm tomato sauce when served.)

○ Spoon the menemen into warm bowls. Garnish with the feta, Aleppo pepper, and chives. Drizzle with some olive oil and season to taste with salt. Serve immediately.

TURKISH EGGS WITH YOGURT AND CHILI CRISP

ÇILBIR

Çilbir, pronounced "jill-bur," is an old Ottoman dish, dating back at least six hundred years. If you ask for it in Turkey, it will be poached eggs with yogurt and a pepper-infused butter, but we (of course) needed to make our own version. I like fried eggs instead of poached, and instead of the pepper butter we created a Turkish take on the amazing Chinese condiment chili crisp. We make an oil out of Aleppo chilies and add crispy onions, garlic, and spices. The recipe on page 30 is more than you'll need for the çilbir, but be sure to make a whole recipe (or even double it) because you'll want to put it on everything—eggs, fish, vegetables, meat—or eat it straight out of the bowl!

Serves 4

1 whole pita

½ cup Greek yogurt

3 tablespoons extra-virgin olive oil

½ teaspoon kosher salt

Freshly ground white pepper

4 large eggs

3 tablespoons Harissa Chili Crisp (page 30)

Leaves from 2 sprigs fresh thyme

1 teaspoon sumac

Flaky sea salt

○ Preheat the oven to 375°F. Split open the pita, tear it into 1-inch pieces, and scatter on a parchment-lined baking sheet. Bake for 10 to 12 minutes, or until the bread is golden brown and crispy.

○ Whisk the yogurt, 1 tablespoon of olive oil, and salt in a mixing bowl and season to taste with white pepper. Continue whisking until smooth and easily spreadable. If the yogurt is too thick, whisk in 1 to 2 teaspoons of water.

○ Put the remaining 2 tablespoons of olive oil in a medium nonstick pan over low heat. Crack the eggs into a small bowl, then slide the eggs into the pan,

increase the heat to medium-low, and cook until the whites just begin to set and the yolks remain runny, about 2 minutes. Cover the pan, and remove from heat. Let the eggs sit for about 3 more minutes, until the egg whites have set.

○ To serve, divide the eggs among plates and spoon the yogurt around the eggs, then spoon a tablespoon or more of the chili crisp around the eggs. Top each with a few pieces of toasted pita, fresh thyme, and a pinch of sumac. Season with flaky salt and serve warm.

06

VEGETABLES

Many of you know by now that I am on a mission to change the way people think about vegetables. I believe one of the roles I'm supposed to play on this beautiful earth is to encourage you to put more vegetables on your table and help elevate them to greatness, where they belong! Vegetables are fascinating, they are dynamic, they are delicious. Their range of textures and flavors is so big, and they have so many possibilities to explore. All of my restaurants focus heavily on vegetables, following the seasons and connecting with farmers and our local farmers' markets—perhaps none more so than Zaytinya.

In Eastern Mediterranean cooking, vegetables are the heroes, and eggplant might just be the star. This humble vegetable epitomizes everything I love about the vegetable preparations from this part of the world. Its unique qualities captivate you from the moment you spot one at the farmers' market: stacks of them piled high in baskets, their rich, beautiful midnight-purple skin glowing in the sunlight, challenging you to make something special. You cannot resist bringing one or two of them home with you. Once in the kitchen, they continue to surprise you with their subtle flavor and meaty texture. Salted and braised in olive oil, charred and pureed, or dusted in flour and fried, eggplant soaks in all the surrounding flavors and gives so much in return.

So it goes for many of the vegetables found in Mediterranean cooking, vibrant, beautiful creatures that transform into something even more astonishing as soon as the elements of olive oil, spice, and heat are added. Throughout Turkey, Greece, and Lebanon, vegetables are often the main dish of weekday meals, along with grains and legumes, leaving meats for a special occasion or as a side dish or seasoning. Seasonal vegetables and greens are easily found around the Mediterranean, while meats, and even seafood, were traditionally expensive or hard to find. Some animals were needed more for milk, cheese, and eggs, and not for dinner. Add to that the Christian teachings that limit eating meat around religious holidays for many in the region and it's no surprise that vegetables are the foundation of these food traditions.

Depending on the season, vegetables will come in several styles. They may be stuffed with rice or bulgur and maybe some meat; they may be sautéed with butter or deep-fried, or stewed with tomatoes, onions, and garlic—a style definitely

influenced by Spain's sofrito! The classic variation for mezze is vegetables cooked in olive oil and served at room temperature or cold. There's an entire family of Turkish dishes of vegetables cooked in olive oil called zeytinyağlı, which take their name from the Turkish word for olive oil, "zeytinyağı"—the inspiration for Zaytinya's name. In Greece, this sort of cooking in olive oil is known as ladera and in the Middle East it's called bil zayt. These olive-oil-based seasonal vegetable dishes, dolma (stuffed vegetables), sarma (stuffed vine leaves), and imam bayıldı, are classic forms of zeytinyağlı. No matter how you like to slice, dice, simmer, or fry, there is plenty of inspiration in this chapter to bring more delicious vegetables into your life.

BRAISED ARTICHOKES AND SPRING VEGETABLES

ZEYTINYAĞLI ENGINAR

I have loved artichokes since I was a little boy. Growing up in Spain, you could find them in stores, already cleaned down to the hearts and ready to cook. My mother would slice the hearts and fry them with a little olive oil. The magic of artichoke and olive oil is nearly perfected in this dish, one of the most classic zeytinyağlı-style combinations. Be sure to use high-quality extra-virgin olive oil for this recipe, because anything zeytinyağlı deserves the best. Look for baby artichokes in spring, when they are tender and flavorful and have less time to develop thick outer leaves, making them much easier to prepare. Many people will tell you to keep trimmed artichokes in lemon water, but I find the juice gives these tender vegetables a bitter taste; a bunch of parsley will do the job just fine.

Serves 4

1 bunch flat-leaf parsley

6 medium whole artichokes, with stem if possible

4 tablespoons extra-virgin olive oil, divided, plus more for serving

Kosher salt

½ pound baby Yukon Gold potatoes, cleaned and halved

2 small carrots, peeled and cut into ½-inch rounds

1 teaspoon honey

¼ cup English peas

10 sugar snap peas, strings removed, cut into ½-inch pieces

1 to 2 tablespoons thinly sliced preserved lemon rind (page 34)

Zest from half a lemon

Fronds from 4 sprigs fresh dill

Flaky sea salt

○ Fill a 2-quart bowl with cold water and add the parsley sprigs. Clean each artichoke by cutting off the top half with a serrated knife. Break off and discard all of the exterior leaves until you reach the pale green, tender center leaves.

○ Next, using a sharp knife or a peeler, remove the tough green exterior around the artichoke bottoms and stem, leaving the heart and 1 to 2 inches of the stem exposed, then immediately drop into the parsley water and hold there until ready to cook.

○ Over medium heat, warm a tablespoon of olive oil in a pot wide enough to hold the artichoke bottoms in one layer. Sauté the artichokes for 3 minutes, then add water to cover and a large pinch of salt. Cover and simmer until the artichokes are tender, about 15 minutes.

○ Remove the artichokes from the water and increase the heat to medium-high. Add the potatoes and boil until almost tender, about 8 minutes, then drain.

○ When the artichokes are cool enough to handle, slice in half through the stems, then remove the furry center choke with a spoon, removing the outer leaves as well so you're left with only the bottoms and stems. Cut each artichoke half into 2 to 3 wedges, depending on how large your artichokes are.

○ Warm the remaining 3 tablespoons of olive oil in the pot, again over medium heat. Add carrots and sauté 3 minutes, then add the honey and water to almost cover. Simmer until the water is almost gone, then stir in the potatoes, artichokes, and English peas.

○ The vegetables should be tender or almost tender. Add water and continue cooking if needed, then add the sugar snap peas and cook for one last minute. Season to taste with salt.

○ When ready to serve, spoon the cooked vegetables into a serving dish. Garnish with the preserved lemon, lemon zest, and dill. Drizzle with lots of olive oil and season with flaky sea salt.

TURKISH STUFFED EGGPLANT

İMAM BAYILDI

Who was the famous imam who fainted when he tasted this dish? And why? Maybe we'll never know, but the iconic eggplant dish imam bayıldı ("the imam fainted") forever secures his memory. Perhaps he fainted out of pure delight or maybe from the shock of how expensive the ingredients were in those days. Turkish in origin, it's a zeytinyağlı-style dish that is beloved around the Eastern Mediterranean, and is traditionally served at room temperature. Our version adds a hint of color and freshness with a drizzle of our Green Mint Oil (page 31).

Serves 4

2 eggplants (about ¾ pound each), preferably Holland

About 4 teaspoons kosher salt

5 tablespoons extra-virgin olive oil, divided

1 pound ripe tomatoes, chopped, juices reserved

4 sun-dried tomato halves, chopped

1 medium Spanish onion, thinly sliced

1 yellow bell pepper, seeded and diced

1 green bell pepper, seeded and diced

1 red Fresno chili, seeded and diced

2 garlic cloves, minced

1 star anise

¼ teaspoon Urfa pepper

½ teaspoon sumac

⅛ teaspoon sweet smoked paprika

¼ teaspoon granulated sugar

½ teaspoon fresh lemon juice

1 teaspoon pomegranate molasses

1 teaspoon honey

¼ cup Green Mint Oil (page 31)

2 tablespoons pine nuts, toasted

1 tablespoon fresh mint leaves

Flaky sea salt

○ Slice each eggplant in half lengthwise, cutting through and leaving the stem attached. Score the cut sides in a diamond pattern about 1 inch deep, then sprinkle each half with 1 teaspoon of salt, gently pulling the halves open so the salt falls into the cross sections. Set the eggplant cut side down in a colander and let drain for 30 minutes. Rinse off any extra salt, then pat dry.

○ Preheat the oven to 350°F and line a baking sheet with parchment paper.

○ Rub the eggplant all over with 2 tablespoons of the olive oil and place cut side down on the baking sheet. Roast for 20 to 25 minutes, or until tender and easily pierced with a knife. Once cool enough to handle, use a spoon to scrape out about 2 tablespoons of flesh from each half, leaving a shallow well.

○ While the eggplant roasts, put the tomatoes and their juices in a small pot set over medium heat, until just beginning to simmer. (Add a little water if there's not enough liquid to simmer.) Remove from the heat, stir in the sun-dried tomatoes, and let them sit for 10 minutes to rehydrate.

○ Warm 1 tablespoon of the olive oil in a large pan over medium-high heat. Add the onions and large pinch of salt and cook, stirring often, until the onions begin to soften and turn golden,

about 10 minutes. Reduce the heat to medium-low and continue to cook, stirring frequently, for 20 minutes, or until the onions have caramelized; deglaze the pan with a little water if the onions are getting too dark and sticking to the pan.

○ Add the diced peppers, increase the heat to medium, and continue to cook until the peppers soften and begin to brown, about 15 minutes. Stir in the chili and garlic and cook for 1 more minute. Add the tomatoes, eggplant flesh, star anise, Urfa pepper, sumac, smoked paprika, and sugar, stirring well, then add the lemon juice, pomegranate molasses, honey, and 1 tablespoon of olive oil. Continue cooking for about 5 minutes, or until any excess liquid evaporates. Remove from the heat.

○ To serve, drizzle four plates with 1 tablespoon each of the Green Mint Oil, then place an eggplant half on each of the plates. Gently flatten each eggplant, sprinkle with a pinch of the flaky salt, and evenly divide the onion-pepper mixture among each eggplant, spreading to cover the halves (removing the star anise as you go). Drizzle the remaining tablespoon of olive oil over the eggplants and garnish with the pine nuts, mint, and a sprinkle of flaky sea salt.

CRISPY BRUSSELS SPROUTS AFELIA

These crispy, tangy Brussels sprouts are far and away our most requested vegetable dish at the restaurant, including by my wife and daughters, for good reason: they're fried to a dark golden brown, then served with a creamy, coriander-studded dressing and rich garlic yogurt, topped with dill and sweet-tart barberries. It's a dish that you won't find on menus in Greece, though it's inspired by Cypriot dishes made with coriander seeds. Make sure to cut the Brussels lengthwise to keep them attached at their base so the leaves stay connected. You may not use up all the coriander dressing here, so try it on salad greens or roasted vegetables. This dish is really all about the fried Brussels sprouts, but if you prefer, you can broil them instead with a coating of olive oil.

Serves 4

For the coriander dressing:

1 tablespoon coriander seeds

2 tablespoons Greek yogurt

2 teaspoons honey

2 tablespoons fresh lemon juice

½ cup extra-virgin olive oil

For the Brussels sprouts:

Canola oil

1 pound Brussels sprouts, trimmed and quartered lengthwise

Flaky sea salt

2 tablespoons chopped fresh dill

2 cloves Garlic Confit (page 29)

⅓ cup Greek yogurt

2 teaspoons fresh lemon juice

Kosher salt

Freshly ground white pepper

¼ cup barberries, soaked (see box)

○ To make the coriander dressing, put the coriander seeds on a cutting board, cover with a dish towel, and use a rolling pin or the side of a chef's knife to coarsely crack the seeds. Brush the cracked seeds into a mixing bowl and whisk in the yogurt, honey, and lemon juice. Continue whisking and slowly add the olive oil to form a creamy dressing. You'll have about ¾ cup.

○ To make the Brussels sprouts, pour 2 to 3 inches of oil into a large, deep saucepan set over medium heat and warm the oil to 350°F. Line a large plate with a few paper towels and have a splatter screen ready. To avoid crowding the pan, add half the Brussels sprouts, and fry until dark golden brown and outer leaves are crispy, about 5 minutes, using the splatter screen if needed. Remove the sprouts using a wire skimmer and transfer to the plate to drain. Allow the oil to return to 350°F, then fry the remaining sprouts. Season the drained sprouts generously with flaky sea salt and half of the chopped dill.

○ To serve, mash the garlic cloves in a small mixing bowl. Add the yogurt, the lemon juice, a pinch of kosher salt, and a pinch of white pepper. Whisk together vigorously, then spread the garlic yogurt on a serving platter and top with the Brussels sprouts. Spoon some of the coriander dressing over the top and garnish with the barberries, remaining dill, and flaky sea salt.

CHEF MOVE

Be sure to pick through your dried barberries and rinse them well before using. While you can use them as is, we like to rehydrate them and add a touch of sweetness. Stir 2 tablespoons sugar with 2 tablespoons hot water in a small bowl to make a quick simple syrup. Stir in 2 tablespoons of lemon juice, add ¼ cup barberries, and cover with a ¼ cup more warm water. Let sit for at least 30 minutes—overnight is even better—and drain before using.

GREEK ZUCCHINI FRITTERS
KOLOKYTHOKEFTEDES

It's a mouthful, and many of our diners won't attempt to say the name of this dish, and instead just point to the menu. But take the opportunity to learn a little Greek: "kolokythi" (zucchini) plus "keftedaki" (meatball). No matter how you say it (or not!), it's one of our favorites—light fritters with a crunchy exterior and a sweet, creamy inside. I first tasted this dish in Santorini, where the rich volcanic soil of the Greek island makes for superb zucchini and tomatoes. If you can use in-season farmers' market vegetables, the dish will be at its peak, but grocery-store zucchini will get you most of the way there. If you can't find Kefalograviera, Manchego cheese can be substituted; just add a pinch more salt as Manchego is less salty than Kefalograviera.

Makes 16 fritters

For the caper-yogurt sauce:

⅔ cup Greek yogurt

1 teaspoon caper brine, plus 1 tablespoon capers

¼ teaspoon orange blossom water

Pinch kosher salt

¼ teaspoon dried mint

Extra-virgin olive oil

For the fritters:

2 cups shredded zucchini

3 scallions, thinly sliced

1 tablespoon chopped parsley

2 teaspoons chopped mint

1 teaspoon dried oregano

⅓ cup panko bread crumbs

2 ounces Kefalograviera cheese, grated or shredded

2 tablespoons all-purpose flour

¼ teaspoon freshly ground white pepper

½ teaspoon kosher salt

2 large egg whites

2 tablespoons canola oil, plus more if needed

○ To make the sauce, whisk together the yogurt, caper brine, orange blossom water, 2 teaspoons of water, and a pinch of salt in a mixing bowl until smooth. If the sauce is too thick, add another teaspoon of water. Cover and refrigerate until ready to use.

○ For the fritters, stir together the zucchini, scallions, parsley, mint, oregano, panko, cheese, flour, pepper, and salt in a large bowl.

○ Whip the egg whites in a medium bowl until firm peaks form, then fold into the zucchini mixture.

○ Heat about 2 tablespoons of canola oil in a large nonstick sauté pan over medium-high heat. Spoon 1 heaping tablespoon of zucchini batter onto the hot pan to form each fritter, using a spoon to pat them out to about 2 inches wide, and cook, turning once, until nicely browned, about 1 to 2 minutes per side. Transfer the fritters to a paper-towel-lined plate to drain. Continue with the remaining batter, being careful not to crowd the pan, until you have 16 fritters. If you need to add a bit more oil to the pan, be sure to let it get hot before adding more batter.

○ To serve, remove the caper-yogurt sauce from the refrigerator, give it a good stir, then spread it in a shallow serving bowl set on a serving platter. Top the sauce with the whole capers, sprinkle with dried mint, and drizzle with a little olive oil. Arrange the fritters around the sauce.

CARROT FRITTERS WITH PISTACHIO SAUCE
HAVUÇ KÖFTESI

Makes 18 fritters

For the sauce:

1¼ cups shelled pistachios, plus 1 tablespoon, chopped, for garnish

1 tablespoon plus ¾ cup extra-virgin olive oil

½ yellow onion, thinly sliced

½ small garlic clove, minced

¼ cup fresh lemon juice

¼ bunch parsley, chopped

1½ teaspoons kosher salt

¼ teaspoon black peppercorns

For the fritters:

1 tablespoon extra-virgin olive oil

5 medium carrots (1¼ pounds), peeled, trimmed and thinly sliced

½ cup panko bread crumbs, plus more if needed

3 dried apricot halves, chopped

½ small garlic clove, minced

¼ teaspoon sweet smoked paprika

¼ teaspoon cayenne pepper

1½ teaspoons kosher salt, plus more to taste

¼ teaspoon freshly ground black pepper

2 scallions, thinly sliced

½ bunch parsley, chopped

1 tablespoon chopped dill

1 tablespoon chopped mint, plus small whole leaves, for garnish

1 large egg

3 tablespoons pine nuts

Canola oil

These Turkish carrot fritters are part of a family of vegetable köfte (like the Kolokythokeftedes, page 189). They are thought to date back to the Ottoman palace kitchens, where dried fruits and nuts were combined into meat and vegetable dishes. Another clue to their palace birthplace: they're not often found outside of Istanbul. From my first bite of these sweet-and-savory fritters in a small shop in Istanbul, I knew we needed them on the menu. The pistachio sauce (which, you should know, is worth the price of this book alone) can be made ahead of time, and the balls of carrot mixture can be kept in the refrigerator—just bring them to room temperature before frying.

○ To make the sauce, preheat your oven to 375°F. Spread the pistachios on a baking sheet and roast, tossing occasionally, until fragrant and lightly golden, 8 to 10 minutes.

○ Meanwhile, warm the 1 tablespoon of olive oil in a sauté pan set over medium heat. Add the onions and cook until soft and lightly golden, about 5 minutes.

○ Put the roasted pistachios, onions, garlic, lemon juice, parsley, salt, and peppercorns in a blender and pulse to chop. With the motor running, pour in the remaining ¾ cup of olive oil and continue blending for about 2 minutes until totally smooth and emulsified. If needed, add water, a few tablespoons at a time, to achieve a smooth, saucy texture. (You will have about 2 cups of sauce; keep in the refrigerator for up to one week).

○ To make the fritters, warm the olive oil in the same sauté pan over medium heat. Add the carrots and cook for about 5 minutes, until just beginning to soften; stir often so the carrots do not begin to brown. Add 2 tablespoons of water and cover the pan. Allow the carrots to steam for 5 to 10 minutes, adding more water

if needed, until they are easily mashed with a fork. Remove from the heat and let cool slightly.

○ Put the carrots in a food processor and add the panko, apricots, garlic, paprika, cayenne, salt, black pepper, scallions, parsley, dill, mint, and egg. Pulse several times, stopping to scrape down the sides, until the carrots are mashed and the mixture holds together when pinched. Add a little more bread crumbs, up to 1 tablespoon, if mixture looks too wet. Add the pine nuts and pulse once or twice, just to mix.

○ Heat 2 inches of canola oil in a medium pot to 350°F. Scoop 1-ounce portions of the carrot mixture (about 2 tablespoons) to create round balls, setting them on a plate as you go. Carefully drop half of the carrot balls into the hot oil and fry until golden brown, 3 to 4 minutes. Remove with a wire skimmer and put on a paper-towel-lined plate to drain. Let the oil return to 350°F, then repeat with the remaining fritters. Sprinkle with a little salt.

○ To serve, spread the pistachio sauce on a serving plate, scatter the fritters on top, and garnish with chopped pistachios and mint leaves.

GOLDEN SPICE CAULIFLOWER

Frying cauliflower is a traditional preparation around the world, and has a deep history in the Levant, where it is known as zahra mekleyah. Our version starts with a quick steam to ensure that the cauliflower is tender, then it's fried to a beautifully burnished golden brown. The spice blend is our take on the classic Yemeni hawayej, meaning "mixture" in Arabic, which is flavored with cumin, black pepper, and turmeric and traditionally used in soups. The final dish—golden spiced cauliflower with a green herbed tahini sauce, preserved lemon, pine nuts, and capers—is nutty, earthy, savory, and tart. If you prefer not to fry, you can coat the cauliflower with a tablespoon or so of oil and roast it in a 375°F oven for 25 to 30 minutes, then toss with the golden spice.

Serves 4

1 medium head cauliflower, cored and broken into 1-inch florets

Kosher salt

Canola oil

1 teaspoon Hawayej (page 27)

Flaky sea salt

¾ cup herbed tahini sauce (page 67)

1 tablespoon salt-cured capers, rinsed and dried

1 tablespoon thinly sliced preserved lemon rind (page 34)

1 teaspoon sesame seeds

2 teaspoons minced chives

2 tablespoons pine nuts, toasted

○ Bring a large pot of water fitted with a steamer basket to a boil over medium-high heat. Add the cauliflower to the basket and steam for 4 to 6 minutes, until it begins to soften. Remove from the heat, then season lightly with kosher salt and let cool.

○ Warm 2 to 3 inches of canola oil in a deep pot over medium heat until it reaches 350°F. Have a splatter screen nearby in case you need it. Fry the cauliflower in batches until nicely golden brown, about 4 minutes, letting the oil return to 350°F after each batch. Remove the cauliflower from the pot using a spider or slotted spoon, shake off excess oil, and put in a mixing bowl. Once all the cauliflower is in the mixing bowl, toss with the Hawayej, then arrange the cauliflower on a rack or paper-towel-lined plate to finish draining. Season to taste with flaky salt.

○ To serve, spread the tahini sauce on the bottom of the plate. Arrange the cauliflower on top and sprinkle with the capers, preserved lemon, sesame seeds, chives, and pine nuts.

OKRA AND TOMATO STEW
BAMYA

This is our take on a classic Lebanese stew featuring okra ("bamya" in Arabic) that are harvested very young—under an inch—and cooked whole. At most U.S. grocery stores and farmers' markets, we get our okra quite a bit larger. Even if you can't find small okra, make sure to find pods that are as fresh and tender as possible—after they're caramelized, they will maintain a bit of crunch, which gives the stew great texture alongside the fried chickpeas. This dish is perfect for summer when okra is in season, but if you can find frozen whole baby okra, known as Okra Zero, in Middle Eastern grocery stores or online, try them—they're the perfect size for an authentic bamya. Even frozen sliced okra can work, but you'll need to thaw and drain it before adding them to the pan to sear.

Serves 4

¾ cup dry chickpeas

Pinch baking soda

¾ pound okra, cut in ½-inch-thick pieces (about 3 cups)

Kosher salt

Canola oil

¼ teaspoon Urfa pepper (or other dried smoky chili pepper)

1½ cups Spiced Tomato Sauce (page 74)

¼ teaspoon ground cardamom

½ teaspoon ground cumin

2 tablespoons microgreens, such as cilantro or parsley (or chopped parsley)

○ The day before you want to prepare the dish, combine the chickpeas and baking soda in a bowl and cover with double the amount of water. Set aside to soak overnight, or for at least 8 hours.

○ If using frozen cut okra, set the okra out on a sheet pan lined with paper towels to thaw completely, then pat dry.

○ Drain the chickpeas and transfer to a large saucepan and cover with 4 to 5 cups of cold water. Bring to a boil over high heat, then reduce to maintain a simmer and cook for about 1 hour, until the chickpeas are completely soft but still hold their shape. Skim off any foam. If the water reduces too quickly, add ¼ cup of cold water to slow down the cooking. The water should barely cover the chickpeas when completely cooked through. Remove from the heat and season to taste with salt.

○ Drain the chickpeas, setting half in a bowl and the other half on a paper-towel-lined plate. Pat dry.

○ Pour about 2 inches of the oil into a medium saucepan set over medium-high and heat to 300°F. Have a splatter screen ready in case you need it. Fry the dried chickpeas until very crispy and golden, 10 to 15 minutes. You don't want them to brown, only to be extremely crispy. Transfer the fried chickpeas to drain on a paper-towel-lined plate and season with ¼ teaspoon salt and the Urfa pepper.

○ Warm 1 tablespoon of the oil in a large sauté pan over medium-high heat. When the pan is very hot and the oil starts to smoke, add the okra in one layer, cut side down if possible, and allow to quickly caramelize, about 3 minutes on each side (it will take longer if using defrosted cut okra; cook until the liquid evaporates). Reduce the heat to medium, add the reserved cooked chickpeas, tomato sauce, cardamom, cumin, and a pinch of salt, then stir and cook until warmed through, about 5 minutes.

○ To serve, spoon the saucy okra on a serving plate, then top with the fried chickpeas and microgreens.

CRISPY FRIED EGGPLANT WITH YOGURT

BATIJAN BIL LABAN

The combination of eggplant ("batijan" in Arabic) and yogurt (laban) is a classic dish found throughout the Levant, particulary in Lebanon. By combining crispy fried eggplant with cool, savory yogurt, we get an incredible dish of textures and flavors. The eggplant gets crispy on the outside and creamy on the inside; the toasted walnuts give a satisfying nutty crunch; and the cardamom apricots offer a pop of acidic sweetness that brightens the whole thing up. In Turkey and Greece, you'll find a similar version where the eggplant is simply sliced into thin rounds before frying.

Serves 4

3 thin eggplants (about ¼ pound each), preferably Chinese or Japanese

Kosher salt

3 cups buttermilk

2 cloves Garlic Confit (page 29)

⅓ cup Greek yogurt

2 teaspoons fresh lemon juice

Pinch freshly ground white pepper

Canola oil

2 cups all-purpose flour

1 tablespoon fine sea salt, plus more for seasoning

6 Cardamom Apricots (page 36), cut into ¼-inch slices

¼ cup roughly chopped walnuts, toasted

2 tablespoons mint leaves

1 teaspoon sesame seeds, toasted

Flaky sea salt

○ Peel the eggplants and cut into ¾-inch-thick rounds, discarding the stem ends. Salt the eggplant pieces and let them drain in a colander for about 15 minutes, then stir together the eggplant and buttermilk in a large mixing bowl and let soak for 30 minutes.

○ Meanwhile, mash the garlic cloves in a small mixing bowl. Whisk in the yogurt, lemon juice, a pinch of kosher salt, and a pinch of white pepper. Taste and adjust seasoning as needed.

○ A few minutes before the eggplant is done soaking, heat 3 inches of oil in a deep pot over medium heat until it reaches 325°F. Mix the flour and sea salt in another large mixing bowl. Using a slotted spoon, and working in batches, transfer the eggplant pieces to the seasoned flour and toss until well coated.

○ Carefully drop the eggplant pieces into the oil and fry for 3 minutes. Do not crowd the pot. Using a spatula or tongs, flip the eggplant pieces over and fry for another 3 to 4 minutes, until golden brown. Transfer the eggplant to a paper-towel-lined plate to drain and season with sea salt. Continue with the remaining eggplant pieces, being sure to let the oil temperature return to 325°F.

○ To serve, put a large dollop of the garlic yogurt in the center of a serving plate. Arrange the eggplant around the plate, garnish with apricots, walnuts, mint leaves, and sesame seeds, and season with flaky salt.

GRILLED ASPARAGUS WITH SMOKED LABNEH

These roasted asparagus are a Zaytinya original: you won't find asparagus served like this in the Eastern Mediterranean. But we wanted to use a few iconic ingredients of the region—labneh, za'atar, and preserved lemons—and have them complement asparagus, one of our springtime favorites. We like to give the dish extra depth by smoking the labneh (see the note on smoking, and how to make your own stove-top smoker, page 205), but a simple seasoned labneh will work fine. I like to grill the asparagus—I'm always looking for an excuse to light up my grill—but you can also broil the asparagus in the oven (see note below) if you need to keep things indoors.

Serves 4

1 cup labneh

Kosher salt

6 tablespoons extra-virgin olive oil, divided

1 preserved lemon (page 34)

1 bunch asparagus, woody ends removed

2 tablespoons za'atar, divided

Flaky sea salt

○ To smoke the labneh, put it in a shallow heatproof bowl. Prepare a stove-top smoker according to manufacturer's instructions (we like to use cherrywood for labneh). Once the wood chips are smoking, remove the smoker from the heat, put in the labneh, and cover. Smoke for 30 to 40 minutes, then remove the labneh, stir in 1 teaspoon of kosher salt and 2 tablespoons of olive oil, cover, and set aside.

○ Cut the lemon into quarters, remove and discard the flesh, then rinse the peel. Finely dice and add to a small mixing bowl, then stir in 3 tablespoons of the oil.

○ Prepare your grill, preferably a charcoal grill. Toss the asparagus with the remaining tablespoon of olive oil to lightly coat, and season to taste with kosher salt. When the grill is hot, arrange the asparagus across the grill grates, close the lid, and cook until lightly charred, 5 to 10 minutes, depending on the asparagus's thickness. Occasionally roll the asparagus across the grates to cook on all sides. Remove the asparagus from the grill and season with 1 tablespoon of the za'atar.

○ To serve, spread the smoked labneh across the bottom of a serving plate. Lay the asparagus on top of the labneh and spoon the preserved lemon and olive oil over the asparagus and labneh. Sprinkle the remaining tablespoon of za'atar on top and season with sea salt.

CHEF MOVE To cook your asparagus in the oven, heat a rimmed baking sheet under the broiler for 3 minutes, then carefully spread the seasoned asparagus on the hot baking sheet and set it under the broiler for 2 to 3 minutes, until tender and lightly browned. Shake the pan to rotate the asparagus and broil for another 3 minutes, until tender and lightly charred. Placing the asparagus on a hot sheet pan will help it cook evenly.

CYPRIOT-STYLE POTATOES WITH CORIANDER AND WINE
PATATES ANTINAHTES

This specialty of Cyprus, where "tossed" baby potatoes are combined with wine and spices, was taught to us by Greek food writer and mentor Aglaia Kremezi. She told us it's important to not only crack the coriander seeds—the telltale spice of Cypriot dishes—but the potatoes as well, so they can absorb all the flavor from the simmering wine and then develop a crispy crust from the olive oil. The semisweet rosé wine commonly used can be difficult to find, so we like to use dry rosé and a touch of honey. We also like to add cilantro, which lends color and echoes the flavor of the traditional coriander seed in this dish.

Serves 4 to 6

2 pounds baby gold potatoes

¼ cup olive oil, plus more for drizzling

Kosher salt

2 tablespoons whole coriander seeds

½ cup dry rosé wine

1 teaspoon honey, preferably Greek

¼ cup cilantro leaves, minced

○ Place the potatoes in a pot large enough to hold them in one layer with a little room to spare. Pour in the olive oil, season with a large pinch of salt, and add water to halfway cover the potatoes. Bring the potatoes to a simmer over high heat, then cook until the water has evaporated and the potatoes start to gently fry, about 10 minutes.

○ Meanwhile, put the coriander seeds on a cutting board, cover with a dish towel, and use a rolling pin or the side of a chef's knife to coarsely crack the seeds. Brush the cracked seeds into a small mixing bowl and set aside.

○ As the potatoes fry, reduce the heat to medium and gently crack them one by one with the back of a ladle or potato masher; you want to slightly crush them while still keeping most of their shape. Continue frying until the exposed potato begins to brown and get crispy.

○ Once the potatoes are browned, add the coriander seeds and toss until aromatic, about 1 minute. Add the wine and honey and continue cooking until the liquid is absorbed and concentrates, about 2 minutes. Stir in the cilantro, season to taste with salt, and serve warm.

SMOKY MUSHROOM KAPNISTA

This dish gets its name from the ancient Greek word kapnós, meaning "smoke." Smoking foods, by cooking over wood-fired pits and stoves, has been part of Greek culinary tradition for thousands of years, and it gives certain ingredients a profound, primordial character. Here we smoke cremini mushrooms, deepening their meaty flavors and making them a perfect match for the creamy labneh, the nutty toasted walnuts, and the rich, sweet dates. You want to brown these mushrooms before and after smoking to get the most flavor. If you don't have an outdoor or stove-top smoker, see page 205 for a tip on making a simple one yourself. You can always skip the smoking and just sauté the mushrooms, they will be delicious, but why miss out on all the fun?

Serves 4

1 pound cremini mushrooms, cleaned

1 tablespoon canola oil, plus more if needed

Kosher salt

2 tablespoons extra-virgin olive oil

4 to 5 dates, chopped (about ⅓ cup)

½ cup walnut halves, toasted

⅓ cup Whipped Labneh (page 60)

Flaky sea salt

1 tablespoon minced chives

Pinch ground cumin

○ Trim the mushroom stems flush with the caps and make sure the mushrooms are dry. Set a large sauté pan over high heat and add the canola oil. Once the oil smokes, add the mushrooms and cook, tossing gently, until nicely browned, about 5 minutes. Add a teaspoon or more of oil if needed to keep the mushrooms sizzling. Remove from the heat and season with a generous pinch of salt.

○ Prepare a smoker according to the manufacturer's instructions, or make your own stove-top smoker (see page 205). Transfer the sautéed mushrooms to the smoker and smoke for about 30 minutes.

○ Return the large sauté pan to the stove top, add the olive oil, and warm over medium-high heat. Add the smoked mushrooms and cook until nicely browned, about 5 minutes, then add the dates and toasted walnuts and continue cooking to warm through, a few minutes more.

○ To serve, spread the labneh around the center of a platter. Spoon the mushroom mixture on top of the labneh. Garnish with flaky sea salt, chives, and cumin.

THE SMOKING SECTION

We love the complexity and earthiness that smoking gives to humble ingredients. Meats have long reigned supreme over the smokers and grills of backyard barbecues; marathon days of low-and-slow cooking give pork, beef, and lamb that elemental taste of wood and fire. But it's the simplicity of vegetables and smoke that I find so fascinating and inspiring. If you take mushrooms and smother them with wood smoke or bury tomatoes or beets in hot embers, they can become something astonishing. Think of smoke as just another seasoning, like salt, herbs, and spices.

A stove-top smoker is an easy and affordable way to season vegetables, olives, nuts, and even labneh and yogurt. Leave the large meat smokers outside and try a kettle- or dome-style stove-top smoker in your kitchen. These shapes have more space for a variety of ingredients compared to a smoker box, and they are a bit less complicated than using a smoking gun. If you don't have space to add another tool to your kitchen, you can follow some easy steps from our friend Aglaia Kremezi to craft a kitchen smoker using the pots and tools you likely already have on hand.

On one of her visits to our restaurant in Washington, Aglaia fell in love with the smoked olives on our horta salata. When she returned home to Kea, she experimented with how to get that smoky flavor in her kitchen. Here's what you can do: Find a large pot with a tight-fitting lid, then line the bottom of the pot with a couple sheets of aluminum foil. Spread about ⅓ cup of wood chips or wood pellets on top of the foil. Put a metal steamer basket into the pot, making sure it sits above the wood chips.

Place the mushrooms (olives, beets, or walnuts) in the basket, spreading them out to allow some smoke to flow around them. Cover the pot with another piece of aluminum foil, then fit the lid tightly on top. Crimp more foil around the seal of the lid to keep any smoke from escaping. Set the pot over medium heat until you smell smoke from burning chips in the pot, about 5 minutes. Then turn the heat off and let the mushrooms (or olives or nuts) rest in the pot to continue smoking for 30 to 40 minutes to absorb the wood flavor. If you want to smoke labneh or yogurt, first heat the pot with the steamer basket, covered tightly, until you begin to smell smoke. Turn off the heat, quickly uncover the pot and place a heatproof bowl with the labneh or yogurt in the steamer basket, then return the cover and tightly seal the edges with foil. Allow to smoke for 30 minutes. Be sure to turn on your vent hood or open a window if you don't want the smell to overpower your kitchen.

When you're ready to remove the ingredients from your smoker, consider taking the pot outside to remove the lid and aluminum foil covers and release the smoke that has gathered in the pot. Carefully remove the bowl or steamer basket and set the ingredients aside to use in your recipe.

For the wood chips, smaller chips or extra-fine chips will perform better on a stove top as they will burn more quickly and easily. Leave the hickory and mesquite varieties for meats and instead look for the fruit woods and oaks commonly found in Greece and Lebanon. For labneh, we like to use chips of cherrywood, and for olives and walnuts, we prefer applewood.

TOMATO SAGANAKI

Saganaki is best known in America as a flaming fried cheese dish, but the saganaki extended universe goes far beyond torched cheese. We make saganaki—whose name refers to the two-handled pan used to serve it—with vegetables and seafood. In fact, we're pretty sure you could "saganaki" almost anything. Below you'll see recipes for tomato, broccoli, and mushroom saganaki, and you can find oyster and shrimp (page 232) in the Seafood chapter. Extra credit if you douse everything in a shower of ouzo and light it on fire (safely, people!). If you can't find Kefalograviera, Manchego cheese can be substituted; add a pinch more salt as Manchego is less salty than Kefalograviera.

Serves 4

1 pound cherry or grape tomatoes, blanched and peeled (page 37, step 1)

1 teaspoon sugar

1 teaspoon kosher salt

4 tablespoons extra-virgin olive oil, divided, plus more for drizzling

8 sun-dried tomato halves, preferably Turkish

1 small garlic clove, minced

2 scallions, trimmed, green and white parts finely chopped

2 tablespoons ouzo

1 cup Spiced Tomato Sauce (page 74)

½ cup grated Kefalograviera cheese

¼ teaspoon Urfa pepper

½ teaspoon ground cumin

1 ounce feta

1 tablespoon minced chives

1 teaspoon dried oregano

1 teaspoon Aleppo pepper

Flaky sea salt

○ Preheat the oven to 200°F. Toss the peeled tomatoes with the sugar, salt, and 2 tablespoons of the olive oil, then spread the tomatoes on a rimmed baking sheet lined with parchment. Roast until the tomatoes begin to dry and slightly shrivel, about 1 hour and 15 minutes. Do not let the tomatoes brown.

○ Meanwhile, cover the sun-dried tomatoes with a little boiling water and set aside to hydrate for 15 minutes, then drain and dice.

○ Warm the remaining 2 tablespoons of olive oil in a sauté pan over medium heat. Add the garlic and cook for 2 minutes, then stir in the scallions and slow-cooked cherry tomatoes. Cook for 1 more minute to meld the flavors, but do not brown the tomatoes. Pour in the ouzo and deglaze the pan, scraping up any brown garlic bits.

○ Stir in the tomato sauce, Kefalograviera cheese, Urfa pepper, and cumin and continue to cook until the cheese has completely melted, 3 more minutes.

○ Spoon the tomato mixture into a shallow serving dish, preferably with two handles. Crumble the feta over the tomatoes and sprinkle with chives, dried oregano, and Aleppo pepper. Drizzle with olive oil and season with flaky sea salt.

FOR BROCCOLI SAGANAKI:

Substitute 1 pound broccoli florets. Blanch the broccoli in boiling salted water for 1 minute, then drain well, add to the sauté pan with the garlic and scallions, and proceed with recipe.

FOR MUSHROOM SAGANAKI:

Substitute 1 pound cleaned, trimmed cremini mushrooms. Cut any larger mushrooms in half or quarters, to keep all the mushrooms about the same size. Heat 3 tablespoons of canola oil over medium-high heat in a sauté pan. When the oil begins to smoke, add the mushrooms in one layer and cook until well browned, turning the mushrooms to cook on all sides, about 5 minutes. You may need to work in batches depending on the size of your pan. Then add the garlic and scallions and continue with the recipe.

07

SEA
FO

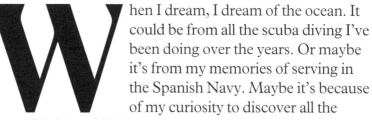

When I dream, I dream of the ocean. It could be from all the scuba diving I've been doing over the years. Or maybe it's from my memories of serving in the Spanish Navy. Maybe it's because of my curiosity to discover all the beautiful things hidden underwater. Or maybe it's just my love for all the delicious creatures that swim in the sea.

Whatever the reason, I find that I'm immediately pulled to the fish stalls at any market. There's something so exciting about exploring the stacks of plump fish and ancient-looking crustaceans, in all the colors of the rainbow, piled high on shelves of ice that soak the floors beneath you. Not long ago I walked the aisles of Varvakios Agora, Athens Central Market (*left*), with Chef Costa and our dear friend Aglaia. We watched as shoppers came to select their sea bass and skoumbri, a kind of mackerel, for that night's dinner. They would point to the squid and shrimp of all sizes, then sellers would scoop them into cones of thick paper to carry home. I was so jealous; I wanted to take one of everything. I decided we needed to eat. We needed to taste some of the wonders laid out before us, and with Aglaia's help, we convinced the owners of the Hasapika food stalls right there in the market to let us cook up all our shopping for an amazing lunch. We bought bushels of glorious langoustines, or cigalas as they are known in Spain—my family's favorite—and steamed them to perfection. We had a few striped bass and a bucketload of tiny crayfish known as karavides, which we tossed with pasta and a fresh tomato sauce. It was the perfect way to celebrate the treasures of the Mediterranean Sea.

Greece is one of the few countries in the world whose identity is so closely tied to the sea. With thousands of miles of coastline and hundreds of islands (more than 150 inhabited!), seafood is at the heart of Greek culture. The Greeks are a people who take great pride in preparing fish and sharing it with love. I learned this lesson many years ago from my friend Chef Costas Spiliadis of Estiatorio Milos, one of the finest Greek restaurants in the world, dedicated to the beauty and versatility of Mediterranean seafood. When I first visited his New York restaurant in the early 2000s (he now has several restaurants around the world), I saw the passion he and his team had for presenting Greek cuisine in new and exciting ways. I immediately knew that what we planned to do at Zaytinya would be amazing: taking traditional ingredients, learning their history and treating them with respect, then reimagining them in our own new style.

THE ULTIMATE SEAFOOD

made from bonito or ling, as well as the many years as a chef tasting pastas or eggs seasoned with shaved bottarga. But it was on a trip to Greece, in the early days of Zaytinya, when a plate of thinly sliced, saffron-colored, creamy avgotaraho from the Trikalinos family was first laid in front of me, simply drizzled with a little olive oil. With one bite, in that moment, I was changed.

This was one of the most incredible, intensely flavored delicacies I had ever tasted, rich and savory but not overly salty. I would learn that the Trikalinos family has been producing avgotaraho in Greece since 1856, using only wild grey mullet roe and a natural beeswax coating to preserve it; their unique process keeps the roe soft, moist, and rich in healthy omega-3s inside the protective coating. I returned to Washington determined that we needed to celebrate this astonishing taste of the Mediterranean at Zaytinya.

Considered a rare product even in Greece, Trikalinos's avgotaraho was not available in the U.S., so we connected with our friends at Rogers Collection, an East Coast import company, who were also blown away by its refined sea flavor, to help bring it to America. I could not have been prouder when Zaytinya was the first restaurant in the United States to serve this very special avgotaraho. Soon after, we welcomed my good friend Zafeiris Trikalinos, the fifth-generation leader of the family business, to Washington to share his amazing story with our team and our guests. Today, they sell their product all across the U.S. And at Zaytinya, just as we did in the very first days, we like to serve the avgotaraho very simply: thinly sliced, still in its beeswax, to be peeled off at the table and drizzled with a little olive oil (*left*).

I am going to surprise you here. The most amazing seafood from Greece is not the beautiful silver-tinted fish or mysterious octopus that fishermen pull from the sea every day, filling markets and village shops. To me, it is the delicate, golden, glistening cured roe known as avgotaraho. It is the ultimate essence of the sea. It's the food of the gods.

Avgotaraho is a specialty of the Eastern Mediterranean, made from the cured roe of grey mullet, and known outside of Greece mainly as bottarga. It is a treasured food, dating back to ancient Egypt, where the roe sacs from grey mullet and other fish from the Mediterranean waters would be salted, dried, and pressed into cakes for preserving. I knew the briny flavor of cured roe, from growing up in Spain, where we have several varieties

Zafeiris and I have now been friends for nearly two decades, and I cannot visit Greece without him insisting on taking me; my wife, Patricia; and Aglaia out to visit the amazing and talented chefs of Athens to show us new and interesting ways they are experimenting with this centuries-old delicacy of the sea. For that, I am forever grateful.

AVGOTARAHO AND SQUID INK PASTA

Sometimes when you have a big, bold ingredient, you want to balance it out—rich with acidic, salty with sweet. Other times, you want to double down, make it bigger, more powerful. This is one of those times, when we take briny, intense avgotaraho and pair it with something that tastes deeply of the ocean: squid ink. Create a creamy sauce by adding a fresh egg yolk to the pasta, stirring the yolk into the hot pasta to gently cook the yolk as it is mixed in. You can find squid ink pasta in specialty stores or online, or just use regular pasta. Look for Trikalinos's Greek avgotaraho and avgotaraho powder online, where it is often named bottarga. A little goes a long way here; serve it with slices of citrus, fried eggs, wilted greens, even a simple slice of crusty bread and butter.

Serves 4

1 wax-covered avgotaraho

Kosher salt

1 pound squid ink pasta

1 tablespoon olive oil, plus more for drizzling

1 garlic clove

4 egg yolks, divided (optional)

¼ cup avgotaraho powder

○ Remove the avgotaraho from the refrigerator and allow to rest for 1 hour, until the wax begins to slightly soften. Cut a 3-inch piece from the avgotaraho, then carefully peel off the wax, keeping the dried roe sacs intact. Using a sharp knife, slice the roe into 10 thin pieces. Separate the two sac roe pieces and remove any membrane from around the sacs. Set the sliced pieces of avgotaraho aside. Cover the exposed side of the stick of avgotaraho tightly with plastic wrap and store in the refrigerator for another use.

○ Bring a large pot of salted water to a boil, add the pasta, and cook until al dente, about 8 minutes. Reserve about ½ cup of the pasta water, then drain the pasta.

○ Meanwhile, heat the olive oil in a large skillet or pot over medium heat. Grate the garlic clove on a Microplane or finely mince and add to the pan. Cook until golden, about 3 minutes. Add the pasta and about ¼ cup of the reserved cooking liquid and toss to coat.

○ To serve, divide the pasta among four bowls and gently top each with an egg yolk, if you like. Lay 5 to 6 pieces of avgotaraho around each plate. Drizzle with olive oil and generously sprinkle with avgotaraho powder.

OCTOPUS SANTORINI

The inspiration for this dish is the island of Santorini and the beautiful Aegean Sea that surrounds it. Smoky charred octopus tentacles swim in a sea of saffron-infused split pea puree, with hits of salty capers and punchy pickled onions bringing brightness to the dish. Santorini, famous for its rich volcanic soil, is home to an ancient pea called fava Santorini—they are not like the favas you find elsewhere, but actually much closer to the texture and flavor of yellow split peas, which we use here. For the octopus, while you only need the tentacles, we like to braise it whole, reserving the head for stock. The vinegar braise is a necessary (and flavorful) step to tenderize the meat before searing it. It's a much easier way than the Greek fishermen's age-old tradition of beating the octopus on the shoreline rocks to soften the muscular tentacles. Frozen octopus is easy to find and prepare; all you need to do is thaw it in the refrigerator (this could take a day or two) and rinse well.

Serves 2 to 4

1 4- to 6-pound cleaned octopus, thawed

2 cups red wine vinegar

1 tablespoon black peppercorns

3 bay leaves

Extra-virgin olive oil

1 cup fava Santorini (page 61), warmed

½ cup pea tendrils or flat-leaf parsley

1 tablespoon ladolemono (page 60)

Flaky sea salt

2 tablespoons salt-cured capers, rinsed and dried

¼ cup pickled onions (page 32)

○ Preheat the oven to 300°F. Thoroughly rinse the octopus with cold water and pat dry. Put the vinegar, peppercorns, and bay leaves in an ovenproof Dutch oven with a lid. Bring to a simmer over medium heat. Lower the octopus into the pot, head side up, and spread out the tentacles in the vinegar. Once the vinegar returns to a boil, cover the pot and transfer it to the oven.

○ Cook the octopus for 1 hour to an hour and 15 minutes, or until tender. To check the octopus for doneness, remove the pot from the oven and carefully lift the lid (avoid the steam that is released so as not to burn your hands). When the octopus is done, the purplish skin will fade somewhat and shrink to reveal the white flesh where the head and tentacles meet. The tip of a sharp knife will also easily pierce the thickest part of the tentacle.

○ Using tongs or a meat fork, remove the octopus from the pot and drain in a colander, then put it on a platter and refrigerate to cool, about 1 hour. Once cool, remove the tentacles from the head and trim off any webbing between the tentacles with a paring knife. Discard the head or reserve for stock.

○ Heat up a grill, preferably charcoal. When the grill is hot, brush the octopus tentacles with olive oil and place them in a grill basket used for whole fish, or arrange them on the grill grate over direct heat. Cook on each side for 4 to 5 minutes, or until the octopus is browned and the suckers are nicely charred. Transfer to a cutting board and divide the tentacles into pieces or slice into medallions.

○ To serve, spread the fava Santorini across a serving plate and place the octopus on top. Toss the pea tendrils with the ladolemono and a pinch of flaky salt, then place alongside the octopus. Garnish the plate with capers and pickled onions, then drizzle with olive oil and season to taste with more flaky salt.

FRIED SQUID

Who doesn't love fried squid? This absolute classic from Greece, where it's known as kalamarakia tiganita, is served as mezze in most restaurants, but it's especially good in the tavernas along the coasts, where the squid is super fresh. When shopping, look for fresh squid if possible, though depending on where you live, you might be more likely to find thawed, previously frozen squid. We like to serve ours with a splash of lemon as well as a garlicky, tangy toum-yogurt sauce—so much better than the tartar sauce at your local pub.

Serves 4

For the toum-yogurt sauce:

¼ cup Toum (page 68)

¼ cup Greek yogurt

For the squid:

2¼ teaspoons coriander seeds

½ tablespoon black peppercorns

½ tablespoon caraway seeds

1 cup all-purpose flour

½ tablespoon kosher salt

1 teaspoon chopped thyme

Canola oil

1 pound fresh small squid, bodies and tentacles separated

Fine sea salt

1 tablespoon chopped fresh dill

1 lemon, cut into wedges

○ Whisk the toum and yogurt together in a mixing bowl.

○ Toast the coriander seeds, peppercorns, and caraway seeds in a small, dry sauté pan over medium-low heat until fragrant, about 2 minutes. Transfer to a spice grinder and finely grind, then combine with the flour, salt, and thyme in a medium bowl.

○ Heat about 3 inches of oil in a medium pot over medium-high heat to 350°F. Line a plate with paper towels.

○ Rinse the squid under cold water. Cut along the seam of the squid bodies and pull out the cartilage. Lay the squid body down flat and cut into 1-inch triangles. Separate the tentacles in half.

○ Toss the squid triangles and tentacles with the seasoned flour. Shake off any excess flour and, working in batches, fry the squid in the hot oil until they have tightened up and turned golden and crispy, 1 to 2 minutes. Transfer the squid to the lined plate to drain and season with sea salt.

○ Sprinkle with dill and serve with the toum-yogurt sauce and lemon wedges.

LOBSTER TZATZIKI

Lobster and apples might not be a pairing you've tried before, but I think it's a beautiful one—the natural sweetness of the lobster speaks to the sweet-tart flavors of the green apple, and the textures dance together. This dish has been a special on our menu for nearly two decades, a taste of the Atlantic and the Mediterranean together. The way we serve this dish makes it something special—I like to clean out the lobster head and use it as part of the final dish, but if that's too much of a project, it will look and taste just as good in a bowl or on a platter.

Serves 2

Kosher salt

1 whole live lobster
(1¼ to 1½ pounds)

1 small clove Garlic Confit
(page 29)

½ cup Greek yogurt

½ cup labneh

1½ tablespoons extra-virgin
olive oil, plus more for
drizzling

1 Granny Smith apple,
peeled, cored, and diced
(1 cup)

1 small seedless cucumber,
peeled and diced (1 cup)

2 tablespoons minced
fresh mint leaves

2 tablespoons minced dill
fronds

2 tablespoons minced chives

Freshly ground white pepper

2 tablespoons ladolemono
(page 60)

Pinch Aleppo pepper, for
garnish

Flaky sea salt

○ Fill a large pot with water and season heavily with salt (it should taste like ocean water). Bring to a boil over medium heat. Carefully place the lobster in the boiling water and cook for 8 to 12 minutes, depending on size. The lobster shell should be a rosy red color.

○ Transfer the lobster to a plate and set aside to rest for 10 minutes, or until cool enough to handle.

○ Meanwhile, put the garlic in a mixing bowl and smash into a paste with a fork or the back of a wooden spoon. Whisk in the yogurt and labneh, then slowly drizzle in the 1½ tablespoons of olive oil while continuing to whisk. Fold in half of the diced apple, half the cucumber, and half the mint, dill, and chives. Season the apple tzatziki to taste with salt and white pepper.

○ Put the remaining apples, cucumbers, mint, dill, and chives in another mixing bowl. Stir in the ladolemono and season the apple salad to taste with salt and white pepper.

○ Return the lobster to a cutting board and, using a sharp knife, cut the head away from the body, then split the head in half lengthwise. Reserve half of the head for garnish and discard the other half. Clean the reserved head by scooping out the greenish paste

(tomalley) and rinsing with cold water. Let the shell dry.

○ Place the lobster tail shell side down on the cutting board. Using sharp kitchen scissors or a knife, carefully cut along both sides of the underside of the tail from end to end, then peel off the underskirt from the outer shell. Gently lift out the tail meat. Place the lobster tail on the cutting board and slice into medallions about ¾-inch thick, along the natural lines of the tail sections, and reserve any extra tail meat.

○ Hold the lobster claws in a kitchen towel and separate the knuckles from the claws. Pull the claws apart and crack the shell, then pull out the claw meat. Crack the knuckles and pull out the knuckle meat.

○ Chop the knuckle and claw meat and any reserved tail meat into a small dice and divide between the apple tzatziki and the apple salad, stirring the meat into the mixtures until well combined.

○ To serve, spread the lobster-apple tzatziki onto the center of a serving plate. Lay the empty lobster head at the top of the plate and spoon the lobster-apple salad into the shell, then garnish with Aleppo pepper. Arrange the lobster tail pieces on top of the tzatziki. Drizzle olive oil over the plate and garnish with flaky sea salt.

BUTTERY SHRIMP WITH DILL
GARIDES ME ÁNITHO

Shrimp like these are served in tavernas throughout Greece, along with a glass of ouzo. This dish has been on our menu since we opened, and all these years later it's still one of our most popular dishes—shrimp (garides) swimming in butter and sautéed with aromatics, then showered with dill (ánitho) before serving. To give a twist on the classic dish, we add a touch of grainy mustard. Be sure to have lots of warm pita or crusty bread nearby to soak up all the amazing sauce. Something to remember when shopping: look for shrimp marked 21/25, which indicates their size—twenty-one to twenty-five of them make up a pound.

Serves 4

1 stick (8 tablespoons) unsalted butter, divided

1 small shallot, minced

1 garlic clove, minced

Kosher salt

1 pound large shrimp, peeled and deveined

3 tablespoons fresh lemon juice

1 teaspoon whole-grain Dijon mustard

1 tablespoon chopped fresh dill, plus more for garnish

Extra-virgin olive oil

Flaky sea salt

○ Melt 3 tablespoons of the butter in a large sauté pan over medium-low heat, then add the minced shallots and garlic. Cook until soft, but not browned, about 5 minutes, then season with salt.

○ Season the shrimp with salt and add them to the pan in one layer. Increase the heat to medium and sauté until the shrimp begin to color, about 1 minute. Flip the shrimp over, then add the lemon juice and mustard to the pan. Simmer for 20 seconds, then immediately reduce the heat to low. Add 1 tablespoon of the butter and swirl the pan to form a sauce. Continue to swirl the pan and add the remaining butter, 1 tablespoon at a time, until each tablespoon melts, to create a creamy, emulsified sauce, about 2 minutes.

○ Once the shrimp are cooked through, remove from the heat and stir in the tablespoon of dill.

○ Spoon the shrimp and sauce into a serving bowl and drizzle with olive oil. Season with flaky sea salt and garnish with dill.

CRAB CAKES WITH GARLIC-YOGURT SAUCE

Makes 16 small crab cakes

For the yogurt sauce:

1 tablespoon Garlic Confit (page 29)

⅓ cup Greek yogurt

⅓ cup labneh

2 tablespoons extra-virgin olive oil

1 tablespoon fresh lemon juice

Pinch kosher salt

Pinch freshly ground white pepper

For the crab cakes:

½ tablespoon whole-grain mustard

½ cup mayonnaise

3 cloves Garlic Confit (page 29), smashed

½ tablespoon minced shallot

3 tablespoons thinly sliced scallions, divided

1 tablespoon finely chopped fresh dill, plus 2 tablespoons dill fronds

½ teaspoon Aleppo pepper, plus more for garnish

Pinch freshly ground white pepper

Kosher salt

1 pound jumbo lump crab meat, picked over

¼ cup coarse bread crumbs, such as panko

1 tablespoon extra-virgin olive oil, plus more for drizzling

½ teaspoon fresh lemon juice

Flaky sea salt

Okay, so crab cakes aren't entirely Greek. So what! Even though Zaytinya is a Mediterranean restaurant, we still wanted to honor our mid-Atlantic roots—and what better way to do that than with crab cakes? I've lived near the Chesapeake Bay for over thirty years and absolutely love the blue crabs we can get here, so of course we wanted to put a crab cake on the menu. I know it's hard to beat a classic Maryland crab cake, but this one comes pretty close.

O To make the yogurt sauce, put the garlic into a medium bowl and smash into a paste with a fork or the back of a wooden spoon. Whisk in the yogurt and labneh, then slowly drizzle in the olive oil and lemon juice while continuing to whisk. Season to taste with salt and white pepper.

O To make the crab cakes, whisk the mustard and mayonnaise together in a mixing bowl. Add the Garlic Confit, shallots, 2 tablespoons of the scallions, chopped dill, ½ teaspoon Aleppo pepper, white pepper, and ½ teaspoon of the salt and continue whisking until well combined. Gently fold in the crabmeat and bread crumbs.

O Line a plate with paper towels and heat 1 tablespoon of olive oil in a large nonstick sauté pan over medium heat. Scoop the crab mixture into 1-ounce balls (about 2 tablespoons) using a portion scoop, then use your hands to gently shape into discs. Place them in the pan in batches, to avoid crowding, and cook until golden brown on both sides, about 5 minutes per side. Transfer to the lined plate to drain.

O Toss the remaining 1 tablespoon of scallions and whole dill fronds with a drizzle of olive oil, the lemon juice, and a pinch of salt.

O To serve, spread a layer of yogurt sauce on a serving platter. Place the crab cakes on the sauce and top each crab cake with some of the scallion-dill salad. Sprinkle with a pinch of Aleppo pepper and flaky sea salt.

SEARED SCALLOPS WITH TZATZIKI

The creamy yogurt in tzatziki brings out the natural sweetness in scallops. In the fall, we like to pair them with an apple cacik, a Turkish cousin to tzatziki. Even fava Santorini (page 61) makes for a delicious combination. Season the scallops with our Sumac Rose Spice (page 27) and you'll find an unexpected aroma and tartness. When shopping for scallops, look for 10/20 size (ten to twenty make up a pound) and make sure they're dry-packed, meaning they haven't been artificially plumped up with water and additives. When cooking them, get a good hard sear and don't cook them beyond that—you want to make sure they don't get chewy.

Serves 4

1 small red radish, trimmed

3 tablespoons canola oil

Kosher salt

12 scallops, cleaned and side muscle removed

1 cup Tzatziki (page 52)

¾ teaspoon Sumac Rose Spice (page 27)

¼ cup pea tendrils (or leaves from 2 sprigs fresh flat-leaf parsley)

1 tablespoon extra-virgin olive oil

Flaky sea salt

○ Thinly slice the radish, preferably using a mandoline or box slicer. Place the slices in a bowl of ice water.

○ To prepare the scallops, warm the canola oil in a skillet over medium-high heat. Line a plate with paper towels. Gently dry the scallops with a paper towel and season with salt. Add the scallops to the hot pan and sear on both sides until dark golden brown, 2 to 3 minutes per side. Transfer the scallops to the lined plate to drain.

○ To serve, divide the tzatziki among four plates and spread across the bottoms. Set 3 scallops on each plate and sprinkle with Sumac Rose Spice. Garnish each plate with radish slices and pea tendrils, then drizzle with olive oil and season with flaky salt.

FRIED MUSSELS WITH WALNUT TARATOR SAUCE
MIDYE TAVA

Fried mussels are one of the most amazing gifts from the sea that no one outside of Turkey seems to knows about! I once dragged my wife, Patricia, all over Istanbul trying different versions. Our favorite was at the Kadıköy Market—crispy on the outside, juicy in the middle, with a briny flavor like a fried bite of the ocean. They're even better with walnut tarator, an Ottoman-era sauce that's creamy and a little garlicky. Spread it on a soft roll and fill with fried mussels for a classic street snack of Istanbul. Extra sauce can be used as a dip, with vegetables, or fried fish.

Serves 4 to 6

For the mussels:

2 tablespoons extra-virgin olive oil, divided

1 medium shallot, thinly sliced

2 garlic cloves, thinly sliced

2 pounds mussels, cleaned and debearded

Canola oil

2 cups all-purpose flour

1 teaspoon fine sea salt

2 tablespoons chopped fresh dill fronds

1 lemon, cut into wedges

For the walnut tarator sauce:

2 tablespoons extra-virgin olive oil

½ cup diced yellow onion

1½ cups walnut halves

2 tablespoons fresh lemon juice

2 teaspoons minced garlic

Kosher salt

Freshly ground black pepper

○ To prepare the mussels, warm 1 tablespoon of the olive oil over medium heat in a large, wide pot with a lid. (You want the mussels to be in one layer in the pot.) Add the shallots and garlic and cook until the garlic starts to color, about 2 minutes.

○ Add the mussels and 1 cup of water and immediately cover the pan. Cook for 3 minutes, then take off the lid. Remove any mussels that opened and place them in a bowl, then cover the pot and continue cooking until the remaining mussels open, about 2 more minutes. Discard any that do not open and reserve the cooking liquid.

○ When the mussels are cool enough to handle, carefully remove them from their shells with your fingers and place in a small storage container; discard the shells. Pour the reserved cooking liquid through a strainer over the mussels. Season with some salt, if needed. Cover and refrigerate the mussels for at least 2 hours or overnight.

○ To make the sauce, warm the olive oil in a medium pot over medium heat. Add the onions and cook until soft and translucent, about 5 minutes. Add the walnuts and continue cooking until the walnuts are toasted and aromatic, about 3 minutes.

○ Transfer to a blender and add ¼ cup of water, and the lemon juice and garlic. Season with a pinch of salt and pepper. Blend until smooth, about 1 minute, adding more water if needed to form a creamy sauce.

○ To fry the mussels, heat 2 to 3 inches of canola oil in a large pot to 350°F and line a plate with paper towels. Combine the flour and sea salt in a medium bowl.

○ Working in batches, remove the mussels from the cooking liquid, then toss in the flour. Shake off any excess flour and return the floured mussels to the cooking liquid again, then dredge a second time in the flour. Shake excess flour from the mussels and, using a spider strainer, gently lower them into the oil to fry.

○ Fry the mussels until crispy and golden brown, about 3 minutes. Remove with the spider strainer and transfer to the plate to drain. Repeat with the remaining mussels.

○ To serve, spoon the walnut sauce around the serving platter, place the mussels on top, then garnish with dill. Serve with lemon wedges.

OYSTER SAGANAKI

To me, oysters are one of nature's most perfect foods. They can be eaten raw or cooked, completely on their own or with anything bright or rich or salty, and they come in their own compostable shells. They also clean up the waters of wherever they are growing. I'm telling you, they're perfect! This oyster saganaki is a great mezze to start a seafood meal—just make sure to get big oysters so that the shells have enough space for all of the delicious sauce. Saganaki, the famous Greek preparation for cheese, vegetables (page 206), and seafood, gets its name from the two-handled pan the dish is traditionally cooked in. Large pans are called "sagani" and smaller ones are "saganaki." If shrimp is more your style of seafood, this saganaki variation below (pictured on page vi) is just the right amount of big flavor and flames.

Serves 2 to 4

12 large oysters

1 tablespoon extra-virgin olive oil

2 teaspoons minced garlic

1 scallion, trimmed and finely sliced

2 tablespoons ouzo

¼ cup Spiced Tomato Sauce (page 74)

Pinch dried oregano

¼ cup crumbled feta

2 to 3 cups kosher salt or sea salt

2 tablespoons minced chives

◦ Preheat the oven to 350°F.

◦ Place the oysters on a large rimmed baking sheet. Roast in the oven until they begin to open, about 5 minutes. You only want to warm the oysters. Remove from the oven and, using gloves, carefully pry open the oysters with an oyster knife. Reserve the juice from the oysters in a bowl. Discard the top shell and detach the meat from the bottom shell. Place the oysters in their shells back on the baking sheet.

◦ Heat the olive oil in a small pan over medium heat, add the garlic and scallions, and cook until golden, about 3 minutes. Add the ouzo and flambé the mixture by igniting the alcohol with a long matchstick or long-reach lighter. (Keep a large heatproof cover for the pan nearby. Cover the pan if flames need to be put out quickly.)

◦ Add the tomato sauce and dried oregano and simmer until thick, about 3 minutes. Stir in the reserved juices from the oysters.

◦ Spoon the tomato sauce on top of each oyster and sprinkle with feta. Place the oysters under a broiler for about 30 seconds, to lightly brown the feta.

◦ To serve, line a plate with a bed of salt mixed with a little water. Set the oysters in the salt and garnish with chives.

FOR SHRIMP SAGANAKI:

Season 1 pound of large peeled and deveined shrimp with salt. Melt 3 tablespoons of butter in a large sauté pan over low heat, then add 3 minced garlic cloves and 2 thinly sliced scallions and cook until they begin to soften, about 5 minutes. Add the shrimp, increase the heat to high, and stir together. Add the ouzo and flambé the shrimp by igniting the alcohol with a long matchstick or long-reach lighter. (Be ready to put flames out if needed.) Carefully stir the shrimp with a metal spatula until the flames burn out.

Add ¼ cup of ladolemono (page 60), a pinch of ground anise, dried oregano, and Aleppo pepper to the shrimp and toss to combine. Then add 1½ cups Spiced Tomato Sauce (page 74) to the pan and simmer for about 30 seconds. Remove the pan from the heat and stir in ¾ cup of shredded Kefalograviera cheese and 1 tablespoon of capers. Garnish with crumbled feta, minced chives, and a drizzle of extra-virgin olive oil.

SEARED SEA BASS

European sea bass, often called branzino in the United States, is one of the most famous fish exports from the Mediterranean. I love it every way it's prepared, whether it's grilled whole and served with tomato-olive sauce (like on page 286) or, here, pan-seared until crispy and served with fennel, tomatoes, parsley, and black olives. I tasted sea bass this way for the first time with my friend Aglaia on the island of Kea—it's herbal, sweet, savory, briny, and bright. If you can't find sea bass, other great fish that sear nicely are halibut and striped bass. To fully enjoy this flavor of the Mediterranean, serve the sea bass with a cold bottle of Greek Assyrtiko (page 330).

Serves 4

½ small fennel bulb, cored and thinly sliced

Leaves from ½ bunch fresh flat-leaf parsley

3 tablespoons ladolemono (page 60), divided

Kosher salt

1 tablespoon extra-virgin olive oil

4 sea bass fillets, skin on

16 Oven-Roasted Cherry Tomatoes (page 37)

¼ cup Kalamata olives, pitted and halved

1 lemon

Flaky sea salt

○ Put the fennel and parsley in a bowl and toss with 1 tablespoon of the ladolemono. Season to taste with salt.

○ Heat the olive oil in a large skillet over medium-high heat. Pat the sea bass dry with paper towels, then season both sides with salt. Sear the sea bass, skin side down, gently flattening the fillets with the back of your spatula to make sure all the skin is pressed against the hot pan. Cook until the skin is golden brown and the fish is nearly cooked through, about 4 minutes. Carefully flip the fish over and quickly cook the flesh side, about 30 seconds. You don't want it to brown. Transfer the fish to a plate, skin side up.

○ To serve, divide the remaining 2 tablespoons of ladolemono among four plates, spooning it onto the center of each plate. Place a piece of sea bass on top. Arrange the fennel and parsley around the fish. Garnish with tomatoes and olives. Zest the lemon over each piece of fish and season with sea salt.

SMOKED SALMON SKORDALIA

Skordalia, which gets its name from the Greek word skórdo for garlic, is a thick sauce of garlic and potatoes that's traditionally served as a spread next to fried fish (read more about it on page 73). Our version is a fun play on the classic: a perfect addition to a brunch table or a cool summer dinner. The smoked salmon is a lighter take on the fish, and the potato chips add the perfect crunchy fried flavor. Try serving with more crispy chips for scooping up the skordalia—who doesn't love using a chip as a spoon?

Serves 4 to 6

3 tablespoons slivered almonds

1½ cups skordalia (page 73)

12 to 16 ounces smoked salmon slices

½ cup good-quality kettle-style potato chips

1 celery stalk, trimmed and thinly sliced

Leaves from inner celery stalks

1 tablespoon ladolemono (page 60)

1 tablespoon extra-virgin olive oil

½ teaspoon Aleppo pepper

Flaky sea salt

O Preheat the oven to 275°F. Spread the almonds in a single layer on a baking sheet and roast for 3 to 4 minutes, shaking a few times, until golden brown. Immediately pour into a shallow bowl to cool.

O Spread the skordalia on a serving platter, then lay the salmon slices on top. Scatter the potato chips over the salmon, then sprinkle with the celery, celery leaves, and almonds. Drizzle with ladolemono and olive oil. Sprinkle the Aleppo pepper over the platter and season with flaky salt.

COD STEAMED IN GRAPE LEAVES
BAKALIAROS SE KLIMATOFILA

You may know about dolmades, the famous stuffed grape leaves of Greece (see page 154 for our recipe). But vine leaves (klimatofila) have many, many other uses in Greek and Eastern Mediterranean cooking, including in the technique of wrapping fish in grape leaves and then poaching, grilling, or baking it. Ours goes in a different direction, steaming the wrapped fish, which gives it a really light and fluffy texture and infuses the whole thing with the leaves' brininess. The leaves themselves also get super tender, which makes this a lot nicer to eat than the grilled version. We like to use cod for this dish, but mackerel and red snapper are often used in the Eastern Mediterranean.

Serves 4

For the sauce:

1 pound ripe tomatoes

1 medium eggplant, peeled and diced (about 2 cups)

Kosher salt

2 tablespoons extra-virgin olive oil, divided

1 medium yellow onion, thinly sliced

1 yellow bell pepper, seeded and diced (1 cup)

1 green bell pepper, seeded and diced (1 cup)

2 garlic cloves, minced

4 sun-dried tomato halves, chopped

1 star anise

¼ teaspoon Urfa pepper

½ teaspoon sumac

⅛ teaspoon sweet smoked paprika

¼ teaspoon granulated sugar

½ teaspoon fresh lemon juice

1 teaspoon pomegranate molasses

1 teaspoon honey

¼ cup Kalamata olives, pitted and halved

¼ cup green cracked olives, pitted and halved

½ cup fish stock (or water)

For the fish:

4 6-ounce cod fillets

Kosher salt

Freshly ground black pepper

8 to 12 grape leaves, rinsed with hot water

Leaves from 4 sprigs fresh flat-leaf parsley

1 tablespoon pine nuts, toasted

Extra-virgin olive oil for drizzling

○ To make the sauce, slice the tomatoes in half. Grate the cut side of the tomatoes on the large holes of a flat or box grater set over a bowl, then discard the skins.

○ Meanwhile, put the eggplant in a colander set over a mixing bowl, season with salt, and set aside to drain.

○ Warm 1 tablespoon of the olive oil in a large skillet over medium-high heat. Add the onions and a large pinch of salt and cook, stirring often, until the onions begin to soften and turn golden, about 10 minutes. Reduce the heat to medium-low and continue to cook, stirring frequently, for 20 minutes, or until the onions have caramelized; deglaze the pan with a little water if the onions are getting too dark and sticking.

○ Add the eggplant, increase the heat to medium, and continue to cook until the eggplant softens and begins to brown, about 5 minutes. Add the peppers and cook, stirring occassionaly, for 15 more minutes. Stir in the garlic and cook for 1 minute, then add the grated tomatoes, sun-dried tomatoes, star anise, Urfa pepper, sumac, smoked paprika, and sugar. Stir well, then add the lemon juice, pomegranate molasses, honey, and remaining tablespoon of olive oil. Continue cooking for about 15 minutes, or until any excess liquid evaporates. Stir in the olives and ¼ cup of the fish stock (or water) and cook for 5 more minutes. Continue adding the remaining fish stock (or water) until you get a thick, soupy sauce. Reduce the heat and keep warm.

○ To make the fish, set up a steamer—a steam basket on top of a pot with 2 cups of water. (Use a metal pasta strainer if you don't have a steam basket.)

○ Season the fish with salt and pepper on both sides. Lay 2 grape leaves flat on a work surface, vein side up, and trim off any stems. Overlap the grape leaves so they are longer than the piece of fish; use 2 to 3 leaves per fish depending on the size of the fish and the grape leaves. Place the fish in the center of the leaves. Fold the stem end over the top of the fish, then fold the two sides into the middle over the fish. Roll the leaf up tightly around the fish like a cigar to completely cover the fish. Repeat with the remaining fish and grape leaves.

○ Lay the wrapped fish in the steam basket (do not let the fish overlap) and steam for 6 minutes. (You can test if the fish is done by sliding a cake tester, or a thin sharp knife, through the fish. If there is no resistance and the knife easily slides through, the fish is ready.)

○ To serve, remove the star anise from the sauce and discard. Spoon about ½ cup of sauce onto four plates. Place the steamed fish on top of the sauce, garnish with parsley leaves and pine nuts, and drizzle with olive oil. Keep any remaining sauce refrigerated for up to 3 days. Serve remaining sauce with pasta or rice, if you like.

SESAME SALMON

This salmon recipe is inspired by a classic Lebanese dish, samak bi tahini—fish with tahini. We've done a few versions of it over the years at the restaurant. One of my favorites is a very traditional one from the great cookbook author and food historian Claudia Roden, who pours a tahini-lemon sauce over fish and then bakes it, giving it a savory, nutty crust. For ours, we like to coat salmon fillets with sesame seeds and sear them, giving a crunchy surface to the fish, then serve it with an herb-filled tahini sauce. If you prefer, you can substitute another full-flavored fish for the salmon—Mediterranean sea bass would work well.

Serves 4

1 pound salmon fillet, pin bones and skin removed

Kosher salt

½ cup sesame seeds

1 tablespoon extra-virgin olive oil

½ cup herbed tahini sauce (page 67)

2 tablespoons pine nuts, toasted

½ teaspoon Aleppo pepper

2 tablespoons pomegranate seeds

2 teaspoons Green Mint Oil (page 31)

1 lemon

O Preheat the oven to 275°F. Cut the salmon into four equal pieces and season each side with salt.

O Spread the sesame seeds in a shallow dish and press the salmon, flat side down, into the sesame seeds to generously coat one side. Repeat with each piece.

O Warm the olive oil in a large ovenproof, nonstick pan over medium heat until hot but not smoking. Place all four pieces of salmon in the pan, sesame side down. Press the fish with the back of a spatula to make sure all the sesame seeds touch the pan. Cook until the sesame seeds begin to toast and turn golden, about 3 minutes.

O Transfer the pan to the oven and cook until the salmon is just barely warmed through (medium rare), about 7 minutes, then remove from the oven.

O Lift the salmon with tongs or a spatula to ensure that the sesame seeds are nicely toasted. If they have not turned golden brown, return the pan to the stove top to continue to toast the sesame seeds over medium heat.

O To serve, spread the herbed tahini sauce on a serving platter, then arrange the salmon on top. Sprinkle with the pine nuts, Aleppo pepper, and pomegranate seeds. Drizzle with Green Mint Oil and grate some fresh lemon zest over the top.

08

There are days at Zaytinya where I feel like I may have stepped back in time. Walking through the kitchen as my team rolls dough, grills eggplant, stirs pots of stock, and roasts lamb shoulders, this precision operation could be like the army of cooks in the enormous kitchens of the Topkapi Palace in Istanbul hundreds of years ago. Okay, okay, I know our restaurant kitchen is a fraction of the size of those in the Ottoman palace, but to me, it is just as coordinated and calculated, with each team member working together to prepare the many dishes that we serve our guests throughout the day.

This is especially true for the kebabs, köfte, kibbeh, and other meat dishes on our menu. Every day, meat is ground to reach the perfect texture, chicken is trimmed and marinated, lamb is sliced thin. Hundreds of kibbeh (page 257) are formed, filled, and shaped into ovals. Beef, chicken, and lamb are seasoned and threaded onto traditional flat kebab skewers destined for the fire of the grills.

In Turkey, more than in Greece and Lebanon, meat dishes have long played an important role in the cuisine and culture. While lamb is the meat of choice for all of the Eastern Mediterranean, Turkey's size and landscape allowed for raising cattle and meant beef became part of the diet. During the Ottoman period, beef was primarily used for making pastirma (page 261)—dried, cured, spiced meat—and spiced sausage, soujouk (which we like to use on our Turkish pide; page 132). Pork, however, was rarely found due to the Muslim dietary rules that prohibit it.

What I think of most when I think about Turkey's influence on the meat dishes of the region are the sights and smells of the kebab shops throughout Istanbul. Chef Costa and I always seek out a handful of shops when we visit the city to see what new and interesting flavors can be found. Kebapçi Etiler and Dürümzade were stops on Chef Costa's last visit; I explored the Asmalı Mescit neighborhood. I am fascinated by how the tradition of cooking meat on a skewer with fire is embraced in Turkey, Greece, and Lebanon and by all the variations of these classic street foods, whether shish kebabs (skewered meats) or shawarma and gyros, the stacked and rotating meats sliced into warm pita bread or tucked and rolled inside lavash. It's a good thing that at Zaytinya we have our cooks, always standing at the ready, guarding the fire and turning kebabs of spiced köfte, skewers of lamb baharat, and marinated chicken, until perfectly roasted.

MARINATED CHICKEN KEBABS
SHISH TAOUK

I'm telling you right now, this marinade will make its way into your regular rotation—it's amazing with grilled chicken but will work for pork or shrimp if you want to give it a try. Shish taouk might be one of the most famous chicken dishes of the Middle East, but it has its roots in the Ottoman Empire—the name is Arabic borrowed from the Turkish tavuk şiş, or chicken skewer. At the restaurant, we serve it with sumac onions, roasted tomatoes, and lots of super-garlicky toum, as is commonly done in Lebanon, and always with lots of warm pita bread (page 129).

Serves 4

For the marinade:

1 teaspoon cumin seeds

1 teaspoon caraway seeds

1 teaspoon kosher salt

¼ cup Greek yogurt

2 teaspoons minced garlic

2 tablespoons extra-virgin olive oil

2 teaspoons Harissa (page 70)

2 tablespoons fresh lemon juice

For the chicken:

1½ pounds boneless, skinless chicken thighs

Extra-virgin olive oil

Flaky sea salt

12 grilled cherry tomatoes (page 303)

½ cup Sumac Onions (page 32)

½ cup Toum (page 68)

○ To make the marinade: Toast the cumin and caraway seeds in a small dry pan over medium heat, about 1 minute, then transfer to a spice grinder and coarsely grind. Pour into a mixing bowl and add the salt, yogurt, garlic, olive oil, Harissa, and lemon juice, then stir well.

○ Lay the chicken thighs flat on a cutting board and, with a sharp knife, trim off any extra fat and bone fragments, then quarter each thigh into about 2-inch cubes. Add the chicken to the marinade and stir to coat. Cover and refrigerate for at least 2 hours or, preferably, overnight.

○ Heat up a grill, preferably charcoal; a gas grill set to medium-high will work as well.

○ Divide the chicken pieces among four skewers, preferably long, flat metal ones. Be sure to pierce the meat through the center of each piece of chicken so it holds well to the skewer while cooking. Keep the chicken pieces close together on the skewer.

○ To cook over charcoal in the traditional style, see page 302; otherwise, lay the skewers on the grill and cook until browned, about 6 minutes. Turn the kebabs over and cook until the other side is browned and the chicken is cooked through, about 6 more minutes. Transfer the skewers to a clean work surface, drizzle with olive oil, and sprinkle with flaky salt.

○ Carefully remove the chicken from the skewers, using a fork to slide the meat off, then place on a serving platter. Add the grilled tomatoes, Sumac Onions, and large spoonfuls of Toum to the platter, then serve.

247

LAMB BAHARAT KEBABS

Baharat is an all-purpose spice blend from around the Middle East—the word just means "spice" in Arabic. Our Golden Baharat features Aleppo pepper, turmeric, ginger, and fenugreek, giving it a warming and aromatic heat, which goes perfectly with lamb. The best cut of lamb for these kebabs is top round, a relatively new cut on the market, which comes from the inside of the leg and is super tender. Slice it thin and it doesn't take long to cook, which makes it perfect for grilling.

If you can't find top round, a butterflied boneless leg of lamb will work—just trim away as much of the connective tissue and fat as possible.

Serves 4

1½ pounds top round lamb, or boneless leg of lamb

¼ cup Golden Baharat (page 27)

2 tablespoons canola oil

Kosher salt

1½ cups Tabbouleh (page 97)

½ cup Tahini Sauce (page 67)

16 grilled cherry tomatoes (page 303)

¼ cup ladolemono (page 60)

Extra-virgin olive oil

Flaky sea salt

○ Trim any fat and connective tissue from the lamb. Slice the meat across the grain into thin (¼-inch) slices, about 2 inches long by 1 inch wide. Toss the sliced meat with the baharat and oil in a mixing bowl, then refrigerate for 15 to 20 minutes.

○ To prepare the skewers, divide the meat into four portions. Thread the meat slices onto four skewers, preferably long, flat metal skewers, by piercing through one short end, folding the meat back over, and pushing through the skewer on the other end. Push the pieces of meat together on the skewers to form a tight, uniform shape, then season with salt.

○ Heat up a grill, preferably charcoal; a gas grill set to medium-high will work as well.

○ To cook over charcoal in the traditional style, see page 302, otherwise lay the skewers on the grill and cook until browned, 4 to 5 minutes. Flip and continue cooking for another 4 minutes. Remove from the grill and set on a work surface to rest.

○ To serve, spread the tabbouleh on the bottom of a serving plate. Carefully slide the lamb off of the skewers and place on top of the Tabbouleh. Spoon Tahini Sauce along the side of the platter and add the grilled tomatoes. Drizzle the meat with ladolemono and olive oil, then garnish with flaky sea salt.

GRILLED LAMB CHOPS

These chops are our take on a classic found in both Greek restaurants and Greek American taverns, where you will always see lamb with a side of tzatziki—the two flavors just work well together. I love this dish with some heat from the Harissa Chili Crisp (page 30), but our Green Mint Oil (page 31) is also a great pairing. Lamb chops have a lot of fat on them, so it's not a bad idea to cook them a little past rare, toward medium rare or even medium, to give that fat a chance to melt. Searing the back side of the chop, where the fat is thickest, can help. Plan for two to four chops per person, depending on how many other dishes you're serving.

Serves 2 to 4

1 rack of lamb
  (1½ to 2 pounds)
Kosher salt
Freshly ground black pepper
1 cup Whipped Labneh
  (page 60)
1 cup Tzatziki (page 52)
¼ cup Harissa Chili Crisp
  (page 30)
Leaves from 1 bunch mint
Flaky sea salt
Extra-virgin olive oil

O Dry the lamb with a paper towel, then place bone side up on a cutting board. Cut the rack into chops of equal thickness by making a downward cut between the rib bones. Trim any excess fat from each chop if you prefer a leaner chop.

O Heat up a grill, preferably charcoal; a gas grill set on high will work as well.

O Season each chop on both sides with salt and pepper. Grill the lamb chops to medium rare, about 3 minutes per side. Finish by standing the chop upright, so the fatty back side of the chop can cook over the heat to crisp, about 1 more minute. Transfer the chops to a platter.

O To serve, place a spoonful of the labneh and a spoonful of Tzatziki on each plate. Lay 2 to 3 chops on top, then drizzle some of the Harissa Chili Crisp over the meat. Garnish with mint leaves, flaky salt, and a drizzle of olive oil.

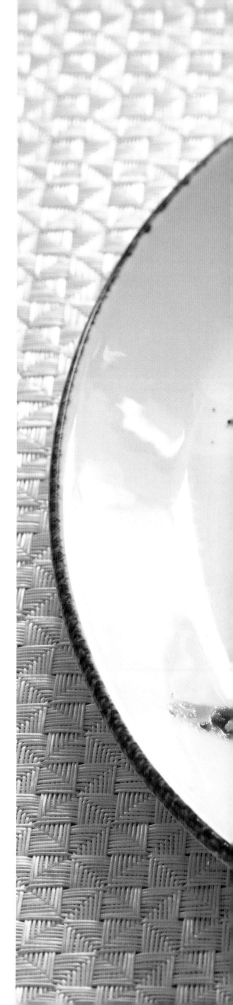

CHICKEN DÜRÜM

This is our tribute to the very famous shawarma, a spit-roasted meat dish that came to be during the Ottoman Empire. In our version, we marinate chicken in the same spices as a traditional shawarma, but we broil the meat—much easier to do at home than stacking it on a vertical spit and grilling it. And while shawarma usually finds its way into pita bread (like gyros found in Greece), we like to roll this chicken in Lavash (page 148), Turkish dürüm-style—a popular street food in Istanbul. Make sure to start a few hours early, or the night before, since the chicken needs some time to marinate.

Serves 4

For the marinade:

¾ cup extra-virgin olive oil

¼ cup white wine vinegar

¼ cup fresh lemon juice

2 tablespoons minced garlic

1½ tablespoons kosher salt

½ tablespoon Aleppo pepper

1 teaspoon chopped parsley

½ teaspoon ground cumin

½ teaspoon sumac

½ teaspoon freshly ground white pepper

¼ teaspoon freshly ground black pepper

¼ teaspoon grated nutmeg

For the chicken:

1 pound boneless, skinless chicken thighs

2 teaspoons kosher salt

1 green bell pepper

1 teaspoon canola oil, divided, plus more if needed

4 Lavash (page 148)

½ cup Toum (page 68)

1 tomato, halved lengthwise and sliced

1 cup shredded romaine lettuce

O To make the marinade, whisk the olive oil, vinegar, and lemon juice in a mixing bowl, then whisk in the garlic, salt, Aleppo pepper, parsley, cumin, sumac, white and black pepper, and nutmeg until well combined.

O Lay the chicken thighs flat on a cutting board and, with a sharp knife, trim off any extra fat and bone fragments, then slice into long, ½-inch-thick strips. Sprinkle the chicken with kosher salt, then toss it with the marinade in a mixing bowl, cover, and refrigerate for at least 2 hours or, preferably, overnight.

O Meanwhile, lightly rub the pepper with ½ teaspoon of the oil. Set the pepper directly on the grate of a gas burner set to medium heat. Using tongs, rotate the pepper to char evenly, 30 seconds to 1 minute per side. (You can also use a broiler, turning the pepper about every 2 minutes.) Transfer the pepper to a mixing bowl and cover so that no steam escapes. Let steam for about 15 minutes, until cool enough to handle, then peel away the charred skin, remove the stem and seeds, and dice.

O Preheat the broiler to high and set a rimmed baking sheet on the top rack of the oven. Once hot, spread the marinated chicken across the baking sheet and broil for 10 minutes. Turn the chicken over, using tongs, if it starts to get too dark on top. Remove the chicken from the oven and set aside to rest.

O Heat a large skillet over medium-high heat. Put the lavash in the dry hot pan, 1 piece at a time, to warm and lightly brown. Spread 2 tablespoons of Toum across each Lavash. Divide the pepper, tomato slices, and lettuce among the Lavash, then top with the spiced chicken and roll lengthwise into large cylinders.

O In the same large skillet, warm the remaining ½ teaspoon of canola oil over medium-high heat. Cook the roll, seam side down, until golden brown, about 1 minute. Carefully flip the dürüm over and cook on the other side until golden, about 1 minute. Transfer to a cutting board and cut in half before serving. Repeat with the remaining rolled dürüm, adding more oil if needed.

BRAISED LAMB WITH CREAMY EGGPLANT
HÜNKÂR BEĞENDI

Our servers will tell you this creamy eggplant and savory lamb combination is one of the most popular dishes in the restaurant, the plate always wiped clean by our guests at the end of their meal. No wonder its name means "sultan's delight." In Turkey you may find this dish made with a chunky eggplant mixture topped with a tomato sauce, but we prefer a combination of smooth textures and meaty, rich flavors. We blend smoky eggplant with nutty Kefalograviera cheese and a béchamel sauce to create a rich and delicious puree topped off with velvety braised lamb. Once you master this eggplant puree, you're going to want to try it with all your favorite roasted meats.

Serves 4 to 6

1 pound eggplant, preferably Italian or globe

1 teaspoon canola oil

2 to 3 braised lamb shanks (about 2½ pounds) and sauce (page 291)

¾ cup heavy cream

¾ cup milk

3 tablespoons unsalted butter

3 tablespoons all-purpose flour

½ tablespoon kosher salt

1 teaspoon freshly grated nutmeg

⅛ teaspoon freshly ground white pepper

¾ cup shredded Kefalograviera cheese

1 tablespoon minced chives

○ Rinse and dry the eggplant, then rub with the oil. Set the eggplant directly on the grate of a gas burner set to medium heat. Cook the eggplant for 20 to 30 minutes, turning with tongs about every 5 minutes. When done, the skin should be charred black and flaky, the flesh collapsing and easily pierced with a sharp knife. (Be sure to turn your vents on to keep your kitchen from getting smoky.) Transfer the eggplant to a cooling rack set over a baking sheet to cool and drain. Once the eggplant is cool enough to handle, slice it in half lengthwise and scoop the flesh into a bowl.

○ Meanwhile, warm the lamb shanks and sauce in a medium pot over low heat. Once the lamb has warmed through, remove the lamb from the sauce and remove the shank bones. Discard the bones (or reserve for stock) and break the meat into large pieces. Stir the warm sauce in the pot until well combined, then return the lamb pieces to the pot. Continue to keep the meat and sauce warm over low heat.

○ Heat the heavy cream and the milk in a saucepot over low heat until warm. Melt the butter over medium heat in a large pot, then whisk in the flour and cook until thick and golden, 3 to 5 minutes. Slowly pour in the warm cream and milk and continue to whisk until the sauce begins to thicken. Reduce the heat to low and simmer gently for 10 minutes, stirring constantly, until thick.

○ Add the roasted eggplant, salt, nutmeg, and white pepper and stir well. Continue to cook, stirring constantly, until the eggplant is warmed through and the mixture is hot, about 3 more minutes. Add the cheese and stir until completely melted.

○ Puree the sauce in the pot with an immersion blender until thick and completely smooth. (Or carefully transfer the hot sauce to a food processor and puree, working in batches if necessary, until smooth.)

○ To serve, divide the warm eggplant puree into serving bowls. Spoon the lamb and sauce over the top and garnish with chives.

KIBBEH

Kibbeh, which comes from the Arabic for "ball," have been on our menu since day one. The great writer on Mediterranean cooking Paula Wolfert described these football-shaped fritters as "one of the most interesting forms of ground meat cookery." I could not agree more! Depending on where you travel, you might see kibbeh made with lamb, but we prefer it with beef. Abdelrazzaq Hashhoush (*below*), the Palestinian-Lebanese chef who was on our team at the very beginning, teaching us the classic dishes of Lebanon and the Middle East (including phyllo making), trained us on how to form meat with our hands to make crisp shells and juicy filling. One unique additional step in making our kibbeh is flavoring the filling with rich bone marrow—it adds a flavor you can't get from anything else. We also don't precook the filling, as many recipes tell you to do, because why would you cook it twice? Serve freshly fried kibbeh with creamy Whipped Labneh (page 60) and a sprinkling of chopped fresh parsley.

For the filling:

1 tablespoon unsalted butter

½ cup minced yellow onion

Kosher salt

1 pound marrow bones, cross-cut (see box)

½ pound ground beef, 80 percent lean

⅛ teaspoon ground cinnamon

¼ teaspoon ground cumin

¼ teaspoon freshly ground black pepper

Pinch ground allspice

¼ teaspoon Aleppo pepper

¼ cup slivered almonds, toasted

¼ cup pine nuts, toasted

2 tablespoons dried currants

For the shell:

¾ cup fine bulgur

Kosher salt

1 pound ground beef, 90 percent lean

½ cup finely minced yellow onion

1 teaspoon ground cumin

½ teaspoon ground allspice

½ teaspoon Aleppo pepper

¼ teaspoon freshly ground black pepper

¼ teaspoon ground cinnamon

Canola oil

Fine sea salt

1 cup Whipped Labneh (page 60)

2 tablespoons thinly sliced fresh parsley leaves

○ To make the filling, melt the butter in a small sauté pan over medium heat. Add the onions and a pinch of salt and cook, covered, until the onions are soft and lightly browned, about 5 minutes. Transfer the onions to a small bowl and chill in the refrigerator until cold, about 1 hour.

○ Meanwhile, remove the marrow from the bones (see box), then finely mince. (You should have about 3 ounces of marrow.)

○ Once the onions are cold, mix them in with the beef, marrow, cinnamon, cumin, black pepper, allspice, and Aleppo pepper in a mixing bowl. Using your hands, mix in the almonds, pine nuts, and currants until well combined. Cover and refrigerate until ready to use.

○ To make the shell, put the bulgur in the bowl of a stand mixer. Bring 1½ cups of water to a boil, stir in 1 teaspoon of salt, then pour over the bulgur. Cover and let sit until all of the water is absorbed, about 30 minutes. Fluff the bulgur with a fork and let cool to room temperature.

○ Once cool, add the beef, onions, cumin, allspice, Aleppo pepper, black pepper, and cinnamon to the bowl. Mix on low with the paddle attachment until smooth, slightly elastic, and slightly stringy, about 10 minutes. (Be sure to knead the shell mixture very well, or the kibbeh may not hold their shape when frying. If kneading by hand, this will take longer.) Cover and refrigerate until ready to use.

○ To prepare the kibbeh, set a bowl of ice water next to your bowls of the filling and shell mixture (A). Pinch off 1 ounce (about 2 tablespoons) of the shell mixture and roll between your hands to form a ball (B). With the ball in one hand, dip the index finger of your other hand in the ice water and insert it into the center of the ball. Using your hand, rotate the ball around your index finger (C) as you press your finger down against the palm of your other hand to create a hollow center with a thin shell (D).

○ Spoon 1 tablespoon of the filling mixture into the shell (E), then continue to rotate the shell in one hand while using the other hand to gently pinch the shell closed. Continue to pinch the edges into the shape of a football (F). Set on a baking sheet (G) and continue with the remaining shell and filling mixtures. If you have any filling left over, sauté it until cooked, maybe add an egg—your treat!

○ Heat 3 inches of canola oil in a large pot to 350°F and line a baking sheet with paper towels. Fry the kibbeh, working in batches, until they are browned and cooked through, 3 to 4 minutes (H). Transfer to the baking sheet and sprinkle with sea salt, then repeat with the remaining kibbeh. Allow the oil to return to 350°F between batches.

○ Serve hot with Whipped Labneh and fresh parsley, if you like.

CHEF MOVE

Look for marrow bones in the meat department of your grocery store; they are also available frozen. Cross-cut bones are best here, not the lengthwise cut. Once thawed, if frozen, use your fingers or the back of a spoon to push the marrow out through the center of the bone. If it does not release easily, use a spoon or a butter knife to scrape out the marrow. Discard the bones or save for stock, although there won't be much flavor left once you've removed the marrow.

KIBBEH NAYEH
CHOPPED BEEF SALAD

The classic kibbeh nayeh is made with raw ground meat and tends to be pureed to a creamy consistency in Lebanon and Turkey. Ours goes in a different direction, coming closer to a classic beef tartare (a recipe first written down by Escoffier himself!), with freshly ground or hand-minced beef combined with bulgur, radishes, and mint—I think it's better to be able to appreciate the different ingredients on their own, instead of as a puree. Freezing the meat before grinding helps the fat combine with the meat instead of turning it into a paste—though if you're mincing by hand, there's no need to freeze it.

Serves 4

For the meat: 1 pound beef sirloin, strip, or tenderloin
• 2 tablespoons fine bulgur • 1 radish, trimmed and minced
• ¼ cup minced red onion • ¼ cup thinly sliced mint leaves
• ½ teaspoon kosher salt • ½ teaspoon ground allspice
• ½ cup extra-virgin olive oil

For the garnish: ¼ small red onion, thinly sliced • 1 small radish, thinly sliced • ¼ cup fresh mint leaves, torn • Extra-virgin olive oil • Flaky sea salt • 1 cup pita chips • 1 head sweet gem lettuce, washed and leaves separated

○ Cut the meat into 1-inch cubes, transfer to a container, and cover. Put in the freezer and chill until almost frozen, about 1 hour.

○ Meanwhile, put the bulgur in a small bowl and cover with ¼ cup of boiling-hot water. Cover and let sit until all of the water is absorbed, about 15 minutes. Fluff the bulgur with a fork and set aside to cool to room temperature.

○ To grind the meat, remove the chilled beef from the freezer. Grind the meat into a mixing bowl using a meat grinder set with a fine die. (The cold meat can also be minced using a sharp kitchen knife.)

○ Add the bulgur, radishes, onions, mint, salt, and allspice to the meat and use a spatula to fold all the ingredients together, taking care not to overmix. Cover and refrigerate up to 1 hour.

○ When ready to serve, spoon the meat mixture onto a serving plate and spread into a large, thin circle. Garnish with the sliced onions, sliced radishes, and torn mint leaves. Season with salt and a drizzle of olive oil. Serve with pita chips and lettuce leaves.

PASTIRMA WITH APRICOTS

Pastirma, a dry-cured spiced meat that's found throughout the Middle East, Balkans, and Turkey, is, yes, you guessed it, a cousin of pastrami. While the name is likely from the Ottoman era, and many consider it Armenian in origin, the dish itself might go back as far as Byzantine times. It's flavored with a fenugreek-garlic-chili spice paste called çemen (make your own; see page 294), and aged for a month or more. It's then sliced very thinly, like jamón in my native Spain, and served either on its own next to other mezze or used to top pide or to flavor sautéed greens. This preparation is beautifully simple, showing off the flavor of the pastirma along with some sweet, spiced cardamom-infused apricots.

Serves 2 to 4

2 to 3 ounces pastirma, thinly sliced • Extra-virgin olive oil
• 6 to 8 Cardamom Apricots (page 36) • 2 teaspoons pine nuts, toasted • ¼ cup baby arugula leaves
• 1 to 2 tablespoons Pickled Anise Onions (page 32)
• 1 teaspoon ladolemono (page 60)

○ Lay the pastirma on a serving plate and drizzle with olive oil. Place the apricots on top of the meat and sprinkle with pine nuts. Toss the arugula and pickled onions with ladolemono, then add to the serving plate.

SHAWARMA SPICE ROAST CHICKEN

I love a roast chicken—I think it's probably programmed deep in humanity's DNA to like it, since there are so many versions of it around the world. This one is a simple one but tastes (and looks) more impressive than it should, considering the amount of work you put in— the secret is the spice mix we use for our chicken dürüm (page 252). Butterflying the bird, also called spatchcocking, makes it easy to get a roast chicken where the breast and leg meat are cooked perfectly. The safest and easiest way is to use kitchen shears or scissors to remove the backbone—and be sure to save it for chicken stock (page 113). You can use the chicken for avgolemono chicken soup (page 110), or our chicken salad (page 108). Or just add some Cypriot-style potatoes (page 201) and a fattoush salad (page 94) for an easy weeknight meal.

Serves 4

1 whole chicken
  (3 to 4 pounds)

3 tablespoons Aleppo pepper

2 tablespoons ground cumin

2 tablespoons sumac

2 tablespoons freshly ground
  white pepper

1 tablespoon freshly ground
  black pepper

1 tablespoon grated nutmeg

1 teaspoon ground turmeric

1 garlic clove

1 tablespoon extra-virgin olive
  oil, plus more for drizzling

1 teaspoon kosher salt

Flaky sea salt

1 lemon, cut into wedges

○ Preheat the oven to 425°F. Set a wire rack over a rimmed baking sheet.

○ Lay the chicken breast side down with the neck nearest you. Remove the backbone of the chicken by using kitchen shears to cut along both sides of the spine, through the ribs. Reserve the backbone for stock. Use the heel of a heavy kitchen knife to cut through the breastbone (but not through the meat on the other side) to open up the chicken.

○ Flip the chicken over and spread out the legs. Push down firmly over the breastbone to crack the wishbone so the chicken lies flat.

○ Transfer the flattened chicken to the wire rack, skin side up, adjusting as needed so the chicken stays flat. Center the chicken and spread out the legs toward the edge of the baking sheet. Tuck the wings under the breast to keep from burning.

○ Stir the Aleppo pepper, cumin, sumac, white and black pepper, nutmeg, and turmeric together in a small storage container. Grate the garlic with a Microplane into a small bowl, then stir in the olive oil.

○ Season the chicken generously all over with kosher salt, then coat with the garlic-oil mixture and sprinkle with 3 to 4 tablespoons of the spice mixture.

○ Roast (middle rack) for 45 minutes, or until the chicken breast reaches 160°F and the chicken is golden brown. (It'll take a little longer for a larger chicken.)

○ Let the chicken rest for about 10 minutes before carving. After carving, sprinkle with additional spice blend and flaky sea salt, then drizzle with olive oil. Serve with lemon wedges.

CHICKEN YOUVETSI

Youvetsi is comfort food made by yiayias, Greek grandmothers. The dish, which takes its name from a clay cooking vessel, is a super easy one-pot dish (clay or not!) that's perfect for a busy weeknight. You may have had orzo before, the small pasta of Italy, but maybe you haven't heard of kritharaki, the Greek version. It's got a similar shape (kritharaki means "little barley") and flavor, but the durum wheat of Greece gives it a nice extra chew—still, you can make it with Italian orzo if that's what you can find. The dish has a subtle spice to it from the allspice, cinnamon, and Aleppo pepper—you don't want them to come across too strongly; they should all blend into the background.

Serves 4

1 pound boneless, skinless chicken thighs

2 tablespoons canola oil

2 tablespoons minced garlic

1 cup orzo, preferably Greek

2 tablespoons tomato paste

2½ cups Chicken Stock (page 113)

½ teaspoon kosher salt, plus more to taste

1½ cups Spiced Tomato Sauce (page 74)

½ teaspoon dried oregano, plus more for garnish

¼ teaspoon ground allspice

¼ teaspoon ground cinnamon

¼ teaspoon Aleppo pepper

1 cup grated Kefalograviera cheese, plus more for garnish

1 tablespoon minced chives

Extra-virgin olive oil, for drizzling

○ Lay the chicken thighs flat on a cutting board and, with a sharp knife, trim off any extra fat and bone fragments. Cut into 1-inch cubes.

○ Warm the canola oil in a medium skillet over high heat. When the oil begins to smoke, add the chicken and brown lightly, about 5 minutes. Reduce the heat to medium, add the garlic, and cook until golden and fragrant, about 2 minutes. Push the chicken and garlic to the one side of the pan, then add the orzo to the opposite side and toast, stirring, for about 2 minutes. Add the tomato paste and cook, stirring the chicken, garlic, and orzo together, until a glaze forms on the bottom of the pan, about 2 minutes. Increase the heat to medium-high and add 2 cups of the stock to deglaze the pan, scraping up any browned bits. Season to taste with salt. Simmer until the stock is reduced by half, about 6 minutes. Stir a few times to avoid sticking.

○ Once the stock is reduced, stir in the tomato sauce, and simmer until the sauce thickens and coats the chicken and orzo, about 10 minutes. Reduce heat if necessary to avoid splatters and scrape the bottom of the pan often to keep the sauce from sticking. Add the oregano, allspice, cinnamon, and Aleppo pepper, stir to combine, and cook for 2 more minutes.

○ When ready to serve, stir in the Kefalograviera cheese, and, if needed to loosen the sauce, add the remaining ½ cup of stock. Spoon into bowls and garnish with a sprinkle of grated Kefalograviera cheese, a pinch of dried oregano, some chives, and a drizzle of olive oil.

SAVORY DUMPLINGS IN YOGURT SAUCE
MANTI

The iconic dumplings of Turkey, mantı are a source of pride for many cooks. To make these tiny parcels, you need patience and practice. But it is worth it once you taste these meat-filled dumplings flavored with yogurt, butter, and chili. We were given the secrets to making Kayseri mantı (or mantısı) by an amazing Turkish home cook named Nejla who showed us how to quickly form hundreds and hundreds of the little dumplings. This style of mantı comes from the city of Kayseri in the Anatolia region of central Turkey, but mantı is believed to have first arrived from Central Asia, traveling the Silk Road with Turkic and Mongol migrants. Mantı became a popular dish in the Ottoman palaces and tiny, delicate kayseri mantı were a favored style; they are my favorite too. According to tradition in Kayseri, a bride would be judged by her mother-in-law on how small she could make her mantı; a good cook should fit at least forty pieces on a spoon!

Serves 4 to 6

For the dough:

2 cups (278 grams)
all-purpose flour

1 teaspoon kosher salt

1 large egg yolk

½ cup cold water, plus more
if needed

For the filling:

½ pound ground beef,
90 percent lean

2 tablespoons minced
yellow onion

1 teaspoon kosher salt

½ teaspoon ground cumin

½ teaspoon freshly ground
black pepper

½ teaspoon ground sumac

¼ teaspoon Aleppo pepper

¼ teaspoon sweet smoked
paprika

¼ teaspoon dried mint

¼ teaspoon dried oregano

For serving:

2 cloves Garlic Confit
(page 29)

1 cup Greek yogurt

Kosher salt

Pinch Aleppo pepper

¼ teaspoon dried oregano

¼ teaspoon ground sumac

¼ teaspoon dried mint

5 tablespoons unsalted butter

¼ teaspoon sweet smoked
paprika

2 teaspoons minced chives

Flaky sea salt

○ To make the dough, combine the flour and salt in a large mixing bowl or on a clean work surface. Make a well in the center of the flour and add the egg yolk. Add the water and, using a fork, gently break up the egg yolk in the water, then stir in the surrounding flour. Use your hands to work the flour into the egg mixture until you get a loose dough, then knead the dough until it becomes soft and elastic, about 8 minutes. If all the flour has not been incorporated, sprinkle with more water and continue to knead the dough. Wrap the dough in plastic and refrigerate for at least an hour.

○ To make the filling, combine the meat, onions, salt, cumin, black pepper, sumac, Aleppo pepper, paprika, mint, and oregano in a mixing bowl and knead thoroughly.

○ Remove the dough from the refrigerator and set on a lightly floured work surface, then dust the dough ball with flour. Roll the dough into a large, thin sheet (A), about 22 by 16 inches.

○ Cut the dough vertically into 1-inch strips using a pizza cutter (B), then cut into 1-inch strips horizontally to make 1-inch squares.

○ Place ⅛ teaspoon of the seasoned meat in the center of each square. It's easiest to do this with your finger; dab the meat onto the squares (C).

○ To fold the mantı, bring two opposite corners of the square together with your fingers and lightly pinch them closed (D), then bring the other two corners together and pinch or twist the dough closed (E). Each dumpling should be about the size of a chickpea (F). If the dough dries and it's difficult to pinch closed, dab the edges with a little water. Set the mantı aside or dust them with flour and freeze (first on a baking sheet, then transferred to a bag) until ready to use.

○ To serve, bring a pot of water to a boil, add the mantı, and cook for 5 to 6 minutes, until all the dumplings float. Drain, reserving the cooking water.

○ Meanwhile, put the Garlic Confit in a bowl and mash with a fork. Whisk in the yogurt and season with a pinch of salt. In another bowl, stir together the Aleppo pepper, oregano, sumac, and dried mint and set the spice mix aside.

○ Heat the butter in a heavy-bottomed medium sauté pan over medium-low heat and cook, stirring, until the butter foams and then browns, 5 to 7 minutes. Remove the pan from the heat and transfer 2 tablespoons of browned butter to a small bowl. Stir the paprika into the small bowl of butter.

○ Add 3 tablespoons of the reserved cooking water to the sauté pan of browned butter and whisk to create a creamy emulsion. Add the mantı and toss to cover in the sauce, adding another tablespoon of cooking water if needed to make the sauce.

○ Spread some garlic yogurt in the bottom of four to six shallow bowls. Spoon the buttered mantı among the bowls, then drizzle with the paprika butter and garnish with chives, flaky salt, and a big pinch of spice mix.

CHEF MOVE You can make these ahead of time, maybe with a friend or two, and freeze them until you're ready to use. Spread the mantı on a parchment-lined baking sheet and place in the freezer. Once frozen, transfer them to a plastic freezer bag and store for up to two months.

MEATBALLS IN SPICED TOMATO SAUCE
SOUTZOUKAKIA

As you have seen throughout this book, Greece and Turkey have a shared history—people have migrated back and forth, bringing with them ingredients, dishes, and stories. These meatballs—full of cumin and cooked in a rich spiced tomato sauce—come from the ancient town of Smyrna, which is now known as İzmir, on the Aegean Sea in the far west of Turkey. The Greeks who lived there fled in the 1920s to Greece, bringing the dish with them. It survives in Greece as soutzoukakia (a Greek-Turkish mash-up meaning "little spicy sausages") and in Turkey as İzmir köfte—the preparations differ, but the dishes share a recognizable heritage. This is our version, which leans toward the Greek side of the border.

Serves 4

1 pound ground beef, 80 percent lean

2 garlic cloves, grated

1 teaspoon ground cumin

½ teaspoon freshly ground black pepper

Kosher salt

2 tablespoons extra-virgin olive oil

2 cups Spiced Tomato Sauce (page 74)

1 teaspoon salt-cured capers, rinsed and dried

1 ounce feta, crumbled

1 teaspoon minced chives

O Combine the beef, garlic, cumin, black pepper, and 1 teaspoon kosher salt in a mixing bowl and knead with your hands until well combined, or pulse in a food processor. Using your hands, take 1-ounce, golf-ball-size pieces of the meat mixture and roll them into oval-shaped meatballs. You should have about eighteen meatballs.

O Warm the oil in a medium sauté pan with a lid over medium-high heat. Working in batches, sear the meatballs until browned all over, about 4 minutes, then set on a paper-towel-lined plate to drain.

O Carefully pour off any excess fat in the pan and return to the heat. Add the tomato sauce and scrape up any browned bits from the bottom of the pan. Return the meatballs to the sauce and stir to coat. Cover, reduce the heat to low, and gently simmer until the meatballs cook through, 15 to 20 minutes. Stir in the capers and season to taste with salt.

O Spoon the meatballs and sauce into serving bowls and garnish with feta and chives.

09

FAMILY & FIRE

There's something so simple and profound about cooking over fire, as we harness the power of the earth, the air, the spark that makes us human. Since the beginning of time, we have cooked over fire, from prehistoric humans roasting animals over open flames, to the popularity of barbecues across the world today.

Greece has long prided itself on its deep connection with open-flame cooking; we can see its importance all the way back to the time of Homer and the stories of ritual sacrifices to the ancient gods throughout *The Odyssey* and *The Iliad*. The tradition continues and is still central to the celebration of Easter. In a country filled with mountains and hills, roasted lamb, kid, and sometimes pork play the biggest roles in feasts and gatherings. There's a reason that these traditions have lasted through the ages: they are amazing moments to gather with family and friends, for everyone to stand together around the fire, around the meat as it cooks, with a glass of wine in hand and something delicious to snack on as you smell the smokiness of the roasting meat. It's a time of anticipation, that moment before the meal begins, when excitement builds about what you're ready to enjoy. Maybe you have a second glass of wine. Just don't forget to check the meat!

Growing up, my family would go to the mountains outside Barcelona on Sundays and invite our friends to join us. My dad and I would build a fire and set up a big paella pan, and he would cook these great big paellas to feed everyone who came. There was something so beautiful about those days, bringing us all together with the fire and paella at the center. In these moments, my dad taught me one of the most important lessons of my life: if more people join the party, just throw another handful of rice in the pan. Maybe that's why I love the act of roasting a whole lamb or grilling a whole fish. It brings me back to those days, surrounded by family and community, cooking for anyone who showed up.

In the early days at the restaurant, we would set up a spit and roast a lamb weekly, making the entire neighborhood smell amazing. Guests would come and watch us cook, and they would learn where their food came from—it was a way to include them in the process of making their dinner. Today, for special occasions, we sometimes bring back spit-roasting to the restaurant. I always love to see how people follow their nose to the source: a beautiful lamb, roasting over the flames, transforming into something aromatic, tender, and delicious.

This chapter is full of recipes that are made for celebrations with your family and friends. Big roasts, show-stopping rice pilaf with braised lamb, spiced meat kebabs, and whole fish cooked over fire. These are impressive, centerpiece dishes that will bring everyone to the table to celebrate. Some of these dishes take a bit of work—the pastirma-

style rib eyes have you making a traditional Turkish spice paste; the lamb shoulder goes through a roast, a steam, and a second roast; and phyllo needs to be rolled out and layered for Lamb and Eggplant Pie (page 296). But you know that everyone in the kitchen—or around the fire—will be able to savor the extra effort you've put in.

ROASTED LAMB SHOULDER

I'll tell you right now, don't let the length of this recipe intimidate you! It's actually not too hard, and the result more than makes up for the work you put in. Chef Costa created this multistep technique for a juicy, tender, flavorful lamb shoulder, and, to me, each step is necessary. One thing that's key to getting it right is having the proper tools on hand: a pan with a rack, butcher's twine, and peach butcher paper. You may have seen this food-grade, pinkish-orange paper at barbecue restaurants and hardware stores. It offers the perfect amount of breathability and strength to wrap the roast and hold in moisture—but in a pinch, a combination of unwaxed parchment paper and aluminum foil can work.

Serves 6 to 8

For the spice rub:

1 garlic clove

2 tablespoons dried Greek oregano

1 tablespoon freshly ground black pepper

2 teaspoons dried mint

1 teaspoon ground cumin

½ teaspoon ground star anise

1 teaspoon olive oil

For the lamb:

1 boneless lamb shoulder roast (4 to 5 pounds)

1 tablespoon kosher salt

1 cup Chicken Stock (page 113)

¼ cup ladolemono (page 60)

2 tablespoons fresh dill, roughly chopped

Flaky sea salt

2 heads romaine or baby romaine lettuce

Pita bread (page 129)

1 cup Harissa (page 70)

1 cup Tzatziki (page 52)

1 cup Toum (page 68)

○ To make the rub, grate the garlic clove with a Microplane into a small mixing bowl. Add the oregano, pepper, mint, cumin, star anise, and olive oil and mix thoroughly.

○ To prepare the lamb, preheat the oven to 375°F. Cut five lengths of butcher's twine long enough to wrap around and tie the shoulder, about 12 inches each. Tie the twine around the shoulder, with equal spacing between the ties, to keep the roast a tight uniform shape.

○ Place the shoulder on a rimmed baking sheet with a rack and sprinkle all over with salt. Let it rest for about 10 minutes, then generously cover the shoulder with the rub. Roast on a center rack in the oven until browned, about 1 hour.

○ Remove the shoulder from the oven and reduce the heat to 275°F. Cut a 2-foot-long piece of peach butcher paper and lay it flat on a cutting board. (You could instead use 2 feet of unwaxed parchment paper on top of the same amount of aluminum foil.)

○ When the roast is cool enough to handle, but still hot, transfer it to the butcher paper, placing it on one end of the paper, and wrap it like a burrito, folding in the sides as you roll. If you're

using parchment and aluminum foil, wrap the shoulder in the unwaxed parchment first, then tightly wrap it in the foil. You want to make sure it's wrapped tightly so no juices will escape.

○ Remove the rack from the roasting pan and carefully pour off any excess fat, then deglaze the pan with the chicken stock, scraping up any browned bits that stick to the pan. Pour the liquid into a small saucepan and set aside.

○ Put the rack back in the deglazed pan, place the paper-wrapped shoulder on top, and return it to the oven on the center rack. Fill another rimmed baking sheet, or shallow baking pan, with about 2 cups of water, and carefully place it on the lower rack of the oven. (This will create steam for a juicy roast.) Cook the shoulder until it reaches an internal temperature of 190°F on a probe thermometer. Begin checking the temperature after 2 hours; it could take up to 3 hours to reach temperature depending on the size of your roast. If at any point the lower pan dries out, add more water.

○ Remove the shoulder and second baking sheet from the oven and increase the oven temperature to 375°F. Carefully unwrap the shoulder while it's still on the rack, collecting all

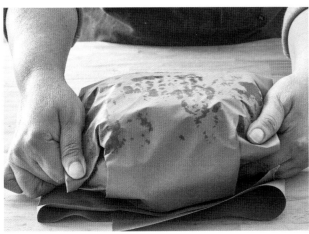

of the juices in the pan. Reserve the paper or foil. Carefully set the rack on a work surface and pour any juices in the pan into the small saucepan with the reserved deglazing liquid.

○ Return the rack to the pan and spray or brush the top and bottom of the shoulder, set on the rack, with olive oil to encourage more browning. If the bottom is less browned than the top, flip the shoulder to brown evenly. When the oven reaches 375°F, return the shoulder to the oven to brown and get crispy, about 10 minutes.

○ Remove the shoulder from the oven and loosely cover with the reserved paper or foil. Allow the roast to rest for 10 minutes.

○ Meanwhile, bring the small saucepan of juices to a boil and season to taste with salt if needed. Simmer until reduced to about 1 cup.

○ Transfer the shoulder to a carving board and remove the twine. Cut the shoulder into nice, even slices, and place them on a serving platter. Spoon the reduced juices over the slices, then drizzle on the ladolemono and sprinkle with dill and flaky sea salt. Serve with lettuce leaves, pita bread, Harissa, Tzatziki, and Toum.

○ Keep any leftover shoulder covered and refrigerated for up to 3 days. Use leftovers for Lamb Kleftiko (page 144) or moussakapita (page 296).

SEVEN SPICE LAMB LEG WITH LEMON POTATOES

If you've ever had lamb shawarma, you already have an idea what this amazing lamb leg will taste like. I love this recipe because it combines the flavor of classic lamb shawarma while being cooked to a beautiful juicy pink medium rare. The lemon roasted potatoes get nice and crispy, then tossed with the juices of the roast. It's meat and potatoes, but for the gods. And if you have any lamb left over, chill it overnight and slice it cold for sandwiches the next day. In fact, you might even want to make two to be sure you have leftovers!

Family & Fire

Serves 6 to 8

For the lamb:

1 boneless lamb leg (about 3 pounds)

Kosher salt

2 garlic cloves, peeled

½ teaspoon dried mint

2 tablespoons Lebanese Seven Spice (page 27), divided

Extra-virgin olive oil

1 cup Chicken Stock (page 113)

For the potatoes:

3 pounds baby Yukon Gold potatoes, halved

Kosher salt

3 tablespoons extra-virgin olive oil, plus more for drizzling

1 teaspoon dried Greek oregano

½ teaspoon ground cumin

½ preserved lemon rind (page 34), cut into fine strips

5 to 6 fresh bay leaves, or ½ bunch flat-leaf parsley, leaves only, thinly sliced

1 lemon

Flaky sea salt

○ Ask your butcher to butterfly the lamb leg for you, or do it yourself: Place the lamb on a cutting board and trim any fat down to about ¼ inch thick. Remove any opaque connective tissue and then slice a long cut through the thickest part of the meat, about ¾ of the way through the meat (be careful to not cut all the way through), then spread open the meat like a book and lay flat. You want the lamb to have a consistent thickness. Season with salt, then, using a Microplane, grate the garlic cloves over the meat. Sprinkle the lamb with dried mint and ½ tablespoon of the Lebanese Seven Spice.

○ Position a rack at the bottom third of the oven and another rack in the middle. Preheat the oven to 300°F and place a rack in a roasting pan.

○ Cut five to six pieces of butcher's twine, each about 12 inches long. You need them to be long enough to wrap around the leg and tie a knot.

○ Beginning with the thinnest end of the meat, roll the leg into a cylinder shape. Starting in the center of the lamb roll, wrap the twine around the meat and tie in a tight knot, then move out to the sides, with equal spacing between the ties. Use more pieces of twine if you need to keep a tight uniform shape. Trim off any excess twine.

○ Generously season the rolled lamb leg with salt and 1½ tablespoons of Lebanese Seven Spice. Spray, or drizzle, olive oil all over the lamb leg. Lay the lamb on the rack and place the roasting pan on the middle rack of the oven. Roast for 45 minutes, then check the temperature of the lamb with a meat thermometer. Continue roasting, checking the temperature every 10 to 15 minutes, until the lamb is browned and reaches 130°F.

○ Meanwhile, to make the potatoes, put them in a large pot and cover with water and 1 tablespoon salt. Bring to a boil and simmer until tender, about 15 minutes. Drain well, then toss with the 3 tablespoons of olive oil and spread them on a sheet pan. After the lamb has cooked for 1 hour, add the potatoes to the oven, on the rack below the roasting pan.

○ When the lamb is done, transfer it to a cutting board to rest and loosely cover with aluminum foil.

○ Increase the oven to 400°F and move the potatoes to the middle rack. Continue roasting, occasionally turning them until they begin to brown, about 20 more minutes.

○ While the potatoes cook, place the roasting pan on the stove top over medium heat and add the chicken stock. Bring to a low simmer and deglaze the pan, scraping up any browned bits with a spatula.

○ Remove the potatoes from the oven and toss with the oregano, cumin, preserved lemon, and bay leaves or parsley to evenly coat the potatoes.

○ When ready to serve, place the potatoes on a serving platter and zest the lemon over the potatoes with a Microplane. Cut the lemon in half and squeeze the juice over the potatoes. Drizzle with olive oil and season with flaky sea salt.

○ Uncover the lamb and remove the twine. Slice the lamb and lay over the potatoes. Pour any juices that collected on the cutting board into the roasting pan with the warm stock. Whisk together, then spoon over the sliced lamb and potatoes. Sprinkle the lamb with the remaining ½ tablespoon of seven spice and some flaky sea salt, then drizzle with olive oil.

GRILLED WHOLE FISH

I love grilling whole fish. It feels so elemental, like you've taken this creature from the sea and introduced it to the fire in order to honor its life and sacrifice. This grilled European sea bass (often seen on menus as branzino) feels like that to me, a simple recipe that lets the nature of the fish really come through. The preparation is inspired by the island of Santorini, in the southern Aegean Sea, where the volcanic soil and dry weather lead to some of the sweetest, most aromatic tomatoes on the planet. The tomato-olive sauce that goes with the branzino is our tribute to those tomatoes. I like using a fish basket to easily grill the fish on both sides—it's a small investment that pays off every time.

Serves 4

For the tomato-olive sauce:

1 large ripe tomato, cored and diced

2 sun-dried tomato halves, diced

Kosher salt

4 Kalamata olives, pitted and diced

1 tablespoon chopped fresh parsley leaves

1 tablespoon extra-virgin olive oil, plus more for drizzling

½ teaspoon Urfa pepper

For the fish:

1 whole sea bass (about 2 pounds), guts, scales, and gills removed

1 lemon

1 bunch fresh thyme

Extra-virgin olive oil

Kosher salt

2 to 3 tablespoons ladolemono (page 60)

Flaky sea salt

½ cup fresh dill fronds

1 cup yellow squash skordalia (page 73)

○ To make the tomato-olive sauce, put the diced tomato and sun-dried tomato in a mixing bowl and season with salt. Stir in the olives, parsley, olive oil, and Urfa pepper, then cover and keep at room temperature.

○ To make the fish, heat up a grill, preferably charcoal; a gas grill set to high will work as well. Score the fish with a sharp kitchen knife under the fins and across the head and tail. (This will make the fish easier to fillet later.)

○ Cut the lemon in half. Thinly slice 1 half, reserving the other. Place the sliced lemon and thyme in the belly of the fish, then rub or brush the skin of the fish with olive oil. Place the fish in an oiled fish basket and put on the grill. Close the grill cover and cook, turning every 5 minutes, until the skin is nicely crispy and the fins are easy to pull out, about 20 minutes depending on the heat of your grill. Remove the sliced lemon and thyme from the belly and allow the fish to rest for 3 minutes.

○ Meanwhile, rub the cut side of the lemon with a little olive oil and grill it, cut side down, until charred and soft, about 7 minutes.

○ To serve, gently lift the fillets from the bones of the fish using an offset metal spatula or a large chef's knife. Lay each fillet on the cutting board and remove any visible bones, being extra careful to remove the small pin bones that run along the spine toward the head.

○ Season the flesh side of each fillet with salt and ladolemono to taste. Move the fillets to a serving platter, skin side up, then sprinkle with flaky sea salt. Garnish with dill and drizzles of ladolemono and olive oil. Serve with the charred lemon half, tomato-olive sauce, and yellow squash skordalia.

CELEBRATION RICE

This is a dish that's meant for something special, and you can decide what occasion is worthy of it! The rice has its roots in a few different Persian dishes, including the incredible jeweled rice that's brought out at feasts in Iran. We added some crispy rice to the top of the dish, with tahdig—the very famous crunchy rice from Iran—as the inspiration. It's definitely not a traditional tahdig, but gives you the crunch that goes beautifully with the sweet-nutty-aromatic toppings and the rich, velvety sauce from the lamb shanks that accompany this dish. You can make the lamb shanks the day before serving, if you'd like—they'll taste even better the next day.

Serves 6 to 8

For the rice:

4 tablespoons unsalted butter, divided

1 large yellow onion, finely diced

6 garlic cloves, minced

2 tablespoons salt, divided, plus more to taste

4 cardamom pods

2 bay leaves, preferably fresh

4 cups basmati rice

2 cinnamon sticks

1 small carrot, peeled and grated

Large pinch saffron threads (about 1 gram)

For the crispy rice:

1 egg white

2 tablespoons cornstarch

1 tablespoon extra-virgin olive oil

1 tablespoon unsalted butter

For the garnish:

4 tablespoons unsalted butter

3 tablespoons chopped pistachios

1 tablespoon sliced almonds

½ cup Chicken Stock (page 113)

1 tablespoon soaked barberries (page 186)

1 tablespoon chopped dried cherries

2 tablespoons turmeric pickled raisins (page 108)

2 tablespoons finely sliced parsley leaves

1 tablespoon minced chives

2 to 3 Lamb Shanks and sauce (opposite page), warmed

2 teaspoons Sumac Rose Spice (page 27)

○ To make the rice, set a large saucepan over medium heat. Add 3 tablespoons of the butter, ⅔ of the minced onions, ⅔ of the garlic, and a pinch of salt. Cook until the onions are translucent, about 5 minutes. Add 3 cups of the rice, 1 of the cinnamon sticks, 2 of the cardamom pods, 1 of the bay leaves and 1½ tablespoons of salt. Continue to cook, stirring, until everything is nicely coated and aromatic, about 1 minute. Add 6 cups of water, increase the heat to high, and bring to a boil. Cover the saucepan and reduce the heat to low. Simmer until all of the water is absorbed and the rice is cooked, about 20 minutes.

○ Let the rice sit for 10 minutes, then fluff with a fork and season to taste with salt if needed. Remove 2 cups of the rice and set aside in a mixing bowl to cool for use in the crispy rice. Keep remaining rice covered in the saucepan.

○ In another medium saucepan, melt 1 tablespoon of the butter over medium heat. Add the remaining minced onions and garlic, and the grated carrots. Season with salt and cook until onions are translucent, about 5 minutes. Add the remaining 1 cup of rice and the remaining cinnamon stick, cardamom pods, bay leaf, and salt. Cook until everything is coated and aromatic, about 1 minute. Add 2 cups of water and the saffron, increase the heat to high, and bring to a boil. Cover the saucepan, reduce the heat to low, and cook until all of the water is absorbed and the rice is cooked, about 20 minutes.

○ Allow to sit for 10 minutes, then fluff with a fork and season to taste with additional salt if needed.

○ To make the crispy rice, lightly whip the egg white, then mix in the cornstarch to form a thin paste. Pour the mixture over the cooled 2 cups

of rice in the mixing bowl and stir with a spoon until well combined. (The mixture should be very sticky.)

○ Warm the olive oil in an 8-inch nonstick pan over medium heat. When the oil is hot but not smoking, add the rice mixture, and using a spatula or the back of a spoon, press the rice flat across the pan. Wet your spatula to keep the rice from sticking as you press it into a thin layer.

○ Cook the rice until it comes together and you can lift an edge to check the bottom without it falling apart, about 5 minutes. Lift up one edge of the rice and add the tablespoon of butter, letting it melt and spread across the pan. Lay the rice back down in the pan and continue cooking until the bottom of the rice is golden brown, about 7 minutes more.

○ Carefully remove the crispy rice from the pan, sliding it on to a paper-towel-lined plate. Set aside in a warm place.

○ To make the garnish, melt the 4 tablespoons of butter in a large pan over medium heat and cook until foaming. Add the nuts and cook until aromatic and browned, about 6 minutes. Add the basmati (white) rice, saffron (yellow) rice, and chicken stock and cook together, stirring until hot, about 3 minutes. Add about ¾ of the barberries, cherries, turmeric pickled raisins, parsley, and chives and stir to mix. Season to taste with salt.

○ Spoon the warm rice mixture onto a large serving dish, sprinkling the remaining garnishes over the top. Place the warmed lamb shanks, still on the bone (opposite page), on the rice and spoon the sauce over the shanks. Garnish each shank with a teaspoon of Rose Sumac Spice. Break the crispy rice into pieces and place them around the plate, standing them in the soft rice.

LAMB SHANKS

If you're not used to cooking lamb, braised lamb shanks are an easy and forgiving way to start. A long simmer in a flavorful sauce will turn this tougher cut of meat fall-off-the bone tender. A perfect partner to the Celebration Rice, braised lamb shanks in a velvety rich sauce are also the irresistible ingredient to our classic hünkâr beğendi (page 254). For a larger 2-pound cut of lamb with more meat on the bone, look for the hind shanks. If smaller fore shanks, at about 1 pound each, are all you can find, double up, and use a pot that allows the lamb shanks to lie flat in one layer. Be sure to brown the meat and shallots very well so the sauce will reach a deep mahogany color.

Serves 4 to 6

2 to 4 lamb shanks (about 4 pounds total), preferably hind shanks

Kosher salt

Freshly ground black pepper

2 tablespoons extra-virgin olive oil

3 shallots, peeled and halved

1 head garlic, cloves separated and peeled

1 tablespoon tomato paste

1 large ripe tomato, cored and diced

2 to 3 quarts veal stock or Chicken Stock (page 113)

1½ ounces demi-glace, preferably classic French veal demi-glace

1 tablespoon unsalted butter

1 tablespoon all-purpose flour

○ Season the shanks with salt and pepper. Warm the olive oil in a large, heavy pot with a lid over high heat. (The pot should be large enough for the shanks to lie in a single layer.) Sear the lamb on all sides until nicely browned, 10 to 15 minutes. Transfer the shanks to a plate.

○ Reduce the heat to medium-high and add the shallots and garlic to the pot. Cook, stirring, until deeply brown, 5 to 10 minutes. Add the tomato paste, stirring to coat. Cook a few minutes more, until a glaze forms on the bottom of the pan, then add the diced tomatoes and season with a pinch of salt. Scrape up any browned bits that have formed in the pan, then whisk in about 1 cup of the stock and the demi-glace. Return the lamb to the pot, then add enough stock to cover the shanks. Bring to a low boil over medium-high heat, then reduce the heat to a simmer, cover, and cook for 1 hour.

○ Uncover and continue cooking, maintaining a steady simmer, until the shanks are tender and the meat begins to pull away from the bone, 1½ to 2 hours. Carefully remove the shanks from the pot, keeping the bone connected to the meat, and set aside to keep warm. Strain the cooking liquid through a fine-mesh sieve into a large heatproof bowl. Allow the liquid to rest and cool slightly, then skim off any fat from the top of the liquid.

○ Return the pot to medium heat and add the butter to melt. Whisk in the flour and cook, stirring, until it starts to turn golden brown and smell nutty, about 5 minutes, then whisk in the reserved cooking liquid. Add the lamb shanks back to the pot and return to a simmer over medium heat. Cook, stirring occasionally, until the sauce is reduced by half and can coat the back of a spoon, about 45 minutes. Taste and season with salt, if needed. Keep warm over low heat until ready to use.

○ If serving the next day, allow the shanks and sauce to cool slightly, then cover and refrigerate overnight. To warm before serving, return the pot to the stove top and simmer slowly over medium-low heat for about 30 minutes, until the sauce and meat have warmed through.

GREEK FISH SOUP
PSAROSOUPA

This beautiful, simple, hearty fish soup ("psari" is "fish"; "soupa" is obvious!) celebrates the flavors of the Mediterranean. It's inspired by an approach taken by our Greek food mentor Aglaia, who makes a soup somewhere between bouillabaisse and kakavia—a classic Greek fisherman's soup made only with finfish. Ours uses European sea bass as well as shrimp and mussels, which we think gives the broth a deeper flavor, along with the herbal sweetness from the fennel and red pepper.

Serves 6 to 8

2 whole sea bass (about 2 pounds each), cleaned and fileted, reserving bones and heads

1 fennel bulb

1 large red bell pepper

¼ cup extra-virgin olive oil, plus more for drizzling

1 yellow onion, coarsely chopped

1 carrot, coarsely chopped

1 stalk celery, coarsely chopped

6 garlic cloves, cut in half lengthwise

2 tablespoons tomato paste

5 sprigs flat-leaf parsley, leaves and stems separated, leaves finely chopped

2 bay leaves

2 star anise

1 whole clove

1 teaspoon whole black peppercorns

4 ripe tomatoes, cored and coarsely chopped

2 cups dry white wine

1 pound large shrimp, peeled and deveined, shells reserved

1½ pounds baby Yukon Gold potatoes

Kosher salt

2 pounds mussels, cleaned and debearded

3 lemons, cut into wedges

○ Rinse the fish heads and bones.

○ Trim the stalk and root from the fennel, peel off the tough outer layer, and reserve for stock. Dice the fennel bulb into ½-inch pieces, about 2 cups.

○ Core and dice the bell pepper into ½-inch pieces, to make about 2 cups. Reserve trimmings for stock.

○ Warm the olive oil in a large pot over high heat, add the onions, carrots, celery, garlic, and the trimmings from the fennel and bell pepper, and cook until the vegetables start to soften, about 3 minutes.

○ Stir in the tomato paste and cook until a glaze starts to form on the bottom of the pan. Add the parsley stems, bay leaves, star anise, clove, and black peppercorns and continue cooking until aromatic, about 30 seconds. Add the chopped tomatoes and white wine and deglaze the pan, scraping up any browned bits from the bottom. Continue to cook until the alcohol evaporates, about 4 minutes.

○ Add the shrimp shells, potatoes, fish heads, and bones, then add enough water to cover, about 10 cups. Bring to a boil over high heat, then cover and cook at a full boil for 30 minutes.

○ Remove the potatoes from the pot with a slotted spoon and set them on a cutting board. Strain the stock through a coarse strainer into a large

soup pot, pushing on the solids with a ladle to release all the liquid, then discard the solids.

○ Once cool enough to handle, peel and roughly chop five of the cooked potatoes, then add them to the strained liquid. Blend with an immersion blender until the broth becomes smooth. Coarsely split the remaining potatoes in half, using the tip of a knife to pry them in half. (The rough sides of the potatoes will help thicken the broth.)

○ Quarter the sea bass fillets by cutting in half lengthwise, then in half again widthwise. Season both sides with salt.

○ Heat the broth to just below a simmer over medium heat. Add the diced bell peppers, fennel, and remaining potatoes and cook for 5 minutes. Add the sea bass and poach for 1 minute, then add the shrimp and gently stir to combine and cover the seafood with the hot broth. Cook for 3 more minutes, until the fish and shrimp are almost cooked through. Last, add the mussels and cover the pot. Cook until the mussels open, about 5 minutes. Discard any mussels that have not opened.

○ Season to taste with salt and freshly squeezed lemon juice from 4 wedges. Stir in the chopped parsley leaves.

○ Ladle the soup and seafood into bowls, drizzle with olive oil, and serve with lemon wedges.

SLOW-ROASTED, PASTIRMA-STYLE RIB EYES

Pastirma, an ancient cured meat from Central Anatolia, gets its distinctive flavor from a spice paste called "çemen," which means "fenugreek" in Turkish—the fenugreek-garlic-chili paste stops any bacteria from growing on the meat as it cures (learn more about pastirma on page 261). For these pastirma-style rib eye steaks, instead of curing them, we rub them in a butter-enriched çemen paste and slowly roast them to a juicy medium-rare perfection . . . the very best of both worlds. If you want, you can marinate the steaks in the paste the day before you plan to grill—just wrap them in plastic wrap and refrigerate them overnight.

Serves 6 to 8

For the steaks:

2 tablespoons cumin seeds

2 teaspoons fenugreek seeds

2 teaspoons dried fenugreek leaves

2 tablespoons Urfa pepper

2 tablespoons Aleppo pepper

2 tablespoons sweet smoked paprika

2 tablespoons boiling water

2 garlic cloves, grated

¼ cup (½ stick) butter, at room temperature

3 tablespoons mild pepper paste (see 341)

1 tablespoon kosher salt

2 boneless rib eye steaks (24 ounces each, at least 2 inches thick)

For the greens:

2 bunches Swiss chard, ribs and leaves separated

¼ cup extra-virgin olive oil, plus more for drizzling

3 garlic cloves, peeled and thinly sliced

4 slices pastirma, cut crosswise into thin strips

2 pounds baby spinach

Flaky sea salt

Freshly ground black pepper

○ Preheat the oven to 300°F.

○ To prepare the steaks, toast the cumin seeds in a small dry pan over medium heat until aromatic, about 1 minute, then put them into a spice grinder. Add the fenugreek seeds to the pan and toast for another minute, then transfer to the spice grinder. Add the fenugreek leaves and the Urfa and Aleppo peppers to the spice grinder and pulse until the spices are coarsely ground. Transfer to a mixing bowl, add the paprika, and stir in the boiling water. Let steep and allow all the water to be absorbed, then stir in the garlic, butter, pepper paste, and salt. Rub this paste over the steaks.

○ Place a flat wire rack in a large roasting pan, or on a large rimmed baking sheet, and lay the steaks on the rack. Roast the steaks in the oven until they reach an internal temperature of 130°F, about 1 hour, and are browned and caramelized. Set the steaks aside to rest.

○ Meanwhile, once the steaks have cooked for 40 minutes, begin to prepare the greens. Thinly slice the Swiss chard stems and tear the leaves into roughly 1-inch pieces.

○ Heat the ¼ cup of olive oil in a large pot over medium heat. Add the garlic and pastirma and cook until garlic is starting to lightly brown around the edges and the pastirma begins to crisp.

○ Add the Swiss chard stems, cover the pan, and cook until the stems are soft, about 8 minutes. Add the Swiss chard leaves and continue cooking, stirring occasionally, until they wilt and begin to soften, about 8 more minutes. Then add the spinach and continue cooking for 3 more minutes, until the spinach wilts. Season to taste with flaky sea salt and pepper.

○ To serve, slice the rib eyes across the grain into pieces about 1½ inches thick. Spoon the greens onto a serving platter and arrange steak slices on top. Pour any of the meat juices from the cutting board over the steak. Garnish with flaky sea salt and drizzle with olive oil.

LAMB AND EGGPLANT PIE
MOUSSAKAPITA

Many Americans know the famous dish moussaka, created by the renowned Greek chef Nikolaos Tselementes—it layers eggplant, potatoes, and lamb with a creamy béchamel before being baked. Ours is a play on the original, entering it into the family of Greek "pitas," or pies. We bake the layered ingredients in a phyllo shell, so the outside gets golden and crispy—and it's beautiful on the table. Lamb shoulder is perfect in this dish, but ground lamb works well too. We use an 11-inch rectangular springform pan so it's easy to cut into slices, and it lets you unhinge midbake to check on how the pie is browning. This is a forgiving recipe, so if you have a round springform or a deep baking dish, it will be just as amazing. You may have filling left over; use it to stir into pasta.

Serves 8 to 10

For the béchamel:

3 cups whole milk

⅓ cup extra-virgin olive oil

⅓ cup all-purpose flour

1 cup Kefalograviera cheese

½ teaspoon grated nutmeg

¼ freshly ground white pepper

Kosher salt

2 large egg yolks

For the pie:

½ cup extra-virgin olive oil, plus more for drizzling

3 eggplants (2 pounds), preferably Italian

Kosher salt

1 head garlic, cloves peeled and stem ends trimmed

¼ teaspoon Aleppo pepper

¼ teaspoon dried oregano

¼ teaspoon ground cumin

1½ pounds russet potatoes, peeled and chopped

2 pounds chopped roasted lamb shoulder (page 280), or cooked ground lamb

2 cups Spiced Tomato Sauce (page 74)

3 to 4 sheets Phyllo (page 141)

Flaky sea salt

○ To make the béchamel, gently warm the milk in a medium pot over medium heat until hot but not boiling.

○ In a medium saucepan, warm the olive oil over medium heat, then whisk in the flour. Cook, stirring constantly, until thickened but not browned, about 2 minutes. Slowly whisk in the hot milk and continue to cook until it becomes a thick sauce, about 10 minutes. Remove from the heat and stir in the cheese, nutmeg, and white pepper, then season to taste with salt.

○ Put the egg yolks in a medium mixing bowl and gently beat them. Whisk 1 cup of the sauce into the eggs to warm them, then add the remaining sauce, stirring until well combined. Set the béchamel aside to cool, covering the top of the sauce with a piece of parchment paper or plastic wrap to keep it from forming a thick skin as it cools.

○ To make the pie, preheat the oven to 375°F and brush a rimmed baking sheet with olive oil. Peel the eggplant, cut it widthwise into ½-inch-thick slices, and sprinkle with salt. Put the eggplant in a colander and set aside to drain for 10 minutes, then blot dry with paper towels.

○ Arrange the eggplant and garlic in a single layer on the baking sheet, overlapping if necessary. Sprinkle with the Aleppo pepper, dried oregano, and cumin. Roast until the eggplant is tender, 30 to 40 minutes, flipping the eggplant halfway through. Set aside to cool.

○ Meanwhile, put the potatoes in a medium saucepan, cover with cold water, add a generous pinch of salt, and bring to a boil. Reduce the heat and simmer, partially covered, until the potatoes are soft, about 20 minutes.

○ Drain the potatoes and return them to the pot. Crush with a fork, then stir in ½ cup of the olive oil, season to taste with salt, and set aside to cool. They should be chunky but not mashed.

○ To assemble the pie, preheat the oven to 400°F. Mix the lamb shoulder or ground lamb with the tomato sauce in a bowl, and season to taste with salt. Brush your baking pan with olive oil. Spray or brush each sheet with olive oil. Lift 1 sheet of phyllo over the pan, then gently press it down into the corners and bottom edges of the pan, being careful not to stretch or tear the dough. Layer on 2 more sheets of phyllo, spraying or brushing with more olive oil between layers, and letting at least 2 inches of phyllo drape over the edges of the pan. Use a fourth sheet of phyllo if needed to patch any tears.

○ Spoon the potatoes onto the phyllo to create the bottom layer of the pie; it should be about 1 inch thick. Spoon the meat on top of the potatoes and press down on the mixture with the back of your spoon. Lay the sliced eggplant and roasted garlic on top of the meat. Finally, ladle the béchamel over the top of the eggplant slices to completely cover with a thick layer of sauce. Fill the pan to about ½ inch from the top. (You will need that gap to allow for the béchamel to puff up when it cooks.) Trim off any remaining phyllo that is draped over the edges.

○ Put the pan on a rimmed baking sheet and place on the middle rack of the oven. Bake until phyllo and béchamel are golden brown, about 1 hour. If the béchamel browns too quickly and the phyllo has not cooked through and turned golden, cover the pan with aluminum foil and continue to cook until the phyllo crust is golden brown.

○ Remove from the oven and allow to rest for 20 minutes. When ready to serve, remove the pie from the pan and transfer to a platter or cutting board. Slice in sections and garnish with flaky sea salt and a drizzle of olive oil.

ADANA KEBAB

Adana kebab, which comes from the city of Adana in Turkey's south, near the Syrian border, is one of the most famous kebabs of Turkey. In fact, laws now govern what can be considered Adana kebabs made in that city, in an effort to protect traditional foodways. There, you will see fresh lamb shoulder and fat from lamb's tail minced together with a curved cleaver known as a zirh (page 65) before being mixed with chilis and spices and shaped onto the extra-wide kebab skewers. There are plenty of opinions across Turkey on what are the best spice mixtures for kebabs, and especially the Adana kebab. We like to keep it pure and simple for this one, and only use Aleppo (or Marash) pepper and smoked paprika to let the most lamb flavor come through. And while you may not be able to find a zirh to mince your meat, I do recommend you invest in some traditional kebab skewers, which are almost an inch across and can be found up to 3 feet long! They are sturdy and work perfectly for other meat and vegetable kebabs. It takes some skill to form the spicy ground lamb around the broad skewers in the traditional style, but don't worry if it takes a few times to get it right. Just make sure your meat is spread out equally on the skewer so it cooks evenly.

Serves 6 to 8

2 pounds ground lamb

1½ tablespoons kosher salt

1 tablespoon Aleppo pepper, plus more for sprinkling

2 teaspoons smoked paprika

Extra-virgin olive oil

Flaky sea salt

24 grilled cherry tomatoes (page 303), or 1 cup Vegetable Ezme Sauce (page 64)

1 cup Sumac Onions (page 32)

1 cup pickled peppers

Toum (page 68)

Harissa (page 70)

Pita bread (page 129), Lavash (page 148), or lettuce leaves

○ Put the lamb, salt, Aleppo pepper, and paprika in a large mixing bowl and stir to combine. Knead the meat and spices together for 2 minutes, or until the mixture is springy, sticky, and coats the side of the bowl. You can also use a stand mixer fitted with a paddle.

○ Fill a bowl with cold water and keep it nearby. Divide the lamb mixture into 8 large balls of equal size—a large handful, about 4 ounces each. Take one ball and shape into an oval in one hand. With your other hand, push the thin edge of the skewer into the center of the oval and squeeze the meat around the skewer, shaping it into a long log. Squeeze the meat out along the skewer, dipping your hand into the water as needed to keep the meat from sticking to your hands, until it is about ½ inch thick all the way around the skewer and roughly 6 inches long. (Pinching indentations into the meat with your fingers every inch as you squeeze the meat is a traditional shape for these kebabs.) Repeat with the remaining meatballs. Depending on the size of your skewer, you may be able to fit two large balls of meat on each skewer.

○ To prepare a grill for kebabs, see page 302. To cook, set the kebabs over the hot coals, or on your grill grates, and cook until browned, about 4 minutes per side.

○ Transfer the cooked kebabs to a work surface, drizzle with olive oil, and sprinkle with flaky salt and Aleppo pepper, if you like it spicy.

○ Carefully slide the meat off the skewers using a fork, tongs, or the back of a chef's knife, then place on a serving platter. Add the grilled tomatoes (or ezme sauce), Sumac Onions, and pickled peppers. Serve with Toum and Harissa, if you like, along with pita bread, lavash, or lettuce leaves.

KÖFTE KEBAB

These meatball kebabs are super-flavorful and juicy—once you try them, they'll be on your grill all summer long. We grind our own meat in the restaurant but that would add a lot of time for a home cook, so feel free to buy ground beef. Just make sure to get 80/20—the high fat content tastes better, but anything more than 20 percent fat tends to flarc up when grilled. If you don't have long, wide skewers, try threading the meat with two thin skewers, or just make little sliders—they'll taste just as good! Grilled tomatoes, pickled peppers or our Tomato Ezme Sauce (page 64) make excellent accompaniments to these kebabs. A tip: to make sure you've properly seasoned the meat before grilling, just pinch off a bit of the mixture and cook it in a pan. Taste and adjust your spices however you like.

Serves 6 to 8

2 pounds ground beef, 80 percent lean

2 garlic cloves, grated or mashed to a paste

1½ tablespoons kosher salt

1½ tablespoons ground cumin

2 teaspoons freshly ground black pepper

2 teaspoons sweet smoked paprika

2 teaspoons dried mint

2 teaspoons Aleppo pepper, plus more for garnish

2 teaspoons dried oregano

Extra-virgin olive oil

Flaky sea salt

24 grilled cherry tomatoes (page 303), or 1 cup Vegetable Ezme Sauce (page 64)

1 cup Sumac Onions (page 32)

1 cup pickled peppers

Toum (page 68)

Harissa (page 70)

Pita bread (page 129), Lavash (page 148), or lettuce leaves

○ Put the beef, garlic, salt, cumin, black pepper, smoked paprika, mint, Aleppo pepper, and oregano in a large mixing bowl. Knead the mixture with your hands until the meat firms up and becomes sticky, about 1 minute. Do not overmix or the kofte will be chewy. (You can also use a stand mixer fitted with a paddle.)

○ Take 1-ounce portions of the meat and roll them into golf ball–size pieces, then slightly flatten to create thick little hamburger shapes. You should have about 32 meatball disks. Thread the meatballs onto skewers, four to eight per skewer depending on length, and push them close together.

○ To prepare a grill for kebabs, see page 302. To cook, set the kebabs over the coals, or on your grill grates, and cook until browned, about 4 minutes per side.

○ Transfer the cooked kebabs to a work surface, drizzle with olive oil, and sprinkle with flaky salt and Aleppo pepper, if you like it a little spicy.

○ Carefully slide the meat off the skewers using a fork, tongs, or the back of a chef's knife, then place on a serving platter. Add the grilled tomatoes (or ezme sauce), Sumac Onions, and pickled peppers. Serve with Toum and Harissa, if you like, along with pita bread, lavash, or lettuce leaves.

TO COOK KEBABS

A kebab rack is a great tool for the most authentic style of cooking meat skewers. The rack suspends the skewers above the grill grates, allowing the kebabs to cook without charring the meat on the hot grates. If you have long, wide kebab skewers, you can lay them across the grill, letting each end rest on the edges of the grill, holding the meat above the fire to cook with radiant heat, as is traditionally done in the Eastern Mediterranean. But don't worry, cooking directly on the grates of a gas grill or even in the oven under a broiler will get the job done.

To prepare your kebabs the traditional way, first make sure your kebab skewers are long enough to lay over the grill, with each end resting on the edge of the grill so the skewer is suspended above the coals. Flat skewers 24 to 36 inches long (*above*) should work on most grills. Depending on the size of your skewers, you may need only 4 skewers or up to 8 to fit all of your meat. Remove the grates from the grill and build a fire using hardwood oak charcoal. To add extra aroma, I like to add a few pieces of apple- or cherrywood. Once the coals are hot and glowing, lay the kebabs over the grill, with the ends resting on the edges of the grill. Cook until browned, about 4 minutes on each side.

TO GRILL TOMATOES

Tossing cherry or grape tomatoes in olive oil and salt and then placing them directly on your grill grates over high heat is an easy way to grill tomatoes. You can also thread them on a skewer if you want to keep them from rolling around the grill (and maybe losing a few to the fire below), but some of their juices will escape where they are pierced. I prefer to put my tomatoes in a metal grill basket and cook them right on the hot coals.

Remove the grates from your grill, and once your coals are hot and glowing, use long tongs to mound some into a little bed on one side of your grill. Put your tomatoes into a grill basket, drizzle them with olive oil, and toss to coat them. Season with kosher salt and toss again. Place the grill basket directly on the coals and cook the tomatoes for about 2 minutes, until they start to blister and brown. (If using a gas grill, place the grill basket right on the grates.) Using an oven mitt and tongs, carefully give the basket a shake to turn the tomatoes and let them cook for another minute or two until charred. Remove the basket from the coals and transfer the tomatoes to a serving bowl. Toss the tomatoes with a little more olive oil and season with flaky sea salt.

10

The first thing I do when I land in Istanbul or Athens—or Barcelona, for that matter—is go for a coffee. While a cortado might be my drink in Spain, when in Turkey, I seek out a spot for a Turkish coffee. It's not just the coffee, always a much-needed jolt of caffeine after a long day of travel. It's not even the satisfyingly thick foam that sits on top. It's the ritual of it. The history. The experience of witnessing a delicious tradition that has shaped the everyday culture of the Mediterranean.

Coffee arrived in Turkey from Yemen in the early sixteenth century and was quickly embraced at the palace of Suleiman the Magnificent, and by the general population. Coffeehouses sprouted throughout the city, and soon they became gathering spots for people to read, play backgammon, and debate new ideas. It wasn't long before Turkish coffee, and its coffeehouse culture, was exported across the Ottoman Empire to Greece and Europe.

To be clear, the "Turkish" in Turkish coffee does not refer to the beans, which are grown elsewhere, but the special method for brewing them. Very finely ground coffee is added with water and sugar to a copper vessel called a cezve, a long-handled pot with a beaked rim for easy pouring. The mixture is then brought to a boil once (and sometimes two or three times by people who insist that this creates the creamiest foam). For me, it's the ratio of coffee, water, and sugar that most affects flavor. At Zaytinya, we serve our Turkish coffee three ways: unsweetened (sade), semisweet (orta şekerli), or sweet (tatlı). Most often our coffee comes from Kurukahveci Mehmet Efendi, one of the oldest coffee makers in Turkey, dating back to 1871. Up to that time, most coffee was sold as raw beans, to be roasted and ground at home or in coffeehouses. They modernized the coffee industry by offering finely ground, roasted coffee for shoppers to brew at home.

I drink mine semisweet. However you order yours, the hot coffee is delivered on trays called askılı kahveci tepsisi, which swing from a tripod handle (*right*). This was another amazing Turkish innovation! You can hold this tray with just one hand. The centripetal swing of the tray prevents beverages from spilling and, in the case of Turkish coffee, helps to settle the grounds before they reach their destination.

As popular as coffee is, people drink even more tea. Tea (çay) is the ultimate symbol of hospitality throughout Turkey, offered to guests in homes and in shops. Visit any bazaar or market in Istanbul and you can see this come to life.

I am amazed at the skill of the people weaving through crowds, swinging trays of hot amber-colored tea to deliver to shopkeepers and tourists on those fascinating round trays. Tea is also served in a special way. The tea is brewed in a Turkish teapot, which is really two pots, one stacked on top of the other. The bottom one holds hot water and the top, the tea—mainly black tea grown in Turkey. The hot water beneath keeps the tea warm and can be used to dilute the tea if it becomes too concentrated. It is served in small, tulip-shaped glasses and never poured to the very top. Otherwise, you will burn your fingers when you pick up the glass!

Some of the recipes you'll find in this chapter are complicated, as desserts can be. For me, sometimes just a little fruit or a few dates can be the perfect ending to a meal. But there is no denying how the skillful combinations of chocolate, cream, and phyllo can make a meal something spectacular. My love of Turkish tea and coffee culture inspired several of Zaytinya's desserts, especially the Turkish coffee chocolate cake, which has been on our menu since the day we opened. The coffee infuses the rich cake with a hint of bitterness. The mastic ice cream that is served with it was a masterstroke from Chef Michael Costa, who, on a visit to Istanbul, had a Turkish coffee brewed with mastic, an aromatic resin from trees that grow on the Greek island of Chios.

I should mention that Turkish coffee isn't called Turkish coffee everywhere. In Greece, it's Greek coffee. In Bosnia, it's Bosnian coffee. In many countries in the Middle East, it's Arabic coffee. I understand the urge for everyone to claim it as their own. But whatever we call it, we all should follow the Turkish approach to coffee. It's more than a drink. It's a way to bring people together. As an old Turkish saying goes: "A single cup of coffee can create a friendship that lasts forty years."

ALMOND COOKIES
AMYGDALOTA

Almonds are the star of these amazing Greek cookies ("almond" in Greek is "amýgdalo"). They are most famous on the Cyclades islands, in the Aegean Sea between Greece and Turkey, where almond trees grow and thrive in the hot dry sun. Almond cookies are reserved for celebrations, especially weddings and baptisms, and represent new beginnings. These ones have a beautiful, unique texture—chewy-crunchy on the outside, light and airy on the inside—with a delicate sweetness. We like to serve them alongside coffee or tea—Greek, Turkish, herbal, whatever you like!

Makes 30 cookies

5 cups (500 grams) almond flour

1 cup plus 1 tablespoon and 1 teaspoon (220 grams) sugar, divided

4 large egg whites

Pinch kosher salt

2 tablespoons amaretto, divided

1 cup blanched almonds

½ teaspoon orange blossom water

○ Preheat the oven to 325°F.

○ Mix the almond flour and 1 cup (200 grams) sugar in a bowl and set aside. In another large bowl, beat the egg whites with the salt and remaining 1 tablespoon and 1 teaspoon (20 grams) sugar, using a whisk, until frothy. Stir in 1 tablespoon of the amaretto.

○ Fold the almond flour mixture into the egg whites until it forms a thick paste. Roll the paste into small balls, about 1 inch in diameter, and slightly flatten on a sheet pan. Brush each cookie with the rest of the amaretto using a pastry brush. Indent each cookie slightly in the center and place a blanched almond in each indent.

○ Bake the cookies 16 to 20 minutes until light golden brown in color. They should be a little crisp on the outside but remain soft on the inside. Transfer the cookies to a cooling rack. Once cool, lightly sprinkle with the orange blossom water.

OLIVE OIL AND HONEY COOKIES
MELOMAKARONA

To many Greeks, the smell of warm spices means Christmas is here. You'll go into a kitchen and breathe in deep the sweet aroma of cinnamon, orange, and brandy and know that the melomakarona cookies are in the oven. It's an interesting history: they're ancient cookies that were originally served after funerals (makaria—the same origin as "macaroni"—was a funeral bread), but during the Byzantine Empire they started to be dipped in honey (meli) and associated with Christmas. We learned to make these slightly egg-shaped cookies from Aglaia, who like her mother before her likes to let the cookies sit overnight before soaking them in honey to keep them crispy. We just can't seem to wait that long and dunk them in the spiced honey syrup straight out of the oven.

Makes about 30 cookies

For the cookies:

6 tablespoons (85 grams) sugar

Zest of one orange

2 cups plus 2 tablespoons (260 grams) all-purpose flour

¾ cup (100 grams) semolina flour

1 teaspoon baking powder

½ teaspoon baking soda

1 teaspoon ground cinnamon

¼ teaspoon kosher salt

½ cup olive oil

6 tablespoons orange juice

2 tablespoons plus 1 teaspoon honey

3 tablespoons brandy

¼ cup walnut halves

For the syrup:

1 cup sugar

3 tablespoons honey, preferably Greek

2 cinnamon sticks

3 cloves

1 strip orange peel

To make the cookies, combine the sugar and the orange zest in the bowl of a stand mixer fitted with a paddle attachment. Set the mixer on a slow speed (number 2 on the dial), add in the all-purpose flour, semolina flour, baking powder, baking soda, cinnamon, and salt, and mix until everything is well combined. Continue mixing and slowly pour in the olive oil, orange juice, honey, and brandy. Mix everything together until a dough forms.

Remove the dough from the mixer, wrap it in plastic wrap, and refrigerate for 1 hour.

While the dough is chilling, make the syrup: combine the sugar, honey, cinnamon sticks, cloves, and orange peel strip with ½ cup of water in a small pot and bring to a boil, then remove from the heat to infuse as it cools. Strain the syrup into a container, discarding the spices and peel, and refrigerate until ready to use.

Preheat the oven to 350°F. Portion the chilled dough into 1-ounce scoops and, using your hands, roll into slightly oval-shaped balls. Place them on a parchment-lined baking tray, slightly pressing down to hold in place.

Bake until golden brown, 16 to 20 minutes. Meanwhile, remove the syrup from the refrigerator. Once the cookies are out of the oven and still warm, use a large fork or slotted spoon to soak each cookie in the syrup for ten seconds. Transfer them back to the baking tray or a cooling rack. Using a Microplane, grate walnut halves over the cookies. Serve warm or room temperature.

GREEK BUTTER COOKIES
KOULOURAKIA

I've read a few stories about the shape of these classic butter cookies. They are ancient, from the Bronze Age Minoan civilization, which worshipped snakes, so maybe the twisted shape comes from the bodies of snakes. Or it could be religious. They are usually made on the Thursday before Easter and served on Easter Saturday, so it would make sense if there's a Christian story behind the three turns—Father, Son, and Holy Ghost, maybe? No matter the history, these cookies are so good, especially with a touch of anise flavor from the ouzo, a generous brush of nutty brown butter, and a sprinkling of sea salt.

Makes about 24 cookies

1¼ cup (2½ sticks) butter, divided

2¾ cups (343 grams) all-purpose flour

1 teaspoons baking powder

¼ teaspoon baking soda

½ vanilla bean

¾ cup plus 1 tablespoon (158 grams) sugar

3 large eggs

2 tablespoons ouzo

¼ cup sesame seeds, toasted

Flaky sea salt

○ Allow 1 cup (2 sticks) of the butter to come to room temperature.

○ Meanwhile, sift together the flour, baking powder, and baking soda in a medium bowl and set it aside.

○ Slice the vanilla bean lengthwise and scrape the seeds into the bowl of a standing mixer. (Reserve the pod for another use.) Add the softened butter and sugar and cream together on medium-high speed until light and fluffy, about 5 minutes. Reduce the mixing speed to medium and add 2 of the eggs, one at a time, making sure each one is fully mixed in before adding the next, then add the ouzo. Reduce the speed to low and slowly add in the flour mixture, a cup at a time, until a smooth dough forms. Remove the bowl from the stand mixer, cover in plastic wrap, and refrigerate for 2 hours.

○ Preheat the oven to 400°F.

○ After the dough has rested, scoop generous tablespoons (about 1 ounce) of the dough and roll them out on a lightly floured surface into about 8-inch-long ropes. Fold each rope in half and twist it together lengthwise a few times until it looks like a braid

(*right*). Place the twist on a parchment-lined baking sheet and continue with the remaining dough. Be sure to space out the cookies; they puff up when baked.

○ Beat the remaining egg in a small bowl to make an egg wash. Gently brush the egg on the cookies, then bake until golden brown, about 15 minutes. Transfer cookies to a rack to cool.

○ While the cookies are baking, make the brown butter. Heat the remaining 4 tablespoons of butter in a small pan over medium heat and cook, stirring often, as the butter foams and begins to lightly brown. Once the foam disappears, the butter smells nutty and is a golden-brown color, remove it from the heat. Be sure to watch the butter closely so it doesn't burn.

○ After the cookies have cooled, brush them with the brown butter and sprinkle with sesame seeds and sea salt.

GREEK YOGURT WITH APRICOTS

A mixture of dry and canned (yes, canned!) apricots is the secret to this sweet and creamy dessert. It's definitely my daughters' favorite, and it's been on our menu since we first opened our doors. Rehydrating high-quality Turkish apricots with a bit of sweet wine (preferably Muscat de Samos from Greece) adds texture and flavor to this dish. There's lots of vanilla in here too, with a whole bean split between each component. This parfait should be made the day before you want to serve it so that it has time to firm up and concentrate its sweet apricot flavor. We dress it up with a topping of apricot gelée, finely ground pistachios, and a scoop of apricot sorbet. A smear of your favorite apricot jam across the top of the yogurt cream and a scoop of vanilla ice cream would also do the trick.

Serves 6

For the apricot compote:

½ cup dried apricots, preferably Turkish

1 (15-ounce) can apricot halves in syrup

⅓ vanilla bean

¼ cup sweet white wine, such as Muscat de Samos

1 teaspoon sugar

Zest of ½ orange

For the apricot gelée:

1 (15-ounce) can apricot halves in syrup

2 teaspoons unflavored powdered gelatin

⅓ cup sweet white wine, such as Muscat de Samos

4 tablespoons orange juice

1½ tablespoons sugar

⅓ vanilla bean

For the yogurt cream:

1½ cups heavy cream, chilled

½ teaspoon unflavored powdered gelatin

⅓ vanilla bean

¼ cup sugar

¼ cup Greek yogurt

3 tablespoons labneh

○ To make the apricot vanilla compote, finely chop the dried apricots or pulse them in a food processor. Transfer to a heatproof mixing bowl. Drain the canned apricots through a strainer set over a medium pot, reserving the syrup. Finely chop the canned apricots and add to the mixing bowl.

○ Slice the vanilla bean lengthwise and scrape the seeds into the pot with the reserved syrup and discard the pod. Add the wine, sugar, orange zest, and 1 teaspoon of water to the pot. Bring to a boil over medium heat, then immediately remove the pot from the heat. Strain the hot liquid over the dried and canned apricots in the bowl and mix well. Cover and refrigerate until ready to use.

○ To make the apricot gelée, put the apricots and syrup in a blender and puree to a smooth liquid. Chill ⅔ cup of puree in the refrigerator, reserving the remaining puree for another use. Once cold, pour the ⅔ cup of puree into a medium pot, sprinkle the gelatin over the surface of the puree, and let sit for 5 minutes to allow the gelatin to bloom.

○ Add the wine, orange juice, and sugar to the pot. Slice the vanilla bean lengthwise and scrape the seeds into the pot. Bring to a boil over medium-high heat and cook, stirring, for 1 minute, until the sugar has dissolved. Strain the hot mixture through a fine-mesh sieve into a heatproof bowl and set aside.

○ To make the yogurt cream, put the cold heavy cream in a medium pot, sprinkle the gelatin over the surface of the cream, and set aside for 5 minutes to allow the gelatin to bloom. Slice the vanilla bean lengthwise and scrape the seeds into the pot, then add the sugar. Bring the mixture to a simmer over medium-high heat and whisk to dissolve the sugar and gelatin, about 1 minute, then remove the pot from the heat.

○ Whisk the yogurt and labneh together in a large mixing bowl. Continue whisking and pour in the hot cream mixture (or blend with an immersion blender). Quickly cool the mixture by setting a medium bowl in a larger bowl filled with ice and strain the hot mixture through a sieve into the empty chilled bowl. Allow the mixture to cool on the ice.

O To assemble the parfait, remove the apricot compote from the refrigerator. Spoon about ⅓ cup of the apricot compote into each of six parfait or serving glasses. Next, give the cooled yogurt cream a brisk stir then divide evenly among the glasses. Place the glasses in the refrigerator to allow the yogurt cream to set, about 1 hour.

O When the yogurt has set, prepare the apricot gelée to top the cream by warming it in a microwave or in a pot over a medium-low heat until it becomes a loose liquid again.

O Pour 2 to 3 tablespoons of the gelée on top of the firm yogurt cream in each of the glasses. Return the glasses to the refrigerator to cool and set, at least 2 hours or overnight. You can keep the parfaits in the refrigerator, covered with plastic wrap, for up to 3 days. Serve with ground pistachios, apricot sorbet, or vanilla ice cream, if you like.

TURKISH COFFEE CHOCOLATE CAKE

To me, Turkish coffee culture is one of the most amazing things about visiting Istanbul. I love the flavor of the rich coffee, of course, but more than that it's the communal aspect, the conversation and hospitality, that I enjoy. This dish is a tribute to that, adding in other flavors from the Mediterranean. If you happen to have a copper Turkish coffee pot (cezve) in your cabinet, you should brew a traditional cup of coffee to use in the coffee syrup. We like to use the finely ground coffee from Kurukahveci Mehmet Efendi, considered the oldest coffee company in Turkey and easy to find in Mediterranean stores and online. Otherwise, a double shot of espresso will work.

Serves 4

For the coffee syrup:

4 tablespoons brewed Turkish coffee or espresso

½ cup sugar

¾ teaspoon lemon zest

For the cakes:

3¾ ounces (106 grams) 70 percent dark chocolate

½ cup (1 stick) butter, plus more for greasing

⅓ cup (71 grams) sugar, plus more for dusting

3 large eggs

⅓ cup (42 grams) all-purpose flour

Extra-virgin olive oil

Flaky sea salt

3 tablespoons pistachios, toasted

Mastic Ice Cream (page 325)

O To make the coffee syrup, strain the brewed Turkish coffee or espresso through a fine-mesh sieve or coffee filter to remove any grinds. Combine the sugar and lemon zest in a small saucepan over medium-low heat. Cook, stirring regularly with a rubber spatula, until the mixture starts to caramelize and take on a deep golden color, about 7 minutes. Carefully stir in the coffee (it will hiss and bubble as it hits the hot sugar) until well combined. Remove from the heat and let cool for 30 minutes. Transfer to an airtight container and refrigerate until ready to use.

O To make the cakes, preheat the oven to 375°F. Put the chocolate and ½ cup of butter in a glass bowl and heat in the microwave for 30 seconds, then stir and heat for another 30 seconds. Stir again; if the chocolate isn't melted, repeat one more time. Be careful not to overcook the mixture. Stir until smooth and set aside to cool.

O Grease four 6-ounce molds with a little butter and dust lightly with sugar. Set the molds on a baking sheet.

O Put the eggs in the bowl of a stand mixer fitted with the whisk attachment.

Beat at medium speed until the eggs are frothy. Pour in the sugar and increase the speed to medium-high. Continue to beat until the eggs have tripled in volume. Scrape the melted chocolate mixture into the eggs. Beat on medium speed until well combined, scraping down the bowl once or twice. Remove the bowl from the mixer. Sift the flour over the chocolate batter in the bowl and fold in gently with a spatula.

O Divide the batter evenly among the molds and bake for 15 minutes. The cakes should be set on the outside but the center should remain soft and look a little underbaked.

O Meanwhile, remove the coffee syrup from the refrigerator and let it come to room temperature.

O To serve, gently unmold the cakes and brush the tops with olive oil and sprinkle with a pinch of sea salt. Drizzle the coffee syrup around each plate, place a cake on each one, and sprinkle pistachios around the plate. Add a scoop of Mastic Ice Cream next to the cake and serve immediately.

OLIVE OIL CAKE

I like to say that I have olive oil running through my veins. It's deep in the DNA of all Mediterranean people and is one of the things that connects Spaniards like me to our neighbors in the Eastern Mediterranean. This cake is one of my favorite ways to serve olive oil for dessert. It's rich but not heavy, sweet but not too much, and has a nice hint of lemon. Make sure to use good extra-virgin olive oil. It doesn't have to be the most expensive stuff, but since there's a whole cup in there, you want to use something high quality that's not too spicy. This versatile cake pairs well with all kinds of fruit; try whatever is in season, like clementines, apricots, figs, or peaches.

Makes 1 cake

1¼ cup (250 grams) sugar, divided, plus more for dusting

1 vanilla bean

4 large eggs, yolks and whites separated

3 tablespoons (42 grams) lemon juice

Zest of 1 lemon

1⅓ cup plus 2 tablespoons (170 grams) cake flour, sifted

1 cup plus 2 tablespoons (240 grams) extra-virgin olive oil, plus more for drizzling

1 teaspoon kosher salt

1 cup heavy cream

½ teaspoon orange blossom water

1 tablespoon powdered sugar

1 to 2 clementines

○ Preheat the oven to 325°F.

○ Put ¾ cup plus 1 tablespoon (160 grams) of the sugar in the bowl of a stand mixer with a whisk attachment. Split the vanilla bean with a sharp knife and scrape the seeds from the bean into the sugar. Add the egg yolks, lemon juice, and lemon zest and mix on medium speed until everything is combined. Gradually add the sifted flour with the mixer running, scraping the sides of the bowl once or twice. After all the flour has been incorporated, keep the mixer running and drizzle in the olive oil in a steady stream, scraping the bowl again. Transfer the batter to a large mixing bowl and set aside.

○ Combine the egg whites and salt in a large mixing bowl and whip on medium speed, using a hand mixer or stand mixer, until a light foam begins to form. Gradually add the remaining sugar (85 grams) to the egg whites and continue to whip until stiff peaks form. Gently fold the egg whites into the batter, in three parts, until just combined.

○ Line the bottom of a 10-inch springform pan with oiled parchment paper, then pour in the airy batter, being careful to not deflate it. Bake for 45 minutes, or until the cake is nicely browned. Test the cake by inserting

a cake pick or paring knife in the center of the cake; if the tester comes out clean, it's done. If not, continue to bake for a few minutes more, and test again. Cool the cake in the pan on a cooling rack, then remove from the springform pan.

○ While the cake is baking, prepare the whipped cream. Combine the heavy cream, orange blossom water, and powdered sugar in a large mixing bowl and whip on medium-high speed, using a hand mixer or stand mixer, until soft, pillowy peaks begin to form, about 4 minutes.

○ Peel the clementines and separate into sections. With a clean dry towel, rub each section to remove as much of the white pith off the membrane as possible. Cut away the white center seam of each segment with a sharp knife or kitchen shears and remove any seeds. Then, using a serrated knife, slice the clementine in half lengthwise through the thick back part of the segment and spread open like a book.

○ Serve the cake warm or room temperature with spoonfuls of whipped cream, clementine segments, and a drizzle of olive oil.

WALNUT DELIGHT

A Zaytinya original, this is a kind of deconstructed version of baklava created by our first pastry chef, Steve Klc. Wanting to honor this classic pastry of the Mediterranean but without the overwhelming syrupy sweetness, we broke down all the flavors and rebuilt it in our own way. There's a reason it has stayed on our menu for twenty years: it is absolutely delicious. While we prefer our house-made phyllo for most dishes, here we make the sweet phyllo crisps with store-bought phyllo. To get the full effect of this dessert, you should make all of the components. I promise you, it's worth it! Just wait and see how your friends and family will lick the plate clean.

Serves 4 to 6

For the yogurt mousse:

¾ teaspoons unflavored gelatin powder

½ cup heavy cream, divided

¼ cup sugar, divided

¾ cup Greek yogurt

2¼ tablespoons dark brown sugar, packed

For the caramel sauce:

6 tablespoons orange juice

½ teaspoon orange zest

6 tablespoons sugar

For the pine nuts:

6 tablespoons sugar

½ cup pine nuts

For serving:

Walnut Ice Cream (page 325)

4 Sweet Phyllo Crisps (see right)

4 teaspoons honey

○ To make the yogurt mousse, combine the gelatin and 2 tablespoons of cold water in small bowl, stir well, and let sit for 5 minutes to allow the gelatin to bloom. Heat ¼ cup of the heavy cream and 2 tablespoons of the sugar in a small pot over medium-low heat. When the cream is hot but not boiling, whisk in the bloomed gelatin until well combined and the gelatin has dissolved. Put the Greek yogurt in a mixing bowl, then stir in the warm cream mixture.

○ Whip the remaining ¼ cup of heavy cream in a separate bowl until stiff peaks begin to form. Fold the whipped cream into the yogurt mixture, then add the remaining 2 tablespoons of sugar and the dark brown sugar and gently mix to combine. Cover the bowl and put it the refrigerator to chill.

○ To make the orange-caramel sauce, put the orange juice, zest, and sugar in a small saucepan and cook over medium-low heat. Let the mixture simmer, stirring regularly, until it reduces by half and becomes a light caramel color, about 15 minutes. Remove from the heat and set aside.

○ To make the caramelized pine nuts, line a rimmed baking sheet with parchment paper. Combine the sugar with 2 tablespoons of water in a small saucepan and cook over medium heat, stirring regularly, until you have a golden-brown caramel, about 6 minutes. Make sure it doesn't burn. Take it off the heat and stir in the pine nuts, then pour onto the lined baking sheet, scraping all of the caramel out of the pot with a spatula. Spread the caramelized nuts in a thin layer across the baking sheet. Let it completely cool to room temperature, then crush into small pieces.

○ To serve, smear a quarter of the yogurt mousse on each of four plates, then drizzle it with the orange-caramel sauce. Add two scoops of Walnut Ice Cream and place a square of sweet phyllo crisp in between the ice cream scoops on each plate. Sprinkle the crushed pine nuts around the plates and drizzle each with a teaspoon of honey.

FOR SWEET PHYLLO CRISPS:
Preheat the oven to 325°F and line a large baking sheet with parchment paper. Combine ½ cup of sugar, 2 cinnamon sticks, and ¼ cup of water in a small pot and bring to a boil over medium-high heat. Remove from

the heat, add 2 tablespoons of butter, and stir until melted. Lay one layer of store-bought phyllo on a baking sheet and brush the cinnamon syrup over the phyllo, then sprinkle about 2 teaspoons of sugar on top. Repeat the same process with two more layers of phyllo. Prick the phyllo all over with a fork. Bake for about 15 minutes or until the phyllo is golden and shiny. Break the baked phyllo into large pieces or gently cut into rectangles, and store in an airtight container until ready to use.

MASTIC ICE CREAM

This recipe uses the famous mastic, a tree resin from the Greek island of Chios (it's also called Tears of Chios). Mastic has been used in cooking and for health reasons for thousands of years, and to me is one of the most distinctive tastes to evoke a sense of place that I've ever had. It infuses this ice cream with a subtle pine flavor and can also be used in breads and pastries, as a flavoring for alcohol, and even as a chewing gum! We began to serve it with our Turkish Coffee Chocolate Cake (page 319) after Chef Costa returned from a trip to Istanbul. There, in the street market of Kadıköy on the Asian side of Istanbul, he watched a street vendor brew Turkish coffee over charcoal and flavor it with mastic. One sip and he was forever changed. Look for mastic in health-food stores or online.

Makes 2 pints

• ¾ teaspoon (3½ grams) mastic gum • 1 cup plus 1 tablespoon (244 grams) whole milk • 1¾ cups (419 grams) heavy cream • ¾ cup (150 grams) sugar • 4 large (60 grams) egg yolks

○ To prepare the mastic, put it in the freezer for one hour, then grind it to a powder (see page 18). Blend the milk and mastic with an immersion blender until well combined. Pour the milk mixture into a small pot, add the heavy cream and sugar, and cook over medium heat until the mixture reaches 175°F. Put the egg yolks in a small bowl and stir a few tablespoons of the hot mixture into the yolks to warm them, then add the tempered yolks to the pot and continue cooking, stirring regularly, until the mixture reaches 183°F, about 3 more minutes.

○ Cool the mixture in an ice bath, then strain it into a container with a lid, and refrigerate overnight.

○ Blend the mixture again the next day, then process in an ice cream machine according to the manufacturer's directions. Store in the freezer until ready to serve.

WALNUT ICE CREAM

Walnuts have their ancient origins in the Eastern Mediterranean and Middle East—they have been traced back nine thousand years to Persia and are thought to have traveled to Greece during the time of Alexander the Great in the 300s BC. They are central to many Greek desserts, including the iconic baklava (and our deconstructed version on page 322). This rich ice cream highlights their nutty sweetness, along with a light tang of buttermilk.

Makes 2 pints

1 cup (125 grams) walnut halves • 1 cup plus 2 tablespoons (250 grams) whole milk • ¾ cup (150 grams) sugar • ½ cup (125 grams) heavy cream • 4 large (60 grams) egg yolks • ⅔ cup (156 grams) buttermilk

○ Preheat the oven to 300°F. Toast the walnuts for 10 to 12 minutes in the oven on a baking sheet. Once cooled, rub the walnuts with a kitchen towel to remove some of their skin.

○ Put the milk, sugar, and heavy cream in a pot and warm to 175°F over low heat. Put the egg yolks in a small bowl and stir a few tablespoons of the hot mixture into the yolks to warm them, then add the tempered yolks to the pot and continue cooking, stirring regularly, until the mixture reaches 183°F, about 3 more minutes.

○ Combine the walnuts and buttermilk in a large container with a lid and strain the milk-egg mix into the same container. Let it sit overnight in the refrigerator.

○ The next day, puree the walnut and milk mixture until completely smooth, then process in an ice cream machine according to the manufacturer's directions. Store in the freezer until ready to serve.

11

WINES, SPIRITS & COCKTAILS

The best friendships begin with a great bottle of wine. Wine has a way of bringing people together, to share in the story each bottle tells us about a place and a people. This was true for me and my friend Serge Hochar, the legendary winemaker from Chateau Musar in Lebanon, and a bottle of his Chateau Musar Blanc, which he shared with me decades ago, opening my eyes to a part of the world and a winemaking tradition that seemed to have endless possibilities. Serge is no longer with us, but his heart and his smile, and his willingness to share his knowledge with me and everyone on my team, always remain with us. His family continues in that tradition at Chateau Musar, bringing the story of Lebanon's wines to the world.

Before we even wrote the first menu for Zaytinya, we were planning our wine selections. My partners, Rob Wilder and Roberto Alvarez, and I traveled through Greece, Turkey, and Lebanon tasting wines and learning about the regions. We wanted the wines to be exclusively from the Eastern Mediterranean, a necessary and authentic way to bring to life the characters and flavors that inspired our approach to honoring Greek, Turkish, and Lebanese cooking. Chateau Musar was at the top of our list, already well-known for producing world-class wines. Founded in 1930 by Serge's father, Gaston, Chateau Musar grew to international fame under Serge's leadership and talent for winemaking. His red wines made from the French varietals growing in the Bekaa Valley were bold and delicious, but it was his whites, made with native grapes Obaideh and Merwah, that were extraordinary. He said it himself: "My best red wine has always been my white wine."

I first met Serge when he came to Washington, D.C., in the early 2000s to showcase his wines. Sitting and talking with him, tasting that first bottle together (followed by many more!), I saw that he was a proud man—proud of wines, of his family, and of his country. He came back to Zaytinya, year after year, for special wine dinners, tastings, and seminars, always sharing and always teaching. Serge was the ultimate ambassador of the people of Lebanon! He asked me every year, "José, when will you visit Lebanon with me?" I always replied, "Soon, soon!" Sadly, I did not make it there before he died at the end of 2014. It would be several years later that I would get there, and in the cellar he had some wines with my name on them that he was holding for me for the day I would visit him. Today, his son Marc continues the tradition of coming to Zaytinya to teach our

staff and guests about Chateau Musar and Lebanon's Bekaa Valley, and I've returned to Lebanon to visit the winery (*left*) and see his son Gaston, who oversees the winemaking. We celebrate Serge and the important influence his wines have had on me and on Zaytinya with a special selection of vintages from Chateau Musar on our wine lists. It is part of how we stay united, not through business, but through friendship and respect.

EVERY TIME I OPEN A BOTTLE OF WINE, IT IS AN AMAZING TRIP SOMEWHERE.

Wines from the Eastern Mediterranean can seem overwhelming if you don't know what you're looking for. While it's one of the world's oldest winemaking regions, the varieties and vineyards are not as well known here in the U.S. as their cousins from the western side of the Mediterranean (Italy, France, and of course, Spain). Do not be intimidated, my friends! There are so many amazing styles to explore, so be adventurous. When you sip these wines, it is like traveling across the ocean, where you can taste the land and sea, the history and the tradition of this ancient region. Next time you shop for a bottle of sauvignon blanc, instead look for an Assyrtiko from Santorini, such as Gaia or Sigalas. If you're out at a restaurant with friends, ask the sommelier if they have any Bordeaux-style reds from Lebanon's Bekaa Valley—look for wines from Chateau Musar or Massaya.

My team and I have tasted thousands of bottles of wines from Greece, Turkey, and Lebanon to build the wine menus for our restaurants. We are always evolving and adding new and exciting producers just making their way to the U.S. market, while still giving a special place to the prestigious wineries that have helped us build Zaytinya's wine program over the last two decades. We've been lucky to have talented wine professionals on our team to educate our staff and our guests on the regions, varieties,

and winemakers, and we've welcomed many producers and winemakers, particularly from Greece and Lebanon, to the restaurants for special dinners and events. While the wine lists in our restaurants, with nearly 150 different bottles, give details on taste and flavor, regions, indigenous grapes, and even pronunciations, here I'll keep it simple, with some highlights to help make it easier to explore these astonishing wines for yourself.

GREECE

With five major wine regions—Northern Greece, Central Greece, the Peloponnese (or Southern Greece), Crete, and the Aegean Islands—Greece's diversity of terrain and climate helps to make it the biggest wine exporter in the region. There are several hundred native varieties of grapes used in winemaking in Greece. Many wines are single varietals, while others are made from blending both indigenous grapes and international varieties. An intensive revival of the indigenous regional varieties from the Aegean islands and Crete is also happening, as well as some exciting new retsina—very different from the cheap resinated wines of the past. Wild fermented and minimal intervention wines are also gaining a lot of attention. To set you on the path to discover this exciting world of wines, these are four worth seeking out.

ASSYRTIKO (ah-SEER-tea-koh) is the most celebrated white grape variety, mostly produced on the island of Santorini, and probably my favorite style of Greek wine, rich in flavor and aroma. I like to keep a bottle of Domaine Sigalas or Gaia Thalassitis chilled for me at the restaurant. MOSCHOFILERO (MOH-sko-FEE-le-roh), an intensely floral white wine, is made from pink-skinned grapes grown mainly in high altitudes on the Peloponnese peninsula. AGIORGITIKO (ah-your-YEE-tea-koh) is considered one of the most important grapes in Greece, a widely planted red grape primarily found in the Peloponnese. Referred to as the "blood of Hercules," agiorgitiko was supposedly the wine Hercules drank before slaying a lion. This red comes in a wide array of styles, from soft and silky to tannic and intense. It also blends well with other varieties, such as syrah and cabernet. XINOMAVRO (ksee-NOH-mahv-roh) is a pale-colored red, extensively grown in the northern wine region, and known for its aging potential, with complex aromas and good structure. The grape also makes wonderful still and sparkling rosé wines.

LEBANON

A small country with a big reputation for producing world-class wines, Lebanon is home to some of my favorites. It's believed that wine was first produced there in 7000 BC, and later traded through the ancient world by the Phoenicians (early inhabitants of today's Lebanon), but with a modern history of unrest and civil war, wine production remains relatively limited. Its varied terrain is planted mainly with French varieties, a result of decades of French colonial rule after World War I, with the heart of wine production located in the Bekaa Valley in the northeast. Here you'll find the vineyards of the great houses, such as Chateau Musar and Massaya, as well as Domaine des Tourelles and Château Ksara, both making wine since the late 1800s. New producers working with indigenous grapes are taking hold in the country but are still hard to find here in the U.S. Along with wines made from cabernet sauvignon, merlot, cinsault, and chardonnay, native varietals to seek out include MERWAH (MARE-wha), a rich and nutty white, and OBAIDEH (oy-BAY-duh), another white, with flavors of honey and citrus. Both are commonly found in blends, and the obaideh grape is used to make the traditional spirit arak (page 337).

TURKEY

Winemaking and grape cultivation in Turkey dates back thousands of years in the Caucasus region in the northeast and in the Euphrates valley in the southeast. Today, Turkey is a leading grape-growing country in the world, mainly for raisins and table grapes. More than one thousand native varieties and many international ones grow across the country; however, only a few dozen are used in large production for winemaking. The majority of the country's wines are made near the western coast, closer to the Aegean and Mediterranean seas. Look for varietals such as NARINCE (nah-RIN-djeh), a white grape that produces fresh and fruity wines (and whose leaves are often used for dolmades, like on page 154!); KALECIK KRASI (KAH-le-djic Car-AH-sir), a medium-bodied, peppery red wine; or ÖKÜGÖZÜ (oh-KOOS-guh-zoo), meaning "bull's eye," the most widely planted red variety, which creates wines that are juicy, aromatic, and easy to drink. Wine is not heavily consumed in Turkey, limiting the production of wines to be exported, but if you look for them, you can find them!

LEMONADA

Go to any small town around the Mediterranean and you know you'll be able to find freshly picked local lemons. And you know what they say—if life gives you lemons, make lemonada! This is a very popular nonalcoholic drink all around the region, especially in Lebanon, bright with fresh lemon and the citrus oils of a lemon twist coating the rim of the glass. Here we give you two options; one is simple with some orange blossom water for aroma, the other is a bit more complex from a syrup made with smoky, earthy black cardamom. Both styles are easy to scale up for a crowd.

Makes 1

1 ounce fresh lemon juice • 2 dashes orange blossom water • 1½ ounces simple syrup (page 338) • 4 ounces club soda • Lemon peel

○ Combine the lemon juice, orange blossom water, simple syrup, and club soda with ice in a chilled Collins glass and stir briefly. Squeeze the lemon peel, skin side down, to express the oils over the surface of the drink, then add the peel to the drink.

FOR A COCKTAIL-STYLE DRINK:

Combine 1¼ ounces of fresh lemon juice, 1¼ ounces of black cardamom syrup (see below), and 3½ ounces of club soda with ice in a chilled Collins glass and stir briefly. Squeeze a strip of lemon peel, skin side down, to express the oils over the surface of the drink, then add the peel to the drink. To make it a real cocktail, add 1½ ounces of your favorite gin or other spirit.

FOR BLACK CARDAMOM SYRUP:

Toast 6 black cardamom pods (page 341) in a small dry pan over medium-low heat until fragrant, about 1 minute. Combine 1 cup of sugar, 1 cup just-boiled water, and the cardamom pods in a blender and blend thoroughly. Strain the mixture through a fine-mesh sieve or coffee filter. Let come to room temperature before using. Keep the syrup in the refrigerator, covered, for up to 2 weeks.

SIDECAR TO TANGIER

The classic sidecar, made with brandy, orange liqueur, and lemon, is both a sophisticated drink and a perfect template for more complex cocktails. Our Moroccan-inspired sidecar (*right*) uses a spice-infused Greek brandy to elevate the brandy's floral flavors. We use ras el hanout, a very famous spice blend, which means "head of the shop" in Arabic and refers to being made with only the best spices. The spice mix can include more than a dozen warming and savory spices, usually including cardamom, nutmeg, allspice, cinnamon, and ginger. Instead of simple syrup, we sometimes like to use a honey syrup—it's easy to make and keep in your fridge for adding sweetness to cocktails. Just combine ¾ cup of honey with ¼ cup of just-boiled water, stir to combine, and keep it cool until you're ready to use.

Makes 1

1½ ounces spice-infused Metaxa (see below) • ½ ounce orange liqueur • ½ ounce honey syrup (see above) • ¾ ounce fresh lemon juice • Pinch of saffron

○ Combine the Metaxa, orange liqueur, honey syrup, and lemon juice in a cocktail shaker. Fill the shaker with ice and shake vigorously until chilled, about 10 seconds. Strain through a fine-mesh cocktail strainer into a chilled stemmed glass. Garnish with a pinch of saffron, 4 to 5 stigmas, gently floated on top of the drink.

FOR SPICE-INFUSED METAXA:

Combine 2½ teaspoons of ras el hanout with 8 ounces of Metaxa 5 Star in a sealable container. Reserve the remaining amount of Metaxa from a 750-ml bottle and set aside. Let the spice and spirit mixture steep for 24 hours, then strain through a coffee filter set in a strainer. Combine the strained spiced spirit with the remaining Metaxa in the bottle. This mixture can keep for up to 3 months.

POMONA

Some people tell me that they don't like ouzo because of its strong anise flavor—I think it's tasty, but I know it can be a challenge. Even if you don't think you like ouzo, this Collins-style drink (*left*) is for you. The anise flavor combines beautifully with the lemon and pomegranate juices for a refreshing cocktail. See if you can find ouzo from the famous town of Plomari, on the island of Lesbos, made by Isidoros Arvanitis—it's a complex but inexpensive bottle with more than a century of history.

Makes 1

1 ounce ouzo • ½ ounce fresh lemon juice • ¾ ounce simple syrup (page 338) • 1 ounce unsweetened pomegranate juice • 12 mint leaves • 1½ ounces club soda • Orange peel

○ Combine the ouzo, lemon juice, simple syrup, pomegranate juice, and mint leaves in a cocktail shaker. Fill the shaker with ice, then give 2 to 3 hard shakes until just chilled. Strain through a fine-mesh cocktail strainer into a Collins glass with fresh ice. Top with club soda and stir briefly. Squeeze a strip of orange peel, skin side down, to express the oils over the surface of the drink, then add the peel to the cocktail.

POM-FILI

This is what you get when a Spaniard spends time in Greece and imagines what an Eastern Mediterranean sangría would taste like. The pomegranate juice makes it so tart and refreshing, balanced by the orange liqueur and a little extra kick from the vodka. We like to use young, fruity red blends from Lebanon and Greece for this drink at the restaurant, but a Spanish tempranillo would work well too. I like to make this by the pitcher and have it chilled before a party, so all you need to do is fill some glasses with ice and slices of orange or lemon.

Serves 6 to 8

2 cups chopped seasonal fruit (such as strawberries, peaches, or apples) • 1 orange, sliced into wheels • ⅓ cup sugar • 3 ounces vodka • 5 ounces orange liqueur • 16 ounces unsweetened pomegranate juice • 12 ounces dry, fruity red wine • Lemon peels

○ Combine the chopped fruit, oranges, and sugar in a container, cover, and set aside to macerate for at least 1 hour. Add the vodka and orange liqueur and set aside, covered, for at least 8 hours, or overnight.

○ Strain the liquid into a large pitcher and reserve the fruit. Add the pomegranate juice and red wine and stir until well combined, then chill in the refrigerator. To serve, pour into ice-filled glasses, garnishing each with a reserved orange slice and a lemon peel. Serve the remaining fruit in a bowl to snack on!

LEBANESE SOUR

I love exploring Beirut at night: it's full of some of the most vibrant, exciting bars in the world. Last time I visited I challenged the bartender at the Jerry Thomas Experience (yes, named after the famous nineteenth-century American bartender) to create something new. We talked about one of my favorite cocktails, the New York Sour, and then made a version with a Lebanese twist using Three Brothers Bathtub Gin and Chateau Musar's Jeune red wine, both made not far from the city. I loved it—and I think the guys behind the bar did too!

Makes 1

2 ounces gin, preferably from Lebanon • 1 ounce fresh lemon juice • ¾ ounce simple syrup (page 338) • 1 ounce red wine, preferably from Lebanon

○ Combine the gin, lemon juice, and simple syrup in a cocktail shaker. Fill the shaker with ice and shake vigorously until chilled, about 10 seconds. Strain into a chilled coupe glass. Carefully float the red wine on top, slowly pouring the wine onto a barspoon set at the surface of the liquid to form a distinct layer.

SPIRITS TO SIP: OUZO, ARAK, AND RAKI

As you can see throughout this book, the three cuisines we focus on—Greek, Lebanese, and Turkish—overlap again and again. History and culture are more relevant than political borders in understanding the food and drink of the Eastern Mediterranean. When we talk about the three spirits known as ouzo in Greece, arak in Lebanon (and throughout the Middle East), and rakı in Turkey, this is very clear—they all have their roots in the twelve-hundred-year-old distillation process, first developed by the Arab chemist Jabir ibn Hayyan to make mascara (the word "alcohol" comes from the Arabic word for eyeliner, "al kohl"!).

All three drinks have a very similar process for production: start by fermenting grapes, then distill it with anise—the key ingredient, and most distinguishing flavor, of this family of drinks. It's what makes them so popular and beloved in the region, and maybe I should say a bit of a challenge to those less familiar with a strong licorice taste. Other herbs and spices might make their way into the distillations—sweet spices like cloves and cardamom, as well as mint and thyme. There are differences in the methods of production and ingredients, of course, and individual makers will take their own liberties. But these three drinks have always been part of a close family.

The process of drinking each one is part of the fun. They're usually served with a small glass of water or ice, which you can mix however you like. When you pour water into each of them, you get a very cool chemical reaction: the essential oils from the anise quickly emulsify in the water, making the drink go from clear to milky and opaque. In Turkey, this is known as aslan sütü—lion's milk.

All of them are usually drunk with food. In fact, the Greeks have a word for drinking without eating—xerosfýri, literally "dry hammer"—which is not a good idea! I don't know all the science, but I've heard that since ouzo's sugar content is generally higher than that of other liquors, and sugar delays the body absorbing alcohol, you will drink more of it before you realize you are drinking too much. Food helps this problem, of course! In Greece, you will see mezze as the traditional accompaniment to ouzo—seafood like fried squid (page 221) or salty bites like kolokythokeftedes (page 189). In Turkey, rakı must be accompanied by cheeses and melon, along with hot and cold mezze. Arak is great with baba ghannouge (page 54) or hommus (page 46). Since these drinks are so strong, they match well with other powerful flavors: raw garlic, fresh lemon, fatty meats. They are also interesting when mixed into cocktails, like our Pomona (page 335).

In Turkey, a table full of mezze and glasses of rakı is sometimes known as a çilingir sofrası, or "locksmith's table," because as you drink more of it, conversations get deeper and truths will be unlocked. I love this idea, that we can all sit around a table together, eating and drinking and discovering things about ourselves and one another, late into the night.

MINOAN SOUR

This Greek riff on Peru's famous pisco sour has a surprising addition: peppery Cretan olive oil! Chef Costa wanted to use olive oil in a cocktail (Zaytinya is named for it, after all), so he came up with a tribute to the Minoans, who were the first to grow olives in Crete more than five thousand years ago. Make sure to use the best olive oil you have—Cretan if you can find it. Tsipouro, an unaged pomace (brandy made from grape skins and seeds), might be new to you—look for Katsaros tsipouro without anise. Peruvian pisco will be the closest equivalent.

Makes 1

1½ ounces Katsaros Tsipouro • ¾ ounce lemon juice • ¾ ounce simple syrup (see below) • ¼ ounce extra-virgin olive oil • 1 egg white • Pinch kosher salt • Dried black lime (page 341)

o Combine the tsipouro, lemon juice, simple syrup, olive oil, egg white, and salt in a cocktail shaker, along with a sparing amount of ice (a single large cube, or 2 to 3 smaller cubes). Shake vigorously until chilled and well combined, about 20 seconds. Strain through a fine-mesh cocktail strainer into a chilled coupe glass. Grate dried black lime over the top to garnish.

FOR SIMPLE SYRUP:
Combine ½ cup water and ½ cup sugar in a small saucepan and heat over medium heat. Stir until all the sugar has dissolved. Remove from the heat and allow to cool. Simple syrup can be kept refrigerated for 2 weeks in an airtight container.

MASTIHA AND TONIC

If you know me, you know that I love a gin and tonic—or, as we Spaniards say, "gintonic." This is a fascinating version of the cocktail, using a unique and rare ingredient: the resin of mastic trees from the island of Chios in the Aegean Sea. It's been made for millennia and has a taste that's hard to describe—with herbal notes of mint, lavender, and chamomile, it will haunt you forever once you've tried it. Just like with gin, the liqueur made from mastiha is layered and complex, which makes it a perfect match for tonic, with a bit of citrus to brighten it up. Mastiha comes in sweet and dry varieties—you'll want to use the dry style for this cocktail.

Makes 1

1½ ounces Verino Mastiha Liqueur • ½ ounce fresh lemon juice, strained • 4½ ounces tonic water, preferably Fever Tree Indian Tonic • Orange peel

o Fill a stemless wineglass with ice or, ideally, one large ice cube. Pour the mastiha and lemon juice over the ice and stir in the glass to chill. Slowly pour the tonic down the side of the glass. Garnish with an orange peel.

SIRT / KONTRFİLE
PASTIRMA
880.00 TL / KG

RESOURCES

Grocery stores across America, from large supermarket chains to specialty stores, are now carrying many of the traditional Mediterranean and Middle Eastern ingredients we use at Zaytinya. Take a walk down any international foods aisle and you can find bags of za'atar, bulgur, freekeh, and sumac, along with jars of grape leaves, grilled eggplant, tahini, and pickled peppers.

For items that might be a little harder to find in your neighborhood, a quick search online makes it easy to order what you need to make these recipes as authentic and flavorful as possible. Start with a few special ingredients, then build your pantry as you get more familiar with how to use them in these recipes and other dishes.

For spices and dried herbs, we love the products from Burlap & Barrel (burlapandbarrel.com), particularly their dried Euphrates Mint Leaves and Silk Chili, which is their version of Aleppo pepper made with Turkish Marash pepper. Spice master and chef Lior Lev Sercarz's shop, La Boîte (laboiteny .com), is a great place to find black cardamom, rose petals, Urfa pepper, and fenugreek, not to mention a number of delicious spice blends.

One of my favorite shops in the world is Kalustyan's (foodsofnations.com) in New York. It's easy to order mastic and barberries, as well as dried black limes (known as lemon omani) to grate over cocktails.

Look for Trikalinos's avgotaraho and avgotaraho powder online at Marky's (markys .com) and Amazon, where you will find it named grey mullet bottarga. To learn more about this amazing specialty of the sea, visit trikalinos.gr.

Meats like pastirma and soujouk, along with cheeses such as Kefalograviera and Kasseri, are worth seeking out. Try visiting a specialty cheese shop or Greek market in your town. They can also be found online at Greek and Turkish food websites.

Don't forget the wine! Exploring Greece, Turkey, and Lebanon can be as easy as opening a bottle of wine. Ask your local wine shop to help you find some of the wines we feature here. Online wine shops are a great option for shipping to your home.

ACKNOWLEDGMENTS

Creating a book is like opening a restaurant: It takes a talented, creative, and dedicated team to build the dream and then share it with the world. For this, I'm grateful to my entire Zaytinya family—past, present, and future!

To my partners in this book: Aglaia Kremezi, our guiding spirit, our Greek yiayia, you are a saint; and Chef Michael Costa, the champion of our Zaytinya restaurants. I could not have made this book without you.

To our chefs and cooks at Zaytinya: Hilda Mazariegos, Jose Ayala, Eleftherios Natas, Ana Ybarra Rojas, Selim Topal, Chris Wroblewski, Zach Foust-Meyers, Ariana Montero, Dinora Melendez, Julia Hernandez, Fernando Flores, Paula Barrera, Nancy Perez, and our growing culinary family, thank you for bringing our food, and this book, to life. To our restaurant team: bussers, bartenders, runners, prep cooks, dishwashers, hosts, managers, and more, I'm proud of everything you do to share our dream.

To my R&D team: Charisse Grey, Claudio Foschi, Hector Contreras, Jesus Serrano, Tammy Saunders, and Koji Terano, thank you for always supporting me and for giving your time and talent to get this book done. To Miguel Lancha, Josh Murski, Daniel Grajewski, and Jordi Paronella for keeping our cocktails creative and for turning wine into wisdom.

To Richard Wolffe, who's helped me tell my stories for decades. To Sam Chapple-Sokol, Jane Black, Gabriella Lozano, Oset Babür-Winter, Kara Elder, Samantha Bello, Jim Webster, and Julian Nguyen, you shaped Zaytinya's story in more ways than one. Thank you for your writing, research, testing, editing, and more. And to Ann McCarthy, my sister, from the recipes to the stories to the pictures, your hands and heart are on every page.

To Thomas Schauer, our brilliant photographer, and his lovely wife, Sahinaz Agamola-Schauer, the photos, like you, are beautiful. Pablo Juncadella, Elena Solaz, Ángela Ballén, and everyone at Mucho, you are a creative force.

Zafiris Trikalinos and Lila Kourti in Athens; Aline Kamakian, Bechara Nammour, Kamal Mouzawak, Marc and Gaston Hochar in Beirut; Nazlı Pişkin in Istanbul; Dany and Jenifer Abi-Najm and Grace Abi-Najm Shea in Washington, D.C., thank you for your knowledge and generosity.

My agent, Kim Witherspoon, who is always ready to protect or to push when I need it. Helen Atsma and Gabriella Doob and everyone at Ecco, thank you for believing in this book and for helping us make it amazing.

To Rob Wilder and Roberto Alvarez, we started on this journey through Greece, Turkey, and Lebanon many years ago; thank you for your support and for your friendship. To our friends, wine importers, farmers, producers, partners, and former team members who helped me look back with gratitude for all we have accomplished at Zaytinya: Ruben Garcia, Christopher Vazquez, Sotiris Bafitis, Selçuk Önce, Steve Klc, Alex Zappos, Brian Zaslavsky, Andy Myers, Eric Martino, Joe Raffa, Yannis Tsapos, Bartholomew Broadbent, Abdelrazzaq Hashhoush, Jorge Chicas, Juan Rivera, Hollis Silverman, and so many more . . . you know who you are!

To Sam Bakhshandehpour, Carles Tejedor, Rick Billings, and my team at José Andrés Group, you inspire me to learn and grow, and to make sure we take care of the people around us and at each and every table. Satchel Kaplan-Allen and Marisa Lobo Rioja, you keep my always-expanding world in order.

To my daughters, Carlota, Inés, and Lucía, who grew up sitting at the tables of Zaytinya, you make this book all the more special. And none of my dreams would come true without my wife, Tichi, you are all that I am.

INDEX

(Page references in *italics* refer to illustrations.)

and Roasted Pepper Spread
(Muhammara), *56*, 57
Spiced Smoked, 38, *39*
Tarator Sauce, 230
toasted, 23
Watermelon and Feta Salad
(Karpouzi me Feta), *98*, 99
weighing ingredients for baking, 129
wheat berry(ies), 16, 152
Kisir, 164, *165*
White Bean Stew (Piyaz), 162, *163*
Whole Fish, Grilled, *275*, 286, *287*
Wilder, Rob, 1, 328
wines, 328–31
of Greece, 330–31
of Lebanon, 328–29, 330, 331
of Turkey, 330, 331
Wolfert, Paula, 257
World Central Kitchen, 45, 100
Wright, Clifford A., 7, 97

X

Xinomavro, 331

Y

Yellow Split Pea Spread (Fava
Santorini), 61
Yellow Squash Skordalia, *72*, 73
Yemen, 306
spice mix from (Hawayej), 27,
192
yogurt, 14
with Apricots, Greek, 316–17,
317
Caper Sauce, *188*, 189
Eggplant, Crispy Fried with
(Batijan bil Laban), *196*, 197
Mousse, 322
Sauce, Garlic- 227
Sauce, Savory Dumplings in
(Mantı), *266–67*, 267–68,
269
Soup, Chilled, *118*, 119
Toum Sauce, *220–21*, 221
Turkish Eggs with, and Chili
Crisp (Çilbir), 174, *175*
Tzatziki, *40–41*, 52
Youvetsi, Chicken, 264, *265*

Z

za'atar, 19
Oil, 130
Pide, 124, 130, *131*
zeytinyağlı (Turkish olive-oil-based
seasonal vegetable dishes, ladera
in Greece and bil zayt in the
Middle East), 181
Zeytinyağlı Enginar (Braised
Artichokes and Spring
Vegetables), *182*, 183
zirh knife, *65*, 298
zucchini:
Briami Pide, *136*, 137
Fritters, Greek
(Kolokythokeftedes), *188*,
189

HarperCollins books may be purchased for educational, business, or sales promotional use. For information, please email the Special Markets Department at the email address SPsales@harpercollins.com.

Ecco® and HarperCollins® are trademarks of HarperCollins Publishers.

FIRST EDITION

CREATED BY José Andrés Media

DESIGNED BY Mucho

PHOTOGRAPHY BY Thomas Schauer

MAP ILLUSTRATION BY Laura Rankin, Rockwell Group

Library of Congress Cataloging-in-Publication Data has been applied for.

ISBN 978-0-06-332790-0

24 25 26 27 28 TC 10 9 8 7 6 5 4 3 2 1